SEEDS
OF
EMPIRE

THE WORLD OF WAR

GENERAL EDITOR
Dennis Showalter

SEEDS OF EMPIRE
The American Revolutionary
Conquest of the Iroquois

MAX M. MINTZ

MAX M. MINTZ

✦ ✦ ✦ ✦ ✦ ✦ ✦ ✦ ✦

SEEDS
OF
EMPIRE

THE AMERICAN
REVOLUTIONARY
CONQUEST
OF THE IROQUOIS

✦ ✦ ✦ ✦ ✦ ✦

NEW YORK UNIVERSITY PRESS
NEW YORK AND LONDON

NEW YORK UNIVERSITY PRESS
New York and London

© 1999 by New York University

Library of Congress Cataloging-in-Publication Data
Mintz, Max M.
Seeds of empire : the American revolutionary conquest of the
Iroquois / Max M. Mintz.
p. cm.—(The world of war)
Includes bibliographical references and index.
ISBN 0-8147-5622-0 (cloth : alk. paper)
1. Sullivan's Indian Campaign, 1779. I. Title. II. Series.
E235 .M56 1999
973.3'35—dc21   99-6006
                    CIP

New York University Press books are printed on acid-free paper,
and their binding materials are chosen for strength and durability.

Manufactured in the United States of America

10 9 8 7 6 5 4 3 2 1

CONTENTS

✦ ✦ ✦ ✦ ✦ ✦ ✦ ✦ ✦ ✦ ✦

ACKNOWLEDGMENTS

✦ ✦ ✦ ✦ ✦ ✦ ✦ ✦ ✦ ✦ ✦

The first eight chapters of this book were read in manuscript by Richard Buel, Jr., and the entire manuscript was read by Thomas J. Farnham and Paul Stewart. I am deeply grateful for their criticisms and suggestions. The maps were drawn with superb computer expertise by Paola Rubbo.

My researches at the British Library and the Public Record Office were supported by a John Adams Fellowship at the University of London Institute of United States Studies (Gary L. McDowell, Director) and by an Eccles Centre Fellowship of the British Library (R. A. Burchell, Director).

I was most courteously received as I searched for information at the Chemung County Historical Society, Fort Stanwix National Monument, the Ontario County Historical Society, the Geneva County Historical Society, the Seneca Falls Historical Society, the Historical Society of Pennsylvania, the Haverford College Magill Library, the New-York Historical Society, the New York Public Library, the New York State Library at Albany, the New York State Historical Association at Cooperstown, and the Massachusetts Historical Society. As always, my labors have been sustained by the Yale University libraries and the Hilton C. Buley Library of Southern Connecticut State University, Paul L. Holmer, Interlibrary Loan Librarian.

Many correspondents took the trouble to answer my queries, notably David J. Fowler, Research Director of the David Library of the American Revolution; J. William Frost, Director of the Friends Historical Library of Swarthmore College; Mary Anne Hines, Chief

of Reference at the Library Company of Philadelphia; Scott Mc-
Cloud, Reference Librarian at the Albany Institute of History and
Art; and Linda Stanley, Manuscripts and Archives Curator at the
Historical Society of Pennsylvania.

I have benefited from the insights received in conversations with
John F. Burke, Jonathan R. Dull, and James E. Mooney.

Niko Pfund, director of the New York University Press, has been
a staunch advocate and a champion of excellence. Despina Papazo-
glou Gimbel, managing editor, and Elyse Strongin have been sterling
supporters.

ILLUSTRATIONS

✦ ✦ ✦ ✦ ✦ ✦ ✦ ✦ ✦ ✦ ✦

The illustrations listed below appear as a group following p. 108.

MAPS

* * * * * * * * * * *

PROLOGUE

✦ ✦ ✦ ✦ ✦ ✦ ✦ ✦ ✦ ✦ ✦

The American Revolution was not only a struggle for independence, but also for the lands of the Indians, and the jewel was the upstate New York domain of the Iroquois Six Nations. The fertile Mohawk, Susquehanna, and Allegheny broad river valleys were a magnet for farmers weary of contending with New England's stubborn soil. The route westward along the southern shore of Lake Erie offered a pass through the Appalachian mountain chain and beyond to the Mississippi.

The population of the six tribes (Haudenosaunee, people of the longhouse) totaled approximately fifteen thousand in the eighteenth century.[1] Easternmost were the Mohawks (people of the flint), inhabiting the south bank of the Mohawk River. Westward of them, the Oneidas (people of the standing stone) occupied the shores of Oneida Lake. Beyond them, the Onondagas (people on the mountain) lived on the Onondaga River. The Cayugas (people on the landing) were situated next at Cayuga Lake. Furthest west were the Senecas (people of the great hill), reaching to the Genesee River. Interspersed among the Oneidas and the Onondagas were the Tuscaroras (people of the Indian hemp), refugees from North Carolina who were adopted into the League in 1722 or 1723.

The confederation, originally formed as a spiritual Great League of Peace and Power to eliminate internecine war, had evolved into the League for War and Survival. Composing the General Council of the League were fifty sachems, chosen by the clan matrons from hereditary female lines. Each tribe had one block vote, and unanimity of the total council was required. But decisions could not be binding,

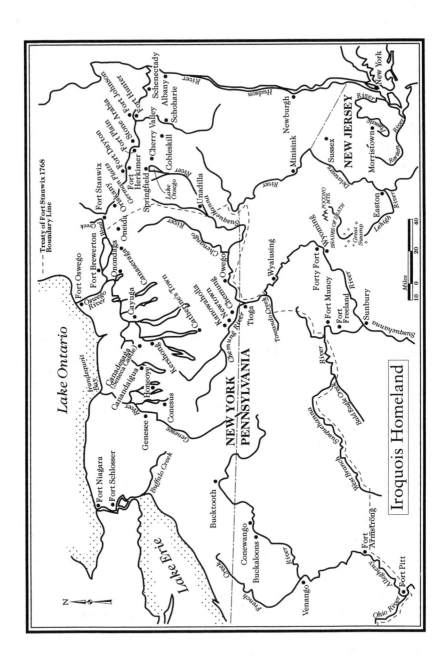

Iroquois Homeland

because member tribes, and even individual villages, retained autonomy. (Some historians speculate that this fluidity was an influence on the formation of the American Constitution.)[2]

Although the General Council mainly regulated intertribal affairs, it could also declare war, and here it came into conflict with the war chiefs. There were two war chiefs, and since the Senecas were the most exposed to attack on the west, both appointments belonged to them. Also chosen by the clan matrons, one chief came from the Wolf Clan and the second from the Turtle Clan. However, an outstandingly brave and sagacious warrior might be elected a nonhereditary "Pine Tree" chief. Furthermore, any individual bellicose chief might recruit his own war party, subject only to refusal of the women to supply it. Yet despite these blurred jurisdictions, during the seventeenth century the League for War, in its contest for the fur trade, had overpowered the tribes to the north and west and inspired a reputation of invincibility and ruthlessness.[3]

In the wars between the French and the British, the League at first had attempted to bargain from strength for a position of imprecise neutrality. But as the conflict progressed, the Mohawks sided with the British and some of the Senecas with the French. By 1759, however, the victories of the British at Louisbourg, Fort Frontenac, and Fort Duquesne gave the tribes no choice. They all opted to ally with the British, and the British in turn sought to pacify them in 1768 by the Treaty of Fort Stanwix, which established a dividing line beyond which white settlers were not to trespass.[4] But the prohibition was not enforced, and as settlers began moving in, the Iroquois saw themselves imperiled.

The outbreak of the Revolution brought a new dilemma. The Iroquois trusted neither side, and their canniest sachems counseled neutrality. The British, however, had too few regular troops to conquer the west without the help of the Indians, and they worked to win them over. In the competition with the undersupplied rebels for their allegiance, they had the advantage of a preponderance of weapons, household implements, and clothing, on which the Indians, after two centuries of contact with the Europeans, had become completely dependent. Torn between the two sides, the Senecas, the Cayugas, and the Onondagas leaned toward the British, while the Oneidas and the Tuscaroras inclined toward the rebels.

The test came in 1777, when the British projected an invasion from Canada of the Champlain-Hudson and Mohawk valleys of New York State. General George Washington had expelled General Sir William Howe from Boston, but Howe had driven him out of New York City. An army under General John Burgoyne was to descend from Montreal to Albany. Howe was to ascend the Hudson to meet him there. A third force under Colonel Barry St. Leger, also from Canada, would sweep westward, past Lake Ontario, capture rebel-held Fort Stanwix on the Mohawk, and unite with the other two at Albany. Control of the Champlain-Hudson corridor supposedly would sever New England from the rest of the country and leave it prey to piecemeal conquest. Occupation of Stanwix would open the way to British control of western New York State.[5]

St. Leger's only hope of manning his army was to recruit Indians. With bountiful gifts, Loyalist commanders lured Senecas, Cayugas, and Onondagas to abandon their neutrality and join him. Even so, his expedition failed, although the rebel militia paid a big price in men killed and wounded. The Iroquois suffered lesser, but never-to-be-forgotten casualties that triggered a campaign of terror against the settlements along the entire frontier.

In response, public outrage forced Washington to dispatch a punitive expedition under General John Sullivan. There are more soldiers' diaries for that campaign surviving than for any other of the Revolution, making possible a uniquely graphic and detailed narrative. The expedition defeated a Loyalist-Iroquois army and left behind a swath of destroyed Iroquois villages, crops, and orchards from which the Indians were never to recover. For launching the expedition, the Indians branded Washington "Town Destroyer." "When that name is heard," Seneca Chief Cornplanter told him, "our women look behind them and turn pale, and our children cling close to the necks of their mothers."[6]

CHAPTER I

✦ ✦ ✦ ✦ ✦ ✦ ✦ ✦ ✦ ✦ ✦

IN HIS STEPS

For two hours in the broiling late-morning sun of July 11, 1774, Sir William Johnson exhorted the Iroquois sachems assembled in the arbor of his Mohawk River mansion not to join the Delawares, the Shawnees, and the Mingoes in their war against the Virginians. In the garb and the language of the Mohawks, who had adopted him as a member of the tribe, he cajoled and implored, gesticulated and promenaded, calling up once more "that influence which has never yet forsaken me." By midday, the ache of the bullet in his hip began to tell, and the dysentery that would not go away became acute. He felt a tightening across the stomach and needed assistance to retire to the library. He took some wine and water, sank down in an armchair, leaned back, and died without a groan.[1]

His like would never come again. Some magic of adaptability had produced in this transplant from Ireland's County Meath a bicultural marvel who moved with equal ease among colonists and Indians. With the Palatinate Germans, he danced in their festivities; with the Indians, he dined in their religious rite on boiled dog and soup laced with lice. As a young man, he had impressed a rich uncle in America, who brought him over to manage his Mohawk Valley estate near the mouth of the Schoharie. The protégé soon set himself up on his own as a trader, land speculator, and politician, and within twenty years he emerged as the undisputed mogul of the valley. An army officer's daughter still remembered him after half a century as "an uncommonly tall, well made man" with "an expression of dignified sedateness, approaching to melancholy" and "the most entire command of temper, and of countenance."

As a reward for protecting the Indians against the speculators, the Mohawks gave him a tract of land sixteen miles by ten on the north side of the river, near Little Falls. As a reward for leading victorious Anglo-Indian armies against the French at Lake George and Fort Niagara, the king confirmed the Mohawk gift, establishing it as a royal patent, and created him a baronet. He had become himself the arch speculator. He was named superintendent of Indian affairs for the region north of the Ohio, including Canada; and the lieutenant governor of New York declared that he had "a greater influence among the Indians than any other Englishman ever had."[2] The Iroquois did heed his deathbed appeal to stay out of what became known as Cresap's War against the Virginians.

Had he lived, would this decorated pillar of the empire have stood with the Patriots or the Tories? Some among the Patriots insisted that he could never have done violence to his neighbors. True, he had supported the Stamp Act and the Townshend Duties. But, after receiving news of the tea disturbances at Boston, averred the Patriots, he had committed suicide rather than take sides.[3] Those who lived closest with him never doubted that they knew better. His Indian consort, his Indian brother-in-law, his only white son, and his two white sons-in-law all believed that he would have remained loyal to the Crown, and they considered it their mission to summon his Iroquois cohorts to aid in the suppression of the unnatural rebellion.

Mary, better known as "Molly" Brant (in her language, Gonwatsijayenni, or someone lends her a flower), was a Mohawk whom Johnson took as mistress after the death of his German wife. He had eight children by Molly, to each of whom he had bequeathed fifteen hundred pounds and three thousand acres. Although not married in English law, she was known as "the Indian Lady Johnson." The mention of her husband's name brought tears to her eyes and a reminder that he had often promised "to live & die a firm Friend to the King of England." Reputed to be descended from the Indian King Hendrick, she became head of the Society of Six Nations Matrons, a position of power in a matriarchy where the mothers chose the sachems. She had a beguiling personality but a violent temper; she did not hesitate to berate a venerable sachem in council for considering peace with the Americans. A British army captain serving with the Indians declared that her influence among them was "far superior to that of all their chiefs put together." One of her sons, William Johnson, went to Canada to fight with the "Sword of my Father" against the invading rebel army. "I kill'd and scalp'd, and kick-d their arses," he boasted.[4]

Molly's thirty-four-year-old brother, Joseph Brant (in the Mohawk tongue Thayendanegea, or two sticks bound together), in time became the best-known chief in the history of the Iroquois. So light-skinned as to inspire a rumor that he was Johnson's son, he was, said an American captive who saw him in 1780, "about the middle size, of a square, stout build." He had dark hair and eyes, an easy dignity, and a lurking sense of humor. Not a hereditary chief on his mother's side, he needed to earn elevation through willpower and achievement, and he began the climb to eminence at thirteen, serving under Johnson at Lake George and later in the fighting to put down Pontiac's Rebellion. When he was fifteen, Johnson sent him to a Congregationalist free school for Indian boys at Lebanon, Connecticut, where he absorbed a smattering of Hebrew, Greek, and Latin. He rejected, however, the rigid New Light doctrine of the schoolmaster, preferring the warmer appeal of Anglicanism, and afterward assisted an Anglican priest to translate the Gospel of St. Mark and a history of the Bible into Mohawk. Before Sir William died, he saw to it that Brant was appointed a Pine Tree chief (a nonhereditary man of distinction) of the Mohawks. Brant also achieved economic solidity. He owned a well-stocked 80-acre farm on the fertile flats of Canajoharie, the chief village of the Mohawks, on the south side of the Mohawk River at the mouth of Nowadaga Creek. Sir William had deeded him another 512 acres across the river.[5]

Of all the Iroquois, Brant was the earliest and most outspoken to take the British side. "It was purely on account of my forefathers' engagements with the king," he said. "I always looked upon these engagements, or covenents, between the king and the Indian nations as a sacred thing." Loyalty would bring its reward. "Every man of us thought," he said years later, "that by fighting for the King, we should insure to ourselves and our children a good inheritance."[6]

His decision also involved a personal factor. Living in 1769 at Springfield, on a six-thousand-acre estate at the head of Lake Otsego, was Augustine Prevost, Jr., a son-in-law of George Croghan, a deputy to Sir William Johnson and a prominent trader and land speculator. Croghan's second wife was an Indian related to Brant's stepfather. Prevost, two years younger than Brant, was a Swiss-born, English-educated, half-pay lieutenant, veteran of the British Sixtieth (Royal American) Regiment in the French and Indian War. A close relationship sprang up between the two young men. According to Brant's Anglican missionary priest, John Stuart, it was a custom among Iroquois men to choose an intimate male friend to share secrets, joys, and sorrows, "carried in practice to an incredible length." Prevost rejoined the Royal Americans in 1771 and the following year was assigned to Jamaica, later to serve against the Americans in Georgia. Brant sent him an Indian costume of the most costly furs, and Prevost kept close by him a portrait of Brant.[7] It would have been traumatic for Brant to fight on the side against his bosom friend.

Sir John Johnson, thirty-three, Sir William's only legitimate son, had an antipathy to his father and cared only to inherit his lands. He visited England in 1765, where he obtained for himself that rarity among Americans, a knighthood to match that of his father. He declined to accept the succession to his father's superintendency of the Indians, and his antipathy carried over to his brothers-in-law, Guy Johnson and Daniel Claus, and to Molly and Joseph Brant. Perhaps the father-son estrangement stemmed from Sir William's acquisition of the Indian consort. Sir John wished to bask in baronial eminence, protected by a corps he had raised of Loyalists and Indians. Sooner than lift up his hand against his king," he vowed, he "would suffer his head to be cut off."[8]

The succession to the management of Indian affairs fell by default to his white brothers-in-law, to each of whose wives Sir William had bequeathed fourteen thousand acres. Guy Johnson, thirty-four, also a distant Irish cousin of Sir William's, was named superintendent of the Northern Indian Department. Bright, personable, and portly, he lived at Guy Park Manor, his square-mile estate at the present Amsterdam. He despised the emerging revolutionary movement in Tryon County, led, he declared, by an "itinerant New England leather-dresser, and conducted by others, if possible more contemptible." If he was to keep his position, he really had no choice but to remain with the Crown, for the Continental Congress appointed its own commissioners of Indian affairs.[9]

Daniel Claus, forty-eight years old, was the deputy for Indians in Canada. Born into the lesser landed gentry of southwestern Germany, at twenty-two he had arrived at Philadelphia to seek his fortune and soon became active in Indian affairs, first with Pennsylvania's Indian agent, Johann Conrad Weiser, and then with Sir William Johnson as his deputy secretary, his colonel of militia, and ultimately as his son-in-law. More than any other of Sir William's white staff, he learned Indian languages, living for a time in the home of Joseph Brant and forming a lifelong friendship with him. He was short and unimpressive and prone to the gout; he compensated for his physical insignificance with a histrionic vanity. He considered the Indians savage and gullible but thought it an "ill judged Delicacy" not to unleash them against the colonists.[10]

Instructions in cipher arrived for Guy Johnson from General Thomas Gage in Boston, directing him to gather his Indians and join forces with Sir Guy Carleton in Canada for an invasion of New England. The order was welcome, for Johnson had reason to fear arrest by the Continental Congress. On May 31, 1774, with Claus and Brant and 120 Loyalists and 90 Mohawks, he left his estate never to return. He held a conference with the Iroquois at Fort Ontario, where he secured their agreement to protect the St. Lawrence River-Lake Ontario supply route. If Puritan missionary Samuel Kirkland interfered, he openly threatened, he would cut his head off "as soon as he would a snakes." At a larger meeting of 1,664 in Montreal on July 26, with Carleton at his side, he obtained their pledge of support.[11]

The pledge, however, came mostly from Canadian Indians, rather than those of the Mohawk Valley. The Oneidas and the Tuscaroras refused to attend the meeting. The Senecas, the Cayugas, and the Onondagas were only sparsely represented, and they were attempting to remain neutral. The Oneidas and the Tuscaroras had closer ties with the Germans and the Dutch than with Sir William's British relatives and retainers.

To the Indians, this war of Britisher against Britisher was difficult to fathom. Among the Oneidas, Kirkland was a major influence, winning over the warriors against the pro-British sachems. A record of his reasoning with warrior chief John Skenandon has been preserved:

> *Kirkland:* "England is the father: we the son. The father heaped burdens upon the son until he was longer unable to bear them and in place of hearing his entreaty for relief, heaped the burdens heavier upon him. Because the son could not stand up under these burdens, the father is trying to whip him. Now, which will you help, father or son?"
> *Skenandon:* "I go for the son."[12]

Only the Mohawks, the easternmost tribe and the one most inundated by white settlement, inclined toward the British. They competed with the Oneidas and the Tuscaroras for the fur trade and were followers of their Loyalist Anglican missionary, John Stuart. Unlike the stern Kirkland, who would baptize only children of regenerate parents, Stuart accepted children of dissolute parents provided a reputable godparent came forward. Yet division existed even among the Mohawks. At a council meeting of the Iroquois Confederacy with the Continental Congress's commissioners for Indian affairs in August 1775 at Albany, the spokesman was a Mohawk sachem, Little Abraham (Tigoransera). The Six Nations, he declared, were determined "not to take any part, but as it is a family affair, to sit still and see you fight it out."[13]

Despite these obstacles, Guy Johnson had a consuming ambition to return to the Mohawk Valley with a conquering army of Indians. In this he met with the opposition on the British side of Sir Guy Carleton, governor and commander of military forces of Canada. Carleton, a forbidding and inflexible man, had, beneath his imperiousness, an insight more perceptive than Johnson's. He declared that he had supreme authority over the Indians in Canada and that they must not be deployed below the forty-fifth parallel. He wished to use them only within Canada, as scouts, in defense against an American invasion then being prepared at Fort Ticonderoga. He even wished to limit the war in the hope that a settlement might be negotiated.

His opposition to Johnson deepened into antagonism. "This gentleman," he wrote, "understands he has the supreme command over all the Indians, and . . . I believe we can manage those of this province better." Carleton had, in fact, already obtained the appointment in London of a new superintendent of Indian affairs for Canada, Major John Campbell of the 27th Regiment, a son-in-law of a brutal Ottawa chief, La Corne St. Luc, who had fought on the side of the French against the British in 1757. Since the border of Canada, according to the recently enacted Quebec Act, now extended south to the Ohio River, Johnson's jurisdiction was severely restricted and Claus's was totally eliminated. When Campbell arrived on September 10, bearing the authority of the royal seal, Johnson was outraged. Claus charged that "after such a Disgrace" he could not "look the Indians in the Face." They determined on an extreme resort: they would take ship to London and plead their case directly with the secretary of the American department, Lord Dartmouth.[14]

They had made a major miscalculation. Happy to see them go, Carleton soon found replacements that would make it all but impossible for them to regain their positions. The principal one was Sir John Johnson. At his Mohawk home at Johnson Hall, he learned that a contingent of Continentals under Colonel Elias Dayton had been sent to arrest him. His adherents were mainly Catholic immigrants from Scotland, anathema to the Protestant Germans from the Palatinate and the Puritans from New England. Against a superior Patriot force, they proved unavailing. He disbanded them and gave his parole that he would remain under the orders of the Continental Congress. Four months later, May 13, he broke his parole, leaving his pregnant wife a hostage and fleeing with 170 supporters to Canada. At Montreal, where he arrived July 16, 1775, Carleton three days later granted him a commission as lieutenant colonel to raise a ranger regiment, the King's Royal Regiment of New York, commonly known as "Johnson's Greens" for the color of their uniforms. Among them were the Catholic Scots of the Mohawk Valley and their Irish chaplain, Father John McKenna, a native, like Sir William Johnson, of County Meath. Sir John was now the prime head of native Canadians, white and Indian.[15]

John Butler replaced Claus as deputy Indian superintendent. A protégé of Sir William Johnson who had migrated from Connecticut to the Mohawk valley, he was not one of the inner circle of relatives. Starting as an interpreter, he had gone on to prove himself a skilled leader of Indians as a captain in the French and Indian War, at Ticonderoga, Fort Frontenac, Fort Niagara, and Montreal. Fifty years old and commissioned a major, he was the very model of a dutiful officer. An undersize, beefy stump of a man with somber, weather-buffeted features, he spoke in rapid torrents, repeating words when excited. He had abandoned his inherited five-thousand-acre estate, Butlersbury, near Johnstown, to join Guy Johnson in the exodus to Canada, taking with him two sons and leaving his wife and other children to be interned by the rebels. To Carleton he seemed "very modest and shy." To the resentful Claus, he was an "illiterate interpreter."[16] In time, however, he was to overshadow Claus.

Joseph Brant accompanied Guy Johnson and Claus on their voyage to England. The Mohawks delegated him to present to the ministry their claim to disputed land at Brant's birthplace, Canajoharie, fifty

miles east of Schenectady, and additional lands in the upper Susquehanna River valley. Although Brant was fluent enough in English to
be employed by the Indian Department as an interpreter, Johnson
appointed Captain Gilbert Tice as a companion to make arrangements for him in London. Tice, a former innkeeper at Johnstown,
had been wounded while leading a group of fifty Indian scouts at the
defense of Montreal. The ship's party, which included Johnson's
three little daughters, Claus's wife and one child, and a second Mohawk, John Hill Oteronyente, departed from Quebec on November
11, 1775, aboard the *Adamant*. In chains in the ship's hold, amid
blackness, stench, and lice, lay Ethan Allen, the taker of Ticonderoga,
who had been captured in a rash attack on Montreal.

The *Adamant* docked at Falmouth December 27 and was greeted
by a crowd straining for a sight of the famed Vermonter. He was to
be imprisoned in Pendennis Castle, but rather than provoke reprisals,
six months later he was returned to America and paroled in New
York City. The *Adamant*'s added attraction was the spectacle of two
authentic American Indians. They and the rest of the Johnson party
proceeded to London, where Johnson and Claus booked lodgings in
Brewer Street, between Mayfair and Soho. Tice, Brant, and Brant's
tribesman took rooms at the Swan-with-Two-Necks in Lad Lane, a
few blocks northeast of St. Paul's Cathedral.[17]

They learned that Dartmouth had been replaced as secretary of the
American department by Lord George Germain. This looked like a
windfall. Germain was a zealous advocate of the employment of
Indians against the American rebels. He was also a political and
personal enemy of Carleton, who, he believed, had been a prime
mover in his court-martial conviction fifteen years earlier for disobe-
dience of orders at the Battle of Minden. Furthermore, he considered
Carleton weak and wavering. He wanted a decisive strike in the
northern colonies that would end the war with a quick victory, and
he chose the combative John Burgoyne as second in command to
Carleton in order to spur him to action.

Johnson promptly requested an interview. Bluntly, he told Germain that if Carleton had permitted use of the Indians the last year,

Canada would not then have been in the hands of the rebels, and he submitted an eleven-page summary of Carleton's obstructive actions. "Without a proper authority the Super-Intendant can be expected to do very little, and without some rank he cannot properly manage or preserve order among his own officers," he declared. Germain was receptive, but he could not yet see his way to removing Campbell, who had so recently been appointed. The best he could do was to confirm Johnson as superintendent for Indian affairs south of Canada, with the rank of colonel. Johnson then offered Claus a renewal of the post of deputy, but at a lower salary than he would accept. Claus decided to remain in England and wait for an improvement in his prospects.[18]

Brant was presented in his Mohawk dress to George III, found him "a finer man than whom I think it wd be a truly difficult task to find," and received from him a watch and a silken banner. On March 14 he had his interview with Germain. "Brother Gorah," he addressed him, "Our late great friend Sr William Johnson who never deceived us," had assured the Mohawks that the king and his ministers would do them justice, "but this notwithstanding all our applications has never been done." Both the government at Albany and private encroachers had cheated them of "the small spots we have left for our women and children to live on." Germain, then deep in plans for an invasion of the Champlain-Hudson valley from Canada, was determined to use the Indians. He replied that the Mohawks "might rest assured, as soon as the troubles were over, every Grievance and Complaint should be Redress'd." Brant, in return, declared that he had not "the least doubt but our brethren the Six Nations will continue firm to their engagements with the King their father."[19]

Londoners were intrigued with the not-so-primitive native of North America who spoke and read English and could bandy subtleties with accomplished diplomats. Viscount George Townshend, master-general of ordnance, gave him a brass rifle. The Falcon Lodge of Masons initiated him into membership, and tradition has it that George III himself handed him his apron. The earl of Warwick commissioned George Romney to paint his portrait, and the finished work, now in the National Gallery of Canada, shows him calm and smooth-faced, with Indian headdress and tomahawk in hand, yet wearing a well-tailored ruffled shirt. James Boswell, meeting him at a subscription ball and taking him for an eminent chief, interviewed him for the *London Magazine* and reported that he promised to recruit three thousand warriors for the king.[20]

Brant was learning sophistication. At a masquerade ball that he attended in full war costume, a nobleman sympathetic to the Americans asked him whether he intended to employ the tomahawk at his side against them, and he imperturbably answered no. Listening to leaders of opposing parties, his old reverence for British authority yielded to a new dedication to the cause of Indian self-determination. The Reverend Stuart, when he next met Brant in America, found him now more a political than a military man—skeptical of people in power and even a questioner of Christian precepts, with a "very high opinion of his own talents" and a conviction that the Indians must form an independent confederacy, at the head of which he "had no doubt but he could place himself."[21]

Early in June, Guy Johnson and Joseph Brant and his tribesman John Hill Oteronyente boarded the brig *Lord Hyde* at Falmouth in a convoy headed for New York. The *Lord Hyde* strayed near Bermuda and fought off a rebel privateer, while Brant used his new rifle to pick off the ship's officers. The voyagers landed at Staten Island on July 29. Johnson's orders were to put his party under General William Howe's command in his campaign up the Hudson to meet the army coming down from Canada. Johnson was to organize a third force, largely from the Six Nations, that would join the other two at Albany. Until then the concerns of the Mohawk Valley would have to wait.[22]

Brant saw action at the Battle of Long Island, but for him that represented only a diversion. Howe chased futilely after George Washington in Jersey and returned to winter quarters in New York, giving up for the year any plan of a push up the Hudson. Brant chafed at the delay. He was also unhappy with Johnson, who would

give him no pay for his services. He asked to return to his people to
rally them to a crusade against the land-grabbing Americans. He had
become a favorite with Howe, who, concerned over the danger of a
journey through rebel territory, reluctantly agreed. Johnson, possibly
to keep Brant under control, delegated Tice to accompany him. Tice,
hitherto a militiaman, was given a captain's rank in Howe's regular
army and entrusted with a fund of one hundred pounds to use as he
saw fit. They set out November 16, disguised as an Oneida and a
militiaman heading home from Washington's army. Traveling often
at night, through rugged country, up the Delaware and over to the
Susquehanna, they arrived within a few days at Oquaga (near the
present Windsor), a village on the Susquehanna where Brant had
settled his family.

Oquaga was an old settlement of mixed Iroquois tribespeople that
served as a way station for north-south Indian migrations. Many
Mohawks who had fled to Canada returned to seek safety there.
Brant's Oneida wife, Susanna, and their two children had left Canajoharie to live on a farm he owned there, with its comfortable house,
fifty acres of cleared land, and an orchard of apple, pear, and peach
trees. Puritan and Anglican missionaries openly proselytized for
American or British allegiance. About seven hundred Indians had
assembled there, and their pro-British sentiment was fueled by resentment at loss of lands to the settlers. Into this milieu Brant plunged
with his call for an Iroquois resurgence under the shield of Britain.
He was an impressive figure, confident and with a self-control that
resisted excess of liquor. He recounted his talks with Germain, his
experiences in England, and his exploits in Howe's campaign at New
York. He conjured all Iroquois to hold fast to the ancient covenant
chain with the king of Britain.[23] As his appeal won supporters, he
saw himself as more than a persuader. He now set about organizing
a military force.

Guns and ammunition were necessary, and he could obtain these
only from the British at Fort Niagara, at the mouth of the Niagara
River where it meets Lake Ontario. He issued a call to the Iroquois
to meet him there for a conference, and with Tice he set out up the

Susquehanna, traveling through the country of the Senecas, whose numbers equaled the other Iroquois tribes combined. They were divided into an eastern wing that had sided with Britain in the French and Indian War and a western wing that had sided with France and had joined Pontiac's uprising against the English in 1763. Brant and Tice passed through the eastern villages of Canadesaga (the present Geneva) at the top of Seneca Lake and Canandaigua at the top of Canandaigua Lake. Westward, they continued to Little Beard's Town (known to the English as Chenussio, the present Cuylerville) on the Genesee River, and thence up to Lake Ontario. Stopping at the smallest settlements, Brant continued his canvass for recruits. The reception was cordial, but he could not obtain a commitment. He had to contend with a second pledge of neutrality that Philip Schuyler had elicited from a grand council of the six Iroquois tribes the previous August at German Flatts, five miles south of the present Herkimer.[24]

They arrived at Niagara on December 28 to find that the commanding officer, John Caldwell, had recently died, and the senior official present was John Butler. He had the previous May organized a force of 200 Indians and 100 troops of the Eighth Regiment, with which he had won a signal victory. In an engagement at the Cedars, a fortification on the St. Lawrence River about forty miles above Montreal, he had captured 300 Americans and a relieving contingent of 120. In his quiet way he had extracted profit from his post at Niagara—he and a merchant, Edward Pollard, together acquired a monopoly of trade with the Loyalists and the Indians there.[25]

He was the perfect public servant, dedicated to a lifetime of obedience to his military superiors. Carleton had directed that the Indians must be restricted to service inside Canada; that meant that forays could not be equipped for the Susquehanna and Mohawk valleys. We have Claus's vitriolic report of Brant's account of his reception by Butler: motivated by "Jealousy & Envy" and attached to Carleton by "flattery & cunning (being bred & born in New England) [Butler originally came from Connecticut]," Butler "in a cold disdainfull Manner told him he could give him nothing without a written order from Authority."[26]

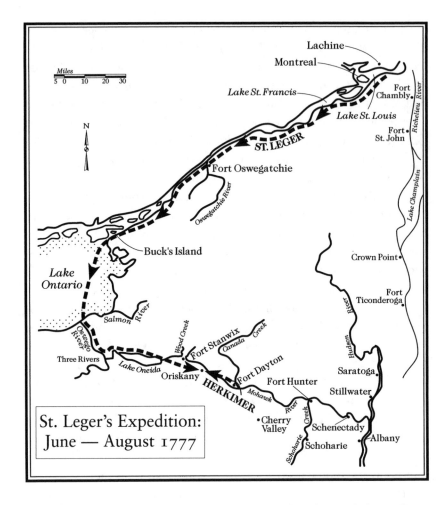

St. Leger's Expedition:
June — August 1777

It did not help that Tice sided with Butler and urged the Indians
to support him. Brant invoked the feared name of the king in censure
of the "notorious" Oneidas and Tuscaroras and warned that Sir
William Howe's army would already have seized the Hudson River
if Albany had contained enough houses to quarter his troops. Several
Indians replied that apparently the king had no need of the Indians
to subdue the Americans. Brant decided that he must carry his message back to the home villages of the Six Nations and campaign to

raise a force unbeholden to Carleton and free to "make war our own way."[27]

During the next few months, he ranged through the entire territory of the Six Nations. The tribes were still divided among themselves. Even the Onondagas, the very symbol of Iroquois unity, remained split. Centrally positioned on the west side of Onondaga Creek, a southern feeder of Onondaga Lake, they were the Fire Keepers and guardian of the Grand Council meetings of the League. They had pro-British, pro-American, and neutral factions. The Cayugas, equal in number to the Mohawks and the Onondagas and residing between Cayuga and Owasco lakes, attempted a precarious neutrality. Although the Oneidas, led by Chief Shenandoah, clung to their Patriot pastor, Samuel Kirkland, their traditional sachems, under Chief Cornelius, continued to be pro-British. Allied to the pro-American Oneidas were the Tuscaroras, some living in a village west of the Oneidas and others in several villages near the Susquehanna, but a minority under Sagwaritha joined the British. Brant had scant success. His hearers stayed largely noncommittal; in the case of the Oneidas they were downright hostile—they refused even to come and meet with him.[28]

He returned to Oquaga, to his Mohawks and to a burgeoning cadre of Loyalists who called themselves "Brant's Volunteers." He levied tribute of cattle, horses, and foodstuffs from the nearby village of Unadilla, at the junction of the Unadilla River with the Susquehanna, and he warned the settlers to declare for the king or leave the county. Real or pretended Loyalists sought safety by posting at their doors the sign of their allegiance, the skull bone of a horse mounted on a stake. Rebel settlers were fearful about where Brant might strike next. From his base at Oquaga, natural geographical pathways led northward up the valley of the Unadilla to German Flatts on the Mohawk, through the valley of the Susquehanna to Lake Otsego and Cherry Valley, and through the valleys of the Charlotte River and Schenerus Creek to the Schoharie valley. A scattering of small forts, some of which were shored-up private homes, could do little more than provide temporary refuge, and the alarmed Tryon County Committee of Safety appealed to the state Committee of Safety for protection.

Schuyler could spare only a force of 150 Continentals under Colonel Gosen (Goose) Van Schaick, and he sent Tryon County militia General Nicholas Herkimer to negotiate with Brant. They knew each other as neighbors. They met near Unadilla toward the end of June 1777, Herkimer with a force of 380 to Brant's 137. In a tense confrontation, a clash was narrowly averted. Despite Herkimer's numerical superiority, Brant remained recalcitrant. Herkimer sensed that he really had no trumps to play. The Indians, for a century, had been dependent for their subsistence on the side that gave them guns, knives, pots, pans, and clothes. The Americans, Brant scoffed, were "not able to afford to put a shirt on their backs." Rather than escalate the hostility, Herkimer conceded to Brant's demands for greater freedom of movement for Mohawks and Tories.[29]

Carleton's policy of Indian restraint vanished May 6, 1777. He received that day a letter from Germain, dated March 26, which dealt a humiliating blow to his personal authority. An invading army under John Burgoyne, not Carleton, was to descend from Canada along the Champlain-Hudson valley to Albany, there to join up with a northward army under Howe, thus sealing off New England from the other states and allowing their piecemeal conquest. Burgoyne's army would include 7,173 British regulars, 3,116 German mercenaries, and "as many Canadians and Indians as may be thought necessary."

To the west, an auxiliary force under Lieutenant Colonel Barrimore (Barry) Matthew St. Leger would sweep around Lake Ontario and Lake Oneida and back eastward to meet Burgoyne's and Howe's armies at Albany. On the way, St. Leger's key target was to be Fort Stanwix, which controlled the strategic portage between Lake Oneida and the Mohawk River, known as the Oneida Carrying Place. His force would consist of 200 British regulars (100 each from the Thirty-fourth and Eighth regiments stationed in Canada), Sir John Johnson's

Loyalist regiment of 133, a Hessian corps of 342 *Jäger*, and "a sufficient number of Canadians and Indians."

Stanwix, situated at the site of the present Rome, New York, was the last outpost at the gateway to the rich potential farmlands of western New York State and to the gap in the Appalachian Mountains that led into the future states of Ohio, Indiana, and Illinois. Some one hundred miles west and a little north of Albany, it stood six hundred feet off the west bank of the Mohawk River, slightly less than thirty miles beyond German Flatts, the farthest frontier settlement. St. Leger, forty-four years old, had served with distinction under Wolfe at Quebec, retired to England at half pay, and then returned with Burgoyne to Canada in 1776 as commander of the Thirty-fourth Regiment. His force was going to require a majority of Indians, yet he had little experience in dealing with them. The commander of the French Canadians who served under him wrote that he alienated his men by "the little consideration that he had for them" and drank to drunkenness, which was "nearly continual."[30]

On June 6 Butler received orders from Carleton to collect as many of the Six Nations as possible to join St. Leger at Oswego about the end of July. He obeyed the new policy with the same fidelity as he had the old. He met with the chiefs and sachems then at Niagara and obtained their support for a grand council at Oswego. There they would rendezvous with Sir John Johnson's Royal Greens and a company of Hanau *Jäger*. He informed Carleton that he was ready and willing to take the field, and he authorized his son, Walter, to raise an independent company of rangers to act with the Indians.[31]

The first essential was to get the Senecas to abandon their neutrality. Many of them had already gathered at Niagara, and Butler chose Irondequoit (near the present Rochester), midway to Oswego, as a stopping place at which to confer presents and exercise persuasion. During a week of councils, he brought out a "flood of rum" and feasts of roasted cattle. See the magnificence of the king, he urged; take up the hatchet against the disobedient rebels. The Senecas adjourned to deliberate among themselves. They were still determined to honor their treaty of neutrality with the Americans. Cornplanter

(Gayentwahga), head of the western Senecas, warned that "war is war, death is death, a fight is hard business." Butler called them back. He painted a picture of British omnipotence. The king's rum, he said, was "as plenty as the water in lake Ontario." His men were "as numerous as the sand upon the lake shore." The Indians "should never want for money or goods." While they debated, a vessel arrived at Irondequoit with a cargo that displayed, to the wonderment of the watching Indians, "Many good things that they never did see before." They met again. Butler produced two wampum belts, one with twenty rows of beads that embodied the Great Old Covenant Chain of the ancient alliance of the Iroquois with the British. With more drinking and more presents, their resolve weakened. They took hold of the hatchet and promised "to make good use of it." They chose two hereditary war chiefs for the campaign. Old Smoke (Sayenqueraghta), almost seventy, over six feet tall and portly, a renowned warrior and orator, was head of the eastern Senecas. His name, originally meaning "morning mist," came to denote his position as the bearer of the smoking brand, the sole custodian of the council fire of all the Senecas. He was "the only Crowned head in America," the inheritor of a crown his ancestors had received from Queen Anne. Cornplanter (also known as John O'Bail, son of an English or Dutch trader and a Seneca mother), although only twenty-five, had already shown himself coolheaded and prudent. The next day each warrior received a fresh outfit of clothes, a brass kettle, a rifle with a supply of powder and lead, a tomahawk and a scalping knife, and a gold coin. They would receive more money for each scalp bought in.

After such a reluctant commitment, there was a report, possibly circulated by Cornplanter's adherents, that the British had said they "did not wish to have them fight, but wanted to have them just sit down, smoke their pipes, and look on." No sooner had the councils been concluded than Butler received from St. Leger an order to send 150 warriors for an advance strike against Stanwix. The next morning, July 20, the war party departed on its mission.[32]

CHAPTER 2

✦ ✦ ✦ ✦ ✦ ✦ ✦ ✦ ✦ ✦ ✦

"Blood over
the Earth"

George Germain was determined that Indians would be used in the war in America. His own reliable appointee, Major John Campbell, was going to lead them in Burgoyne's Champlain-Hudson invasion. He did not feel so certain of Butler, Carleton's man, in the expedition against Fort Stanwix.

Convenient in London was Daniel Claus, a derogator of Carleton, an outspoken advocate of Indian employment, and a supplicant in search of a job. Germain's under-secretary of state, William Knox, approached him. The Stanwix expedition, he said, would be headed by Sir John Johnson, Claus's brother-in-law; Claus could serve under him as superintendent of the Indian contingent. Claus demurred, fearing to function under Carleton's unfriendly eye. Knox replied that upon the certain success of the union of Burgoyne's and Howe's armies, he would find himself under Howe's command. Claus attempted to bargain, requesting army promotion to major. This Knox refused. At last Claus agreed, in truth eager for the position. On February 19, a week before the final instructions were issued for the Burgoyne campaign, Germain wrote to Carleton, appointing Claus, at his old yearly salary of two hundred pounds, to serve in a "secondary expedition" where "the assistance of the Indians will also be highly necessary."[1] Claus did not discover until later that the commander of the expedition was not to be Johnson but, at Burgoyne's request, Colonel Barry St. Leger, who had served with him the previous year in the expedition from Canada, which had gotten only so far as Ticonderoga and turned back.

During the first week in April, Claus departed from Cork for Quebec aboard the *British Queen,* a sixteen-gun warship in a convoy of nine transports, and arrived June 1. Accompanied by Tice, he had his interview with Carleton at Montreal and met with instant hostility. Carleton would not even directly acknowledge Claus's appointment, but merely turned to Tice to inform him that he and the Indians of St. Leger's expedition were now responsible to Claus. Rather than grant him authority to purchase Indian goods, he referred him to Butler. They differed over strategy. Carleton regarded the St. Leger campaign as a foregone capture of a weak fort that Butler had reported as a picket enclosure manned by only sixty defenders. Claus thought Fort Stanwix far more formidable, and he dispatched a reconnoitering party of Captain John Hare and a group of Mohawk scouts from Oswegatchie (the present Ogdensburg) under Chief John Deserontyon. Ignoring orders, he purchased supplies out of his own funds. Finding Sir John Johnson and his regiment camped at the village of Lachine on the island of Montreal, on June 23 he set out with them up the St. Lawrence River to join St. Leger's gathering troops at Buck's Island (now Carleton Island), about five miles above Lake Ontario, a journey of 180 miles.[2]

Outside of Montreal, he stopped at an Indian town, Cassasseny, to appeal for recruits from a group of pro-British Algonquin Mississaugas (Eagle tribe of the Ojibwa, or Chippewa nation) and Iroquois. A half-breed Oneida sachem, Thomas Spencer, spying for the Patriots, hid in the upper floor of the council house and watched. Strutting before his listeners, Claus playacted the conquering commander. Spencer, with some language difficulty, reported the speech: "Ticonderoga is mine. This is true, you may depend on, and not one Shot shall be fired for. The same is with Fort Schuyler, I am Sure, said Col. Claus, that when I come towards that Fort and the Commanding officer there shall see me, he shall also not fire one Shot, and render the Fort to me." The warriors apparently approved the flamboyance, and 150 of them joined the expedition.[3] When St. Leger, as yet some fifty miles to the rear, learned of the recruitment, he felt emboldened. He was willing to accept at face value Butler's report of the weakly defended Fort Stanwix, and expecting an easy victory, he impulsively decided that he would lead the Indians in an advance force for a quick strike. Claus could not convince him otherwise, and himself could only continue with Johnson.

Once past Lake St. Louis, Johnson's regiment had to surmount an eleven-mile stretch of rapids with a fall of eighty-four feet. Beyond Lake St. Francis came the still rougher swells, the nine miles of the Long Sault Rapids, where, a French officer had earlier observed, "the water boils like the sea in a storm." As they neared Lake Ontario, now among the quiet "Thousand Islands," they met Captain Hare, returning from Fort Stanwix with five prisoners and four scalps. On July 3, they had surprised a work party of seventeen three-quarters of a mile outside the fort's walls. The prisoners reported that the fort was a square, strongly constructed enclosure manned by six hundred defenders already alerted to the coming and the size of the approaching British.[4]

St. Leger's two regiments and the newly arrived company of about fifty Hessian *Jäger* commanded by Lieutenant Hildebrand joined Johnson's regiment at Buck's Island July 8. There, on July 12, St. Leger issued for the first time, in general orders, the appointment of Claus as "Superintendent of the Indian Department in this Expedition." Once more, Claus attempted to dissuade him from his advance attack, pointing out that the separate accounts of the prisoners agreed that Stanwix was formidable. Not dissuaded, St. Leger did dispatch to Butler a requisition for a reinforcement of 150 warriors. Planning to meet them on the way, he departed with his detachment on July 19, leaving orders for the British and German forces to proceed to Oswego.

If he would not listen to Claus, the Indians with whom he was marching would be heard. Whatever it was that they had understood from Claus's harangue at Cassasseny, it had not prepared them for strong resistance. St. Leger distributed a quart of rum apiece, which produced a havoc of inebriation but not compliance. When they reached the Salmon River, fifty miles from Stanwix, they adamantly refused to proceed further. He had no choice. He turned westward and joined Johnson, Claus, and the rest of his force at Oswego July 25. But he still would not let go of the project of an advance force. He dispatched Lieutenant Henry Bird with a detachment of thirty men from the King's Regiment and an unnumbered band of Indians, with orders to clear Wood Creek for transport of cannon to Stanwix and seal off the fort from reinforcements and supplies.

Brant had just arrived at Oswego with three hundred needy warriors. Claus equipped them with the supplies he had purchased and others Butler had stored there. Butler and the Senecas from Niagara and some Indians from Detroit also arrived. He was mortified to find himself demoted to Claus's assistant, "the success of all my labours conferred upon another," he wrote Carleton. He had planned another council and had laid up a large supply of rum in preparation. Claus disapproved of these methods. He canceled the meeting, concealed the rum, and admonished Butler that "Indians on a march upon the Enemy could or did not expect formal Meetings & councelling." He later charged that the Senecas were so incensed against Butler as "to be ready to massacre him." Tempers mounted. Claus denounced Carleton, relating criticism he had heard of him in London over his failure to capture Benedict Arnold's fleeing army in Canada in 1776. He sent a censorious report on Butler to the Foreign Office in London, charging that Butler had so confused the Indians that they "declared publicly that they were not called to war, but to a Congress to be held at Oswego, and receive presents."

Brant proved a major asset in winning over the Senecas. He confronted Cornplanter and flatly accused him of being a "very coward man." The watching warriors, shamed to be labeled likewise, declared for the British. One by one, first Brant for the Mohawks, then the chiefs of the Senecas, the Cayugas, and even of the sparsely represented Oneidas and Tuscaroras came forward and accepted the war belt.

St. Leger was anxious to get started for Stanwix, and he set out

July 26. Claus went with him, taking along Brant and his warriors. In order to speed the arrival of the Iroquois coming from the south, Claus sent messages for them to assemble at Three Rivers, twenty-three miles south of Oswego, at the juncture of the Oneida, Seneca, and Oswego rivers. And he instructed Butler, "in the strongest Manner," to meet them there with the Indians he had brought from Niagara, equip them, and hurry them to St. Leger's corps.[5]

If St. Leger had brought sufficient artillery with him, Fort Stanwix could not have held out. Situated on a stony plateau within sight eastward of the Mohawk and northwestward of Wood Creek, the outlet of Lake Oneida, the original fort had been erected by the British in 1758 as a shield against the French, but it was afterward allowed to decay. A fire in 1774 destroyed the barracks. By 1776, with the British now the menace from the north, Congress ordered the fort rebuilt. Under a succession of commanders and engineers, progress had been erratic. Yet, though incomplete, the structure remained formidable. It was of log construction, with an outer wall of sod, measuring 350 feet on three sides and a little less on the east, with a pentagonal bastion projecting from each corner. Surrounding it was a forty-foot-wide ditch palisaded by a six-to-seven-foot-high picket fence. The American armament consisted, however, only of thirteen cannon, including three nine-pounders (one-mile range), four six-pounders (one-half-mile range), a few three-pounders (one-fourth-mile range), and four 4-2/5 caliber Royal mortars. Against this defense, St. Leger brought a meager artillery of two six-pounders, two three-pounders, and four 4-2/5 Royal mortars.[6]

Manning the fort were about five-hundred-odd Continentals of the Third New York and Ninth Massachusetts regiments, commanded by Colonel Peter Gansevoort. Twenty-eight years old and a member of a prominent Albany family, he had served in Montgomery's invasion of Canada, but with only limited experience as a commander. Because he was popular with his officers, many from his old regiment had chosen to go with him when he rose to colonel of the Third

Regiment. A handsome, heavyset man over six feet in height, methodical and efficient, he would relax with music lessons from an instructor in the regiment.

As early as May, reports from Indian scouts brought word of St. Leger's expedition. Although the fort's housing was so inadequate that many enlisted men slept on floors, Gansevoort called for reinforcements for work outside the fort—felling timber to obstruct an attack from Wood Creek, clearing the thirty-mile road from Fort Dayton (the present Herkimer) to open the way for communication with the Americans there, and providing scouting parties. Schuyler could not spare Continentals from the army resisting Burgoyne. He ordered Nicholas Herkimer to supply two hundred men from his militia brigade.

Panic, however, had swept the countryside. Only a few of Herkimer's men would consent to march to Stanwix, and those were obligated to serve for no more than fourteen days. News of the loss of Fort Ticonderoga had deepened despair. "Some declare publickly," Herkimer wrote Schuyler, "that if the Enemy shall come, they would not leave home, but stay with their Families, and render themselves over to the Enemy."[7]

Bird's detachment proved futile. Most of its Indians refused to advance upon the fort, and when St. Leger dispatched Brant with a reinforcement of two hundred more Indians, they were too few and too late. They did not prevent the arrival of two hundred Continentals from Fort Dayton, by way of Wood Creek, bringing the rebels four bateaux with much needed ammunition and provisions. Gansevoort's defenders now numbered more than seven hundred.[8]

The main British force arrived before the fort on the morning of August 3, 1777. The cannon had not yet come up, stalled while the trees were being removed from Wood Creek and from the road connecting Oneida Lake and the Carrying Place (the "Trow Plat" of the Dutch and the "De-o-wain-sta" of the Indians). Work crews from the fort continued to labor in the open on the uncompleted parapet with little interference from enemy sharpshooters. Nevertheless, without artillery and without the Senecas, who had not yet arrived from Three Rivers, St. Leger quixotically thought he could unnerve the garrison into surrender. He reissued under his own name a pretentious proclamation with which Burgoyne, at Lake Champlain, had seven weeks earlier vainly attempted to intimidate resistors on his path to Albany. At three o'clock in the afternoon, Captain Tice appeared before the fort under a flag of truce, bearing the manifesto. If the Americans did not surrender, it warned, they would be punished with "devastation, famine, and every concomitant horror." He was handed a curt refusal to take back.[9]

St. Leger now had to face up to an extended siege. The British and Hessian regulars camped six hundred yards northeast of the fort, in a ravine above the Mohawk. Sir John Johnson's Royal Greens settled six hundred yards south of the fort, on the west bank of the Mohawk. The Indians camped a mile to the east, at the Lower Landing Place, below the bend of the Mohawk. Butler arrived the following afternoon from Three Rivers with two hundred Senecas and some Wyandots, Ottawas, Potawatomis, and Chippewas from Detroit. This brought the total number of Indians to about eight hundred. They dispersed in small groups in the woods around the fort, setting fire to a barracks building that had unaccountably been erected a hundred yards outside the fort, and keeping up a continuous fire that killed one of the men working on the parapets and wounded seven others. Chilling war whoops echoed through the night. Meanwhile, fifty Canadian militiamen under Captain Jean-Baptiste-Melchior Hertel de Rouville and sixty Loyalists under Herkimer's brother, Lieutenant Johan Jost Herkimer, labored in the heat and the rain to remove the felled trees impeding Wood Creek. Another detail of regulars under Lieutenant James Lundy, the quartermaster, worked to clear the wagon road connecting the Carrying Place and Oneida Lake and cut a trail around the clogged portion of the creek. The artillery did not get through until four days after the siege began, and then the few shells lobbed into the fort by the light cannon under Lieutenant James Glennie proved completely inadequate.[10]

*

As late as July, the reality of the British invasion had not taken root in Tryon County. Frederick F. Helmer, a Tryon County committee-man from German Flatts and Kingsland, determined to check with the Oneidas for himself. Taking with him a companion, Melchior Folts, and an Indian interpreter, Thomas Follmer, he journeyed to Oneida and there, on July 15, conferred with the Oneida chief, Thomas Spencer. Spencer, who had just returned five days previously from his listening post at Caughnawaga, informed him that Sir John Johnson and Colonel Claus had seven hundred Indians, four hundred British army regulars, and six hundred Tories camped at Carleton Island, preparing to march on Stanwix and thence to Albany. At Oswego they were to join Colonel Butler, who had called the Five Nations to meet him there and take up the hatchet against the Amer-icans.

On July 17, Helmer delivered his information to the committee. At the same meeting, the committee was informed by Major Stephen Badlam, from Fort Dayton, that no help could be expected from his Continental troops there. (He did, nevertheless, lead the relief contin-gent of two hundred to Stanwix two weeks later.) The committee immediately authorized Herkimer to issue a new call to the militia, with a threat of punishment to the footdraggers. Herkimer promptly posted a proclamation, ordering "every male person, being in health, from 16 to 60 years of age," to repair "with arms and accoutre-ments," to Fort Dayton to prepare to proceed to the aid of Stanwix. The response this time was encouraging, except from Schoharie and Schenectady. The local militia there were needed to protect the settle-ments against a threatening force of one hundred Loyalists under John Macdonell and Adam Crysler, and twenty-five Indians under a Schoharie tribe chief, Seth Henry.

At three o'clock in the afternoon of July 27, two hundred yards from Fort Stanwix, three girls were picking blackberries when four Indians shot them from concealment. Two of the girls were killed, tomahawked, and scalped. The third escaped with two bullets through her shoulder. One of the dead was the daughter of a disabled retired British artilleryman. Plain to see, the Indians would not spare the settlers regardless of which side they took. With this lesson starkly in mind, the Tryon County Committee of Safety received on July 30 another communication from Thomas Spencer, announcing the imminent appearance of St. Leger's army at Fort Stanwix. It would certainly arrive August 4, and probably earlier. "Let the militia rise up," Spencer urged, and do not "make a Ticonderoga of it."[11]

Indecision vanished. The members of the committee themselves enlisted. A formidable total of 760 farmers and tradesmen assembled. Colonel Ebenezer Cox headed the Canajoharie district regiment, Colonel Peter Bellinger the Kingsland and German Flatts regiment, Colonel Jacob Klock the Palatine regiment, and Colonel Frederick Visscher the Mohawk regiment.

On August 4, the march to Stanwix began. The impromptu soldiers, dressed in their everyday homespun, untrained and undisciplined, encumbered with fifteen supply wagons and oxcarts, trudged twelve miles along the north shore of the Mohawk, and that evening they camped west of Stirling Creek. From the start, there was disagreement between the colonels and Herkimer. They upbraided him for having backed down to Brant at Unadilla and distrusted him for the Loyalism of his brother, Johan Jost, and his brother-in-law, Peter Ten Broeck. A dispute arose over which road to take. One ran along the high north shore of the Mohawk and then recrossed at the fort. A second, across the river from Old Fort Schuyler (the present Utica), extended along the low-lying, swampy south side (approximately the present Route 5S, leading to Route 69). The colonels favored the northern route. Herkimer chose the southern, in order to avoid fording the river under fire of the enemy surrounding the fort. It was an uneasy truce.[12]

On the morning of August 5, the militia resumed their trek and crossed the river at Old Fort Schuyler. After a day's march of another ten miles, they bivouacked along two miles between the Sauquoit and Oriskany creeks, eight miles from Stanwix. Here they were joined by a party of some sixty Oneidas led by chiefs Honeyery Doxtater (Thawengarakwen), Henry Cornelius (Haunnagwasuke), and the dependable Thomas Spencer. Herkimer now judged that he must pause

and make contact with the fort. He deputed Adam Helmer and two
scouts with a message to Gansevoort, requesting him to fire three
cannon shots as a signal that communication had been achieved and
to send assistance at the sound of gunfire. Herkimer would then
advance.

The morning of August 6 came and there was no sound from the
fort. The scouts had not yet gotten through to deliver their message.
Herkimer called a council of war. He wished to wait for the cannon
signals, but the scornful colonels, headed by Cox and Visscher, demanded advance. Cox, earlier at Unadilla, had clashed with Herkimer by insulting Brant and almost precipitating a clash with the
Indians that Herkimer barely averted. The colonels accused Herkimer
of Tory disloyalty, and even cowardice. He could not resist. He
started the men forward.[13]

Horse skull bones disappeared from Tryon County doorways. No
Loyalist dared venture, at the risk of rebel detection, into the British
camp to warn of Herkimer's approach. Only unyielding Molly Brant,
obstinately persisting on the lands at Canajoharie deeded to her by
Sir William, boldly sent a messenger to her brother at Stanwix with
word of the gathering of the militia. It confirmed what the expedition's scouts had surmised.

St. Leger recognized that he stood in danger of being caught in a
pincers movement of "a sally from the garrison in the rear, while the
reinforcement employed me in front." Since most of his regulars were
engaged in road duty, he could spare only eighty of those still in
camp, and he had to rely mainly on a contingent of four hundred
Indians to intercept Herkimer. Brant's Mohawks were included, but
the Senecas predominated, and they took their orders from Old
Smoke and Cornplanter. Overall leadership of the Indians was in
dispute, for Butler challenged Claus's appointment and demanded a
confirmation of it from St. Leger. He replied with the admonition
that Butler cooperate with Claus "in carrying on the business of this
Campaign, by an Union of your Interests, and by that harmony I am
confident will subsist from the Opinions and Sentiments you have

severally expressed of each other." In a temporary truce, Butler took charge of the Indian detachment while Claus remained in camp. Sir John Johnson, at the head of fifty of his Royal Greens, volunteered to lead the entire force.[14]

At first the Senecas hung back, arguing that the militia was not really committed to the rebel cause and might be induced to come over to the British side. Brant scorned this as a delusion. Some questioned whether Herkimer's force was too large to overcome. Brant sent out a party to a spot a mile west of Oriskany, thirty feet from the road the militia were taking. A hole was dug for a scout, covered from view with hemlock brush, who counted Herkimer's corps as it passed. The news of the numbers he brought back did not faze Brant. He denounced the Senecas' footdragging and declared that he and his followers would go it alone. As good as his word, Brant, with Sir John Johnson and 280 men, broke camp at dawn while the shamed Senecas watched. Fifteen minutes later they followed. It was a fateful decision, a Seneca warrior named Blacksnake (Thewonyas, or boys betting) recalled years later, to shed "Blood over the Earth."[15]

The road to Stanwix offered itself to ambush. Five miles east of the fort it crossed a swamp in a 150-foot-deep, 500-foot-wide ravine. Overlooking the road's narrow, wooden causeway, the ravine afforded easy concealment in a thickly wooded, tangled mass of underbrush, rotting tree trunks, and fallen branches. In the flats beyond, there was easy hiding in the tall grass, cattails, and calamus. The ambuscade positioned the Royal New Yorkers at the western end of the ravine to meet the militia vanguard, while the Indians waited at both sides of the road at the eastern end to seal off Herkimer's rear.

With the taunts of his colonels still in his ears, Herkimer plunged on without a stop. The Oneida flank guards did not have the time or the visibility to detect the enemy lying in wait. Astride his white horse, he rode in the van with Cox and his regiment; Bellinger's and Klock's were behind, then the train of supply wagons, and Visscher's brought up the rear. They reached the ravine a little after nine o'clock. Down into the hemlock-darkened swamp snaked the procession, over the bridge across the stream at the bottom, and up the western slope of the ravine. About ten o'clock, the van reached the plateau at the top, while Visscher's men had not yet entered the ravine.

The terrifying war cry of the Senecas rang out, and a fusillade raked the ranks of the startled militia. Herkimer ordered Cox to form his regiment in a defensive line. But Cox was killed immediately after, and his men, each for himself, sought cover behind trees. A bullet struck Herkimer six inches below his knee, shattering the bone and also killing his horse under him. The Indians poured down in a melee of swinging bayonets, knives, tomahawks, spears, and clubbed muskets. "The impetuosity of the Indians is not to be described," St. Leger wrote; "they rushed in hatchet in hand and thereby gave the enemy's rear an opportunity to escape." The entrance to the ravine at the east was blocked, and Visscher's men, oblivious to his attempts to hold them (he had a narrow escape when a bullet drew blood from the nape of his neck and tore off a part of his auburn queue), turned and ran, pursued by Brant's warriors, in many cases to be caught and tomahawked.

One report described the scene as a carnage of "mangled Limbs" and "dieing Groans." A wounded Palatine rebel, George Walter, crept out in the open to slake his thirst at a spring and was tomahawked and his scalp torn off, but he lived. "Dat Indian tot I vash tot, but I knows petter," he afterward said. "I tot I would say nodding, so as he would go off." Molly Brant's son, William Johnson, attempting to crawl away with a broken leg, was discovered by a militia captain, an acquaintance, himself wounded in the right arm. Brandishing a sword in his left, he cried out, "One of us must die!" and thrust into him, but Johnson survived. Indian fought Indian. An Oneida sachem, Captain Honyery Doxtater, was wounded in the right wrist while his wife, Dolly Cobus, at his side, reloaded his rifle and fired her own. Thomas Spencer was killed.[16]

Herkimer was carried to a vantage point above the west bank, a little north of the center of the ravine. As he sat on the saddle unstrapped from his dead horse, propped up against a beech tree, his knee was bandaged by Dr. William Petrie. Between puffs on his pipe, reportedly with a pistol in one hand and a sword in the other, he directed the men to fight in pairs, so as to prevent lone militiamen from being tomahawked while reloading. After the initial confusion, Herkimer formed the 150-odd survivors into a compact body on the plateau on the ravine's western side, behind the shelter of a pine thicket and fallen trees. Good shots and resourceful woodsmen, they fought off the Senecas.

Johnson's Greens, led by Johnson's brother-in-law, Major Stephen Watts, launched a bayonet charge that the militia at first took to be a reinforcement from the fort. When they recognized their former Tryon County neighbors, the contest became a savagery of white against white. Fighting hand-to-hand, some throttled each other with their bare hands or stabbed each other with their hunting knives. Watts was wounded and left for dead on the field but two days later was found alive and brought into the British camp.

Three interminable hours passed. Then, just when the attackers were preparing for a final assault, a drenching thunderstorm burst on the valley, bringing the struggle to a halt. The delay proved the militia's salvation. By the time the storm cleared, Hellmer had gotten through to the fort, and Gansevoort had sent out a sortie under his second in command, Lieutenant Colonel Marinus Willett, against the sparsely defended Indian camps. When the Indians facing Herkimer's men learned of the danger to their possessions, they abandoned their ambuscade and returned to their camps. The surviving militia made no attempt to continue the relief mission to the fort. Led now by Majors Samuel Campbell and Samuel Clyde of Cherry Valley, carrying their wounded, they limped back to Old Fort Schuyler and to the refuge of their homes.[17]

Willett's sortie was a skillfully delivered stroke. With 250 Continentals and one three-pound field piece, he emerged from the fort about two o'clock and, without the loss of a single soldier, in two hours returned in complete triumph:

> We totally routed two of the enemy's encampments [he reported], destroyed all provisions that was in them, brought off upwards of fifty brass kettles, and more than a hundred blankets . . . , with a number

of muskets, tomahawks, spears, ammunition, clothing, deer-skins, a variety of Indian affairs, and five colors which, on our return to the fort, were displayed on our flag-staff under the Continental flag.[18]

Among the effects seized were the scalps of the two girls killed on July 27 and papers of Sir John Johnson and St. Leger. On his return trip, Willett encountered a small group of British regulars and Indians in a thicket near where he had positioned his cannon. When the artillery from the fort also opened on them, they dispersed, leaving four prisoners in Patriot hands.

According to the best estimates, the Patriots lost 200 killed, in some cases several in a family—among them an assemblyman, Captain Jacob Snell, and six other Snells. Since the militia could not stop to retrieve all their wounded, many were killed, as Butler reported, "conformable to the Indian custom." The militia did save 155 wounded. At Old Fort Schuyler, Herkimer was carried to a boat and rowed down the Mohawk sixteen miles to his mansion, two miles east of Little Falls. There his leg was amputated above the knee, but he sensed that the primitive surgery would not save him. "I guess you boys will have to take up that leg and bury it with me," he said, looking out at the diggers in his garden, "for I am going to follow it"; he died soon after.

Probably forty-five militiamen, among them a state senator, Isaac Paris, were captured. The morning following the battle, four officers were forced to run the gauntlet and then clubbed to death. According to a fellow captive, Paris, whose son had been killed, was "kicked and abused" by some Loyalists and then turned over to the Indians, who tortured him "barbarously." Although other prisoners also suffered, most survived and were ransomed to the British at Montreal or Quebec. Brant maintained that he captured a man on the field at Oriskany and safeguarded him to his home a mile away.[19]

The British white troops lost five officers and six privates dead and probably an equal number of wounded, a heavy toll considering the small force involved in the battle. Of the approximately 450 Indians, 33 were killed, including 9 chiefs, and 32 wounded. At least 6 of the slain chiefs were Senecas, including Old Smoke's son, Tocenando.

No record exists of Indians captured, a testament, perhaps, to the ruthlessness of the rebels.[20]

In the Iroquois value system, the slaying of the nine chiefs was an infuriating affront that required revenge. The morning after the battle, Old Smoke and Brant proposed to Claus and Johnson that a raid be immediately launched into the demoralized backcountry. St. Leger refused. He met with the chiefs and informed them that he could not spare troops from the siege. He feared atrocities against women and children. He offered them a recompense—once the fort surrendered, they might have a free hand in looting its public supplies. They accepted, on condition that Butler be sent into the fort with an explicit warning that continued hostilities would provoke a blood-bath of retribution.[21]

It seemed that St. Leger found himself in thrall to the demands of the chiefs. Conforming to his agreement with them, on the afternoon of August 8 a roll of drums from the British announced the raising of a white flag with a request that Butler and two officers be admitted to the fort to convey a message to Gansevoort. They were blindfolded and conducted to a dining room that was shuttered and lit by candles. They were seated at one end of a table, facing Gansevoort and two of his officers at the other end. Gathered around were the fort's staff of officers, assembled for all to witness. Wine and cheese were passed around, and then St. Leger's adjutant general, Captain Edward Ancram, began: If the garrison's officers and soldiers and supplies would be delivered up without further resistance, the Indians would pledge that they might keep their personal possessions and "not a hair of the head of any of them shall be hurt." Turning to Butler to confirm this veiled threat of scalping, he asked, "That, I think, was the expression they made use of, was it not?" Butler agreed. Then, if Gansevoort should have missed the point, Ancram bluntly concluded: "Indeed the Indians are so exceedingly provoked, and mortified by the losses they have sustained, in the late actions, having had several of their favorite chiefs killed, that they threaten,—and the Colonel, if the present arrangements should not be entered into, will not be able to prevent them from executing their threats,—to march down the country, and destroy the settlement, with its inhabitants. In this case, not only men, but women and children, will experience the sad effects of their vengeance."

Gansevoort refused personally to reply to an unwritten communication from an adjutant, and Willett, in his stead, delivered a blistering rejoinder:

> You have made a long speech on the occasion of your visit, which, stript of all its superfluities, amounts to this, that you come from a British colonel, to the commandant of this garrison, to tell him, that if he does not deliver up the garrison into the hands of your Colonel, he will send his Indians to murder our women and children. . . . I consider the message you have brought, a degrading one for a British officer to carry. For my part, I declare, before I would consent to deliver this garrison to such a murdering set as your army, by your own account, consists of, I would suffer my body to be filled with splinters, and set on fire, as you know has at times been practised, by such hordes of women and children killers, as belong to your army.[22]

The watching garrison officers applauded. Ancram, seeing that no agreement was forthcoming, then requested a cease-fire of three days. This could provide the British the time for a cadre being organized by Butler's son, Walter, to recruit Loyalists in the countryside, possibly as a counterweight to the Indian numbers. Gansevoort would agree only until nine o'clock the next morning, when he would send his response in writing. He was playing for safe passage for a planned attempt by Willett to set out for the settlements down the river and make a renewed effort for reinforcements.

In the morning, playing for more time, Gansevoort requested a statement from St. Leger in writing before he would reply. St. Leger's letter soon arrived. Ostensibly a peremptory demand for total surrender, it was an abject recitation of his powerlessness in the face of the Indians' belligerence:

> I expect an immediate answer, as the Indians are extremely impatient; and if this proposal is rejected, I am afraid it will be attended with

very fatal consequences, not only to you and your garrison, but the whole country down the Mohawk River—such consequences as will be very repugnant to my sentiments of humanity, but after this, entirely out of my power to prevent.

Gansevoort's response was a curt note: "I say, that it is my determined resolution, with the forces under my command, to defend this fort and garrison to the last extremity." To his officers he declared that he would "eat the leather of his shoes before he gives up."[23]

For all of Gansevoort's bravado, the British threat was very real. The fort's magazine of ammunition was dangerously low, and food spoilage had seriously reduced the store of salted provisions. Gansevoort complained to Horatio Gates that he was "only Supply'd from hand to mouth."[24] Unless reinforcements arrived, the garrison might be starved into surrender. At a meeting of the fort's officers it was decided that, despite the repulse at Oriskany, a second attempt must be made to obtain succor from the militia. Willett, who had proved popular with the militia, should get out into the country and attempt to organize a fresh relief expedition.

At one o'clock in the morning of August 9, Willett and one companion, Lieutenant Levi Stockwell, an experienced woodsman, stole out through the sally port of the fort, carrying no baggage or blankets, with some crackers and cheese in their pockets and a canteen of spirits. Traveling zigzag to avoid detection, they spent a cold night on the ground, which the next day gave Willett a rheumatic limp for several hours, and reached Fort Dayton at three o'clock that afternoon. There they learned that Schuyler had at last decided to send Brigadier General Ebenezer Learned's Massachusetts brigade, then stationed at Van Schaick's Island, ten miles north of Albany, to the relief of Fort Stanwix. Willett abandoned his mission of militia recruitment and sped northward with Stockwell to meet Learned. From him they learned that Major General Benedict Arnold, then at Albany, had volunteered to lead the expedition. They continued to Albany, and with Arnold they returned to Fort Dayton.[25]

In the meantime, Major General Horatio Gates had replaced Philip

Schuyler in command of the Northern Army. The change culminated a bitter contest between Gates, the down-to-earth favorite of the New England foot soldier, and Schuyler, the aristocratic scorner of militia. Gates had similar differences with his commander in chief, General George Washington, a supporter of Schuyler. In Pennsylvania, Arnold had sided with Washington. At Saratoga, Arnold had sided with Schuyler. Now, at Fort Dayton, Arnold might well wonder how much backing he could expect from Gates. Prudently, he waited for the arrival of Oneida and Tuscarora reinforcements. When an Oneida chief who had viewed the British encampment arrived with a report that St. Leger's force numbered 1,000 Indians and 700 whites, Arnold called a council of senior officers to consider what action he should take with his force of 946 Continentals and no more than 100 militia. The council recommended that he request a reinforcement of 1,000 from Gates and wait for an answer. Although his force and Gansevoort's combined totaled 1,746, outnumbering the besiegers, he agreed. Arnold dispatched Willett with the letter to Gates.[26]

The impulsive Arnold did not feel comfortable, however, with a counsel of delay. Lieutenant Colonel John Brooks, who had recently arrived with Learned, suggested a novel tactic. The effort of Walter Butler to recruit Loyalists had been attempted with only ten British regulars and a few Loyalists and Indians; and five days before Arnold's arrival at Fort Dayton, at a nearby tavern, Butler's party had been captured by a detachment of Brooks's Eighth Massachusetts Continentals. Butler was convicted as a spy by a court-martial conducted by Willett and sent to jail in Albany. One of the Loyalists captured with Butler was a young local, Han Yost Schuyler, thought to be retarded and superstitiously held in awe by Indians who knew him. On pain of death, and with his brother held as security, he was instructed to enter the British camp as a pretended escapee and carry spurious intelligence to St. Leger of the coming of an overwhelming rebel relief force of two thousand men and ten cannon. Pistol shots were fired through his clothes to fortify his guise as an escapee, and an Oneida chief who remained on speaking terms with the Senecas was sent to follow him into the camp and confirm his story.[27]

Meanwhile, in the British camp, frustration was growing over the stalemate of the siege. The "popgun" cannon had proved ineffective. The hope of an outpouring of Loyalists in the Mohawk Valley had disappeared with the capture on August 15 of Walter Butler's party. Similarly, an uprising of 125 Loyalists in the Schoharie Valley under John Macdonell and Adam Crysler had been crushed on August 13 by a force of Continentals and militia under Colonel John Harper. St. Leger became more and more apprehensive. He wrote Burgoyne, asking for a diversion that would forestall the Americans from dispatching Continental troops to the aid of Stanwix. On his own, he could think of nothing better than digging a trench from the British batteries on the high ground toward the northwest bastion of the fort in order to provide cover from which to bring his artillery closer. A tunnel might then be attempted to undermine the bastion.

Before these efforts could be completed, scouts brought word of Arnold's marching relief force, estimated at one thousand. St. Leger called a council of the Indian chiefs and proposed an attack similar to the one that had stopped Herkimer, promising to lead it himself at the head of three hundred picked regulars. Despite the chiefs' resentment over having borne the brunt of the casualties at Oriskany, they seemed willing, and the next morning, August 22, they went with him to reconnoiter a site for an ambush.

At this point, Han Yost Schuyler made his appearance. He was hardly the half-wit. He knew the Indians' language and customs. He told an elaborate tale of his supposed perilous escape, embellished with the exhibit of his bullet-riddled garments. The rebel force, he said, numbered two thousand, and he pointed ominously to the leaves of the trees. He was followed by the Oneida, who reported an even greater rapidly approaching army of three thousand and claimed news that Burgoyne's army was "cut to pieces." Also by design, confederates of the Oneida straggled in, seemingly by coincidence, with supporting details. Their Iroquois listeners became thoroughly alarmed. They called their own council and demanded an immediate withdrawal, possibly to regroup at Oswego with more men and increased artillery.

While they were conferring, St. Leger learned that two hundred Indians had already decamped. Not knowing that these were wounded being evacuated, he suspected "cowardice in some and treason in others." Without Indians, his siege became hopeless. But he wished to delay his retreat until night in order to allow the wounded and the artillery to start ahead down Wood Creek. The Indians would not wait. He accused Johnson, who according to Molly Brant had antagonized the Indians with his "hasty temper," of failing to control them. Johnson blamed St. Leger, who, Hertel de Rouville reported, had alienated his men with his "haughtiness," for ineffective leadership. The enraged Indians abandoned all discipline and began seizing officers' liquor and clothes. They "became more formidable than the enemy we had to expect," wrote St. Leger.

In this explosive chaos, a couple of derisive sachems provided the spark with a shout, "they are coming!—they are coming!" A headlong rout of the white troops erupted. Left behind were fifteen wagons, seventeen bateaux, and a large quantity of ammunition, baggage, and camp equipage. The Senecas lingered long enough to wreak vengeance on the nearby Oneida village of Oriska. Houses were burned, crops destroyed, and cattle carried away.

St. Leger afterward said that he managed a phased withdrawal of his white troops to the junction of Canada and Wood creeks, where at three o'clock in the morning boats were brought up that carried them across Lake Oneida to Onondaga Falls.[28] An artillery officer, however, charged that St. Leger was eight miles on his way before the gun crew learned of the retreat. A captured Hessian soldier reported that when the troops were ten miles from the fort, the Indians fell upon them, seized their arms, and stabbed many with their own bayonets. Hertel de Rouville wrote that the British "covered twelve miles without once looking behind them."[29]

Arnold, impatient of delay, on August 23 had set out from Fort Dayton to Stanwix, and on the way he was met with a letter from Gansevoort with the news of St. Leger's flight. He raced to the fort, too late in the evening to catch up with the enemy's rear. The following morning he sent out a pursuit force of five hundred, but a heavy rain forced most of them to return. A small party continued to Oneida Lake and arrived just in time to see the last of the British boats depart. The British reached Oswego August 26.[30]

Most of the embittered Indians dispersed to their homes, leaving Claus and Butler to dispute who now had the titular claim to their leadership. Claus maintained that his authority extended to the remnant of St. Leger's Indians being ordered to the reinforcement of Burgoyne's army on the Hudson. Butler countered that the conclusion of St. Leger's campaign terminated Claus's appointment and reverted the superintendency of the Indians to him. He rushed off to see Carleton at Montreal, taking with him three friendly chiefs to demonstrate his support among the Oneidas. Predictably, Carleton sided with him. He approved the expansion of a body of rangers Butler had organized for the Stanwix campaign into a battalion of eight companies, fifty-eight men each. Two of them, to consist of Indian-speaking recruits, were to receive four shillings a day, and the rest two shillings, extraordinarily high pay. Butler's son, Walter, although then in captivity in an Albany jail, was to captain the senior company. On September 15, Carleton ordered Butler to proceed with his rangers and as many Indians as could be spared from their homes to join Burgoyne's army.[31]

Claus, before following Butler to Montreal, provided Brant with funds to recruit Mohawks in their villages at Canajoharie and Fort Hunter and lead them to Burgoyne. Also, he assembled about seventy Canadian Indians for a rendezvous with St. Leger on the Richelieu River. At Montreal, he found that Carleton had put Brigadier General Allan Maclean in charge of Canadian troops. Maclean was willing to work with Claus and instructed him to recruit more Indians in Canada. Claus took advantage of the order to induce Gilbert Tice and several other former associates to serve with him. With his new appointments, he proceeded at the end of September to the rendezvous with St. Leger at St. Johns and found Carleton there. Carleton refused to acknowledge that the orders Claus had received had accorded him any legitimacy. He brutally informed him that "there was no farther Service for him in Indn. Affairs," and that they were now under the direction of Butler. Neither would Carleton refund to Claus fifteen hundred pounds that he had laid out on his own credit to supply the Indians. He appointed Tice to head St. Leger's Indian contingent and ordered it only to relieve the British garrison at Ticonderoga and then return to Canada.[32]

Neither Brant nor Butler delivered any effective aid to Burgoyne. Brant got through to the British camp on August 28, but after a week there disapproved of Burgoyne's management and decided to return to Onondaga and prepare the Indians for the blow of an impending defeat. Butler had planned to raise his Indian contingent at Niagara without knowing that food and clothing there were insufficient. It didn't matter. News arrived of Burgoyne's surrender. His expedition to the Hudson was pointless.[33]

On his return, Brant found that a general meeting of the Iroquois confederacy had been called for early in October at Onondaga. The way had been prepared for his message by his sister, Molly. She had been driven from her home at Canajoharie by enraged Oneidas, abetted by rapacious whites, who sacked the village in retaliation for the Mohawk destruction of Oriska. St. Leger's debacle and Burgoyne's disaster, accompanied by the British evacuation of Fort Oswego, had aroused fears for the safety of Iroquois villages. Old Smoke himself had begun to waver. Molly, with her enormous prestige and authority, confronted him directly, reminding him of the obligation to preserve the sacred covenant chain Sir William had forged between the crown and the confederacy. Another powerful matron assisted her, Sarah McGinnis, a Loyalist white widow adopted by the Iroquois, who persuaded the Cayuga chiefs to reject a large wampum belt with a war ax worked into it that an Onondaga messenger brought with an offer of alliance from Schuyler. Old Smoke, grieving for the loss of his son, Tocenando, was not hard to convince. He decided that, "the break being too wide," he had "struck his Hatchet deep all about him."

Brant was at his most eloquent. He dwelled on the loss of the chiefs and warriors at Oriskany and Stanwix. He warned of the "subjection & Slavery they must be exposed to" if the rebels won. The confederacy recommitted itself to all-out war. "Our hatchet is dull, on account of being restrained these 2 years," they resolved. They would "take up the Hatchet their forefathers gave them, wch was buried in a deep pit, but very sharp, and would force its way wherever pointed, without controul." Brant completely triumphed. It was the tactic he had been preaching for a year: the Indians must make war their own way. They must launch their own raids on the white settlements in their homeland and eradicate these violations of their birthright.

The war now took a new turn. The Indians would no longer serve as auxiliaries in a British force of professional soldiers fighting an American force of professional soldiers. They were to direct their main offensive against civilian centers, destroy private residences, and take the lives of noncombatants of both sexes and all ages. Ironically, the first blow would be struck against their own brethren. In their fury over the sack of the Mohawk villages of Canajoharie and Fort Huron, they resolved to sack the Oneidas' principal castle, Kanowa-lohale, fifteen miles southwest of Stanwix.[34]

CHAPTER 3

✦ ✦ ✦ ✦ ✦ ✦ ✦ ✦ ✦ ✦ ✦

No Quarter

Brant and Old Smoke made plans for their war. The raids would not begin until the spring, because several of the Indian villages were not equipped to resist winter rebel counterattacks, owing to the failure to stock provisions while the warriors were away at the siege of Stanwix. Also, outlying rebel settlements were protected by troops posted for winter cantonment. "As those people whom we intend to attack in the Spring are now asleep," advised Old Smoke, "we do not choose to awaken them till we strike the blow." When the snows melted, Brant would launch operations in the Mohawk Valley, the Cherry Valley, and the Schoharie. Old Smoke would take for his territory Wyoming and the Susquehanna settlements. In the meantime, to divert the rebels' attention, war parties from the western Senecas' Allegheny towns would harass the western frontiers of Pennsylvania and Virginia.[1]

The Indians might spurn white leadership, but they could not dispense with white supplies. Yet for the Euro-Christian, British government to endorse Indian-style guerrilla warfare was a radical departure. The British government, in fact, did not formally endorse the new thrust. Support for the Indians came rather as a product of the Claus-Butler feud in America and the Carleton-Germain clash in England. Carleton considered himself rejected and overruled by Germain, and he tendered his resignation. While awaiting his replacement, with a total force in Canada of no more than forty-five hundred, he declined to attempt any formal military initiative or to provide direction to the Indians. He was, nevertheless, a supporter of Butler and an opponent of Claus, and he authorized Butler practically unlimited funds to shower the Indians with implements and provisions.[2] Butler saw himself as released from Carleton's previous prohibition of unrestricted Indian warfare, and he set about currying favor with the Indians so as to supersede Claus's popularity with them.

He convened a formal council of the Six Nations at Niagara December 1, and it was carefully planned. In preliminary discussions, he strove to win over the Mohawks from their allegiance to Claus. He persuaded Molly Brant to move with her family from Cayuga to Niagara and exert her influence there among the gathering refugees from Canajoharie and Fort Huron. He promised Brant to write to Carleton, recommending two years' back pay for him. He courted a Loyalist, Adam Crysler, who arrived from the East Branch of the Susquehanna with a party of Schoharie Mohawks. And he obtained beef, pork, flour, and vegetables for twenty-seven hundred Iroquois of all ages who flocked to Niagara. Present were some Tuscaroras and Onondagas, minor factions of their tribes, who recanted earlier support they had pledged to Schuyler at a council in September at Albany.

The meeting opened with an exchange of condolences for Indian and British casualties. "Our revenge," Butler vowed, "shall be in proportion to our former loss." He distributed lavish gifts to all at the council, including reparation for the goods lost at Stanwix and three hundred silver medals for the participants in the St. Leger campaign. He promised to press upon Carleton the need to reoccupy Fort Oswego as a retreat for beleaguered families. He attempted to offset Burgoyne's surrender with the news of Howe's capture of Philadelphia and victories at Brandywine and Germantown. Old Smoke spoke for the Indians, Brant interpreting. The Iroquois, he declared, remained committed to the stand they had taken in September, whether or not the British approved. They were "determined to make the War our own." They would wait until spring and then

launch "a very formidable irruption with their whole collected force
into the frontiers of New York and glut that revenge they so impa-
tiently wish for."[3]

There is no evidence that Butler recoiled from this prospect of
terrorism. He did later obtain a pledge not to harm women and
nonpartisans, but Indian-style hit-and-run warfare inevitably entailed
destruction of homes and crops, murder and captivity of civilians,
and death by torture of captured soldiers. This did not deter a man
smarting from exile, the internment of his wife and youngest children,
the loss of his estate, and the confinement in irons of his ailing eldest
son in an Albany jail. Modern apologists for Butler have maintained
that his purpose was to interdict food supplies for the Continental
armies from the rich Mohawk-Susquehanna granary valleys and si-
phon off American troops from coastal operations. The only general
objective he ever considered, however, was, as he wrote Carleton,
"to join the Southern Army." He and the Fort Niagara commandant,
Lieutenant Colonel Mason Bolton, jointly wrote to General Sir William Howe, asking "how we can be of use."[4] But with Howe in
Philadelphia, Washington at Valley Forge blocked the way to any
union. And when Sir Henry Clinton replaced Howe, he took his army
back to New York; after the defeat at Monmouth, he had no stomach
for a northward expedition up the Hudson. The kind of warfare
Butler advocated was simply devastation of rebel settlements, on the
model of what the western tribes had wrought, as he reported to
Carleton with satisfaction:

> The Indians of the Six Nations and those from the westward have
> exerted themselves in laying waste the country most exposed to them.
> On the east branch of the Susquehannah to the Kiskimenitas Creek
> upon the Ohio, and from there down to Kanahawa River, an extent
> of many hundred miles, is now nothing but an heap of ashes. Such of
> those miserable people as have escaped have taken refuge in small
> forts.[5]

Raids began early in 1778 against the backcountry settlements of
Pennsylvania between the Susquehanna and the Allegheny rivers

north of Forbes Road, led by Seneca, Cayuga, and a few Delaware chiefs. Butler headquartered at Niagara, outfitting war parties and rewarding them with presents on their return. Rum, as in 1777, proved a major factor—two thousand gallons distributed by April's end and fifty-three hundred more planned. The year's first three months yielded seventy scalps and a few captives. On April 28, a band of 125 Senecas and Cayugas attacked Fort Wallace on Conemaugh Creek in Westmoreland County and took fifteen scalps and two prisoners, losing one warrior killed and four wounded. Parties of Senecas and Cayugas, a total of some 150, swept the upper Susquehanna valley. Early in May, twenty people were killed along the North Branch; on a farm on upper Penn's Creek, a woman and her daughter were killed and scalped, and her son was abducted. On the West Branch, fifteen people were killed in the area of the lower Lycoming, the Loyalstock Valley, and Bald Eagle Creek. Fifty-six were taken captive, including a mother, six children, and two grandparents of a family at Wysox. A militia colonel declared that if something were not done "to put a stop to these murders soon, this Cuntrey will be entierly given up to the saviges." There were attacks in 1778 on the frontiers of Virginia. A party of 124 Senecas and Cayugas returned at the end of May with thirteen scalps and two prisoners, at the cost of several of their own casualties.

And yet there was rebel brutality, too. To the west, from Fort Pitt, Brigadier General Edward Hand on February 15, 1778, led a retaliatory expedition of five hundred horsemen that attacked a Delaware Indian village at the present Edinburg, near New Castle, and finding the warriors gone killed one old man, four women, and one boy and carried away two women. Jeering frontiersmen called it "the squaw campaign."[6]

While Old Smoke's warriors carried out their diversion, Butler and Brant were readying their forces for their prime targets. There were unsettling reports of attempts by Schuyler to win back the Six Nations, and he had succeeded in neutralizing the Onondagas. The pro-British Iroquois were now mainly Mohawk, Seneca, and Cayuga. Disturbing rumors circulated of planned rebel attacks on their vil-

lages, but Old Smoke proclaimed that the blood of the veterans of
Fort Stanwix was "still reeking." "My being with them," wrote
Butler, "may be of use to accelerate their departure & direct their
motions." His rangers headquartered at Niagara, but a party of them
wintered in the Wyoming Valley, and twenty-seven were seized there
by rebel militia in January, who sent eighteen to a Connecticut
prison. By the end of March, however, Butler's agent had enlisted
almost one hundred recruits who would join the corps on the road.
Brant returned to Oquaga with thirty Canajoharie Mohawks in late
February and for the next three months recruited Indians and some
sixty Loyalists. He commandeered horses, cattle, and provisions
along the East Branch and the upper Delaware valley but refrained
from violence against settlers.[7]

On May 2, Butler set out with a seventy-man nucleus of his corps
and a large supply of arms and ammunition for a final war council
of the Six Nations at Canadesaga. Oneidas, Tuscaroras, and Onondagas attended, but their neutralist appeals, relayed from a council
Schuyler had convened in March at Johnstown and another he had
called for Onondaga, were brushed aside. The Oneidas felt more
than ever committed to the rebels, and Schuyler had cemented their
allegiance by constructing for them a palisade fort at Kanowalohale
that secured them from the Senecas' intended attack. Butler wished
to concentrate the campaign against his home ground of the Mohawk
Valley, and he held out as inducement a promise never fulfilled of the
occupation of Oswego by Sir John Johnson's regiment. Old Smoke
was adamant for the Wyoming Valley, at the present Wilkes-Barre.
It was the gateway, up the Susquehanna and along its north and west
branches, through which rebel forces from Pennsylvania could invade
Cayuga and Seneca territory from Lake Cayuga to Lake Erie. Butler
could only acquiesce.[8]

As planned earlier, the Mohawk and Schoharie valleys were allotted to Brant. Basing his operation at Oquaga and Unadilla, he had
collected some two hundred Indians and one hundred whites. Disregarding any coordination with the movement of the southbound

force under Butler and Sayenqueraghta, he arrived on May 30 at Cobleskill, on Cobleskill Creek, twenty-two miles south of Fort Hunter, where he aimed to free some of his Mohawks who were being forcibly detained by the rebels. Cobleskill was a community of twenty families, all Patriot, living along a three-mile stretch of the valley, with no fort and defended only by thirty-three Continentals under Captain William Patrick and fifteen militia under Captain Christian Brown. When fifteen or twenty Indians appeared, the inhabitants fled into the woods. The defenders gathered at the settlement's southernmost house (the present Warnerville), home of George Warner, a Schoharie committee member. Brown advised caution, but Patrick demanded attack, and when he charged cowardice, Brown yielded. They chased the Indians for a mile, when the pursuit ran into the main body of Brant's force concealed behind a low ridge. Patrick was fatally shot with a bullet that broke his thigh. Brown led a hasty retreat back to Warner's house, where five men held off the Indians while the rest escaped. Two of them were taken captive and the other three left in the building, which was set afire. One captive was shot. The other was afterward found with his body cut open and his intestines tied to a tree several feet away. Twenty-two Americans were killed, eight wounded, and two captured. The Indians lost only one wounded and one missing. With resistance overcome, the attackers plundered and burned ten of the homes, with their barns and stables. A rain that night saved the rest. Horses that could not be caught were shot in the fields.[9]

After this success, Brant considered Cherry Valley, twenty-two miles to the northwest, as his next target, but that settlement had already been alerted. When he learned from a scout that a Palatine District militia regiment under Colonel Jacob Klock had been sent there, he decided to return to Oquaga and Unadilla and strengthen his force for a later attack, in the meanwhile sending out foraging raids to gather provisions. The settlers of the Mohawk Valley, however, had no respite. During the first days of June, a mixed party of some three hundred Mohawks and Loyalists, coming from Canada, swooped down to the Johnstown area, burning three houses, taking seventeen captives, and retrieving Loyalist wives and children and most of the Fort Hunter Mohawks (a few chose to remain).[10]

To this point, there was lack of coordination and continuing rivalry between the Mohawk and the Susquehanna offensives. With summer coming, it was necessary to resolve the differences. Butler injected himself as the catalyst. He summoned Brant to a conference at the Tioga Point peninsula (the present Athens), and after a week of negotiations he worked out a compromise: First he and his Ranger Corps would unite with Old Smoke and his Senecas and Cayugas in a campaign against the Wyoming Valley. Then he would join with Brant and his Mohawks in an attack on Cherry Valley.[11]

The frontier clamored for protection. Governor George Clinton urged Tryon and Schoharie counties to recruit more militia companies, but they pleaded that their men were tied up with essential local functions and defense of their homes. Gates had no troops to spare from those needed to contain the British army at New York; he was so short of manpower that he had to requisition two thousand New York militia. As early as January 1778, pressure had been mounting for the Continental Congress to authorize a major strike against the hostile tribes of the Iroquois. The commissioners of Indian Affairs proposed it to the Congress on January 12. So did Schuyler, February 8 and March 15. William Duer, a New York delegate to the Continental Congress, also served on the Board of War. On June 10, he wrote the board's report, asserting that "a defensive war would not only prove an inadequate security against the inroads of the Indians, but would, in a short time, be much more expensive than a vigorous attempt to compel them to sue for peace." The report formally recommended an offensive operation against the hostile Indians between Fort Pitt and Detroit and another against the Senecas.

Congress approved the report and appropriated $932,743.33 for the total proposal. Although Gates, as the northern commander, was directed to "take the most expeditious measures for carrying the war into the Senecas' country," the board advised that the expedition was to be led by Major General Thomas Mifflin and Brigadier General John Stark. A partisan element had been injected, for Duer was an open political enemy of Gates. Gates had sided with Ethan Allen and the Vermont separatists, whom Duer and New York land speculators detested. Mifflin was then under a cloud for accusations of misconduct in his recent post of quartermaster general. Thus Stark, a Vermonter who nevertheless opposed the separatists, appeared the real nominee. The Congress rejected the maneuver and resolved merely that Gates be directed to appoint "a suitable officer to conduct the expedition."[12]

Whatever Gates might have known and thought about this machination, he had more pressing reasons to resist the expedition. He was deep in plans to follow up his defeat of Burgoyne with an invasion of Canada, which if successful could end the entire war and more effectually cut off the Indian ravages from their nesting ground. Although New Hampshire was not willing to send troops to the Mohawk Valley, that state's General Jacob Bailey had promised to supply fifteen hundred New Hampshire militia by August 1 for a Canadian invasion, and Colonel Moses Hazen was eager to add his regiment of Continentals.[13]

Determined that nothing must stand in the way of the Canadian venture, Gates countered Congress's directive with delay and deception. On June 17 he informed President Henry Laurens that he had obtained militia reinforcements from New Hampshire and New York for Stark, commander of the northern department at Albany, sufficient to "Secure the Frontiers." An expedition against the Indians, however, "will be unnecessary," for two days earlier he had met with a deputation of Seneca, Tuscarora, and Oneida chiefs who had assured him that "upon the favourable reception of their requests, War shall cease." They would turn over to him Joseph Brant "a prisoner, to be dealt with as I thought proper." In fact, the militia reinforcements were intended for Gates's projected Canadian invasion, and there is no record of an understanding with the chiefs, who in any case could not speak for the majority of the warring Senecas or for any of the Cayugas.

Laurens was not taken in, and he repeated his request for compliance. Gates promised that he would "immediately provide" the expedition but was "somewhat apprehensive, our provision Magazines at Albany, and Fort Schuyler, may not be so well stored as such an Emergency (considered with the many demands our present, and future circumstances) may require." For the command of the expedition, he said, he had first considered Brigadier General Samuel H. Parsons, whom the Board of War, again asserting itself, had proposed to him. But he had declined, pleading, as a Connecticut man, that he was unfamiliar with the country and people of the Mohawk Valley. Having thus placated the Board of War, and gained time, Gates named Marinus Willett as his choice. This was another evasion. Willett had already gone south to join Washington's army at the Battle of Monmouth. "I still wish this Indian War, could, consistent with Wisdom, & sound policy, be, for this Summer at least, delayed," Gates told Laurens.[14]

In the face of this irresolution, Brant struck again. From his base at Unadilla, he moved up Butternut Creek to Springfield, at the head of Lake Otsego, and Andrustown (now Jordanville), seven miles northwest. The two small settlements, caught unaware, were totally destroyed, the horses and cattle driven away, and eight men killed and fourteen taken prisoner.[15]

The Wyoming Valley of the Susquehanna is a twenty-five-mile stretch, about three miles wide, that runs from the northeast to the southwest between two high, parallel, irregular mountain ranges covered with oak and pine. The serpentine river enters and leaves the valley through passes in the jagged western mountain—at the north, the Lackawannock Gap and at the south, the Nanticoke Gap. The river is generally two hundred yards wide, punctuated by two rapids and fed by several tributary streams. Ideal for settlement were "flats" of rich soil on both sides of the river, with sea coal that lined the banks supplying ample fuel. The *Connecticut Courant* of September 29, 1772, publicized the valley as "the best, and the pleasantest land we ever saw." Pennsylvania vied with Connecticut for ownership,

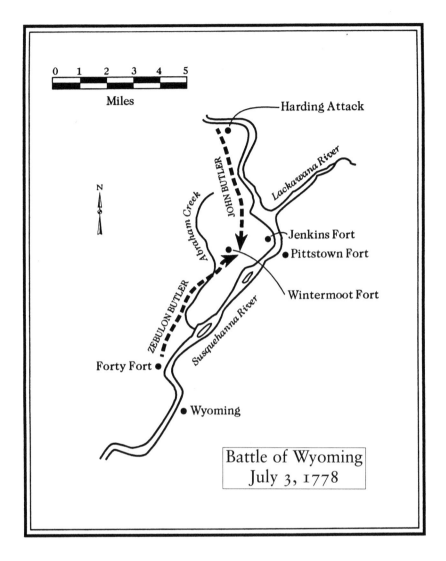

Battle of Wyoming
July 3, 1778

based on their colonial charters and agreements with the Indians.
Connecticut settlers, numbering about three thousand, established
three towns of five-hundred-acre farms on each side of the river,
centering at the present Wilkes-Barre, and they forcibly expelled
"Pennamite" contenders. The Iroquois, however, had conquered the

valley from the Delawares, and they repudiated sales of the land as fraudulent. The sales had been negotiated by unauthorized chiefs with the Susquehanna Company of Connecticut speculators and with the Pennsylvania proprietors in 1754 and again with the proprietors in 1768.[16]

The attack force comprised 464 Indians and 110 of Butler's Rangers. The Indians, under Old Smoke, were mainly eastern Senecas, with some western Senecas, Cayugas, Onondagas, and Delawares. The Rangers, under Captain William Caldwell (the other captain, Butler's son, Walter, had not yet arrived), were principally Loyalists, many of them exiles from the valley and bitter about being dispossessed from their lands. In preparation, the warriors partook of a feast of roasted white dogs, the ceremonial representation of the flesh of captives. On the morning of June 27, the flotilla of fifty canoes and boats started down the Susquehanna, and three days later, thirty-one miles downstream, the invaders beached their craft on the west shore and established a base slightly inland on an elevation west of Sutton Creek. From there they could see the entire valley, with seven "forts," most of them flimsily stockaded homes, strung ten miles along the river.

The settlers had sent scouts up the Susquehanna, but they had gone no further than Wyalusing, a few miles short of the British rendezvous at Tioga, and therefore had not detected the invaders. A little distance on the far side of Sutton Creek, on a farm belonging to Stephen Harding, Jr., twelve unsuspecting field workers, including an eleven-year-old boy and a black servant, were hoeing corn. Two local Loyalists spotted them and directed two Indian scouting parties to the scene. The Indians sprang from ambush and killed four and took four prisoner. Two captives, James Hadsall, whose son had just been tomahawked, and the servant, Quocko Martin, were tortured until they died.

The inhabitants fled to the stockades, and resistance was centered at Forty Fort, the largest of them, on the river's west shore across from Wyoming at a bend a little upstream. The troops there consisted of 60 Continentals of the Third Connecticut Regiment under Lieuten-

ant Colonel Zebulon Butler and 390 Twenty-fourth Connecticut militia under Colonel Nathan Denison. (A call for assistance sent to a
company of 90 Pennamite militia in neighboring Northumberland
drew no reply.) Butler (no relation of the British commander), forty-
seven years old, headed the combined garrison, and he promptly led
it out to seek the invaders. Oblivious of each other's movements, the
two forces passed each other in the woods. The Americans headed
for the east shore of Sutton Creek, where the field workers had been
attacked, and found there, near the two mutilated bodies, two Indians, whom they killed. Finding no other targets, they returned in the
evening to Forty Fort. The British marched to Wintermoot Fort, at
the northern rim of the present Exeter, whose garrison of thirty or
forty, dominated by the Loyalist Wintermoot family, tamely capitulated. The next morning a squad also obtained the surrender of
Jenkins Fort, about a mile and a half to the east, on the west river
bank, with only eight defenders. The terms for both forts promised
that the men, women, and children would not be harmed.[17]

The British now advanced to Forty Fort. Early in the morning of
July 3, under a flag of truce, Lieutenant John Turney, of Butler's
Rangers, and a fifer, John Phillips, delivered a written demand from
Butler for the unconditional surrender of all the remaining forts in
the valley with all the Continental officers and soldiers, promising
the safety of the inhabitants and threatening, upon refusal, to attack
in full force. Colonel Denison, in the absence of Colonel Zebulon
Butler, refused but requested time for consultation. One of the fort's
guards, Lazarus Stewart, derisively offered Turney a drink, which he
declined. The Americans, Stewart hotly responded, would give the
invaders "spirit enough before night." After Turney and Phillips left,
Denison, in order to play for time, sent a messenger with a white flag
to Butler at Wintermoot Fort to request a conference. Prowling Indians fired upon him and on a second messenger, and both had to
return.

The enemy did not attack. Scouts reported that, rather than carrying out their threat, they were collecting the cattle and burning and
plundering the vacated settlements. Some of the fort's officers pro-

posed to stop the depredations by attacking the British at their camp.
Denison wished to wait for reinforcements, but the hotheads would
not wait, and rather than be accused of cowardice he acquiesced.
Zebulon Butler in the meantime arrived from Wyoming, and that
afternoon he and Denison rode out at the head of the full force from
Forty Fort, under the waving new national flag—thirteen stripes, red
and white alternately, and thirteen white stars in a blue field, while
the drummers and fifers played "St. Patrick's Day in the Morning."
Among them were seventy volunteers—old men, boys, and civil officials. They marched two miles northeastward to a high bank at
Abraham's Creek, where they paused to assess the situation. Since
there was still no evidence of enemy activity, a third messenger with
a white flag was dispatched to Fort Wintermoot with a request for a
conference, and again he had to return. He reported that the enemy
was on the move, but he could not say whether they were advancing
to fight or retreating to leave the valley. Zebulon Butler wished to
delay again for fuller information, and behind his judgment was his
service in the French and Indian War and, since the outbreak of the
Revolution, in the Continental Army.

Again the hotheads refused; their spokesman was Lazarus Stewart,
now a lieutenant in the Hanover Company of Captain William
McKerachan (a school teacher who came from northern Ireland) of
the Twenty-fourth Regiment of Connecticut militia. Forty-four years
old, a violent firebrand, he was somewhat unusual among the Wyoming settlers, who had come chiefly from Connecticut. He was the
son of immigrants from northern Ireland who had settled in Lancaster County, Pennsylvania. Intelligent, daring, and physically hardy,
he had organized a company of provincial volunteers during the
French and Indian War and served with distinction under Edward
Braddock at the Battle of the Monongahela. Subsequently, in Pontiac's War, he commanded a company of Paxtang and Donegal
County Rangers, and in 1763, as a reprisal for Indian attacks, he led
a band of fifty-seven of them, known as the "Paxton Boys," in a
massacre of twenty peaceful Conestogas near Lancaster, including
five women and eight children. Although he declared that he person-

ally had shed no blood, he extolled the resort to "our God and our guns." Resentful of the land monopolies of Pennsylvania speculators, he and fifty Paxton Boys offered to drive out the Pennsylvania claimants from the Wyoming Valley in return for land grants from the Susquehanna Company. They were given a six-mile-square township at Hanover. In the clashes that followed, Pennamites were imprisoned and their homes destroyed. Stewart was arrested but broke out of jail and with an ax handle knocked down the deputy constable, Frederick Bullman. Four months later, he fatally shot down a deputy sheriff, Nathan Ogden, who attempted to serve a warrant for his rearrest. A reward of three hundred pounds was offered for his apprehension, and he fled for a time to Connecticut. The Connecticut governor, Jonathan Trumbull, refused Pennsylvania's demand for extradition of Stewart, who was now being seen as an intercolonial social radical. Pennsylvania's Governor John Penn compared the Paxton Boys to the rioting Regulators of North Carolina, and Stewart declared that his Paxton Boys had allies in Virginia and Maryland. He returned to Hanover, where Connecticut's jurisdiction still protected him, but before long he fell out with the Connecticut men. One of them, Ezekiel Peirce, the former major of Stewart's battalion, even threatened to turn him over to the Pennsylvania authorities. Earlier in 1778, he had volunteered for the Continental Army, but the Pennsylvania government prohibited him from leaving the Wyoming Valley.

Among the defenders at Abraham's Creek, the Connecticut-Pennsylvania feud inflamed the dispute over whether to wait or attack. Stewart did not hesitate to challenge Zebulon Butler. Having a wife and seven children, the youngest a daughter a day old, did not deter him. He threatened that if Butler did not advance he would lead a revolt and charge cowardice. Denison, although he had been a personal friend of Stewart, placed him under arrest. At this, Captain McKerachan resigned in protest, and the company immediately elected Stewart to replace him. Finally, Butler gave up his resistance. He released Stewart from arrest, vowing that he would "show the men that I dare lead where they dare follow." At about three o'clock in the afternoon, the Americans resumed their march to Fort Winter-moot.[18]

In forsaking the shelter of Forty Fort, they had exposed themselves to the same hazard that had overwhelmed Herkimer's militia at Oriskany. "This pleased the Indians highly," John Butler noted, "who observed they should be on an equal footing with them in the woods." In order to lure the Americans, he ordered Wintermoot and Jenkins forts set on fire, to create the impression that the British were retreating. East of Fort Wintermoot, bordering on the Susquehanna, his Rangers were concealed behind a log fence along the upper edge of an open field of six acres sparsely covered with pine trees and oak shrubs. At their right, under Old Smoke, the main body of the Indians was strung out in six bands from the field to a thick morass of timber and brushwood. Butler removed his hat, tied a handkerchief around his head, and awaited the assault.

By five o'clock, under a hot sun in a clear sky, the Americans moved forward to within two hundred yards of the fence, so far having encountered only sporadic skirmishing. Now they discovered the enemy lying behind the fence. Zebulon Butler gave the order for a volley, and when this received no response, his line reloaded and fired again, advancing and calling, "Come out if you dare and show your heads." The bravado proved suicidal. When the rebels were within one hundred yards, the Rangers returned the fire and deceptively fell back a short distance. The rebels raised a cheer. Suddenly, to their left, the hitherto undetected Indians jumped up, firing and yelling. The struggle was furious, as the Indians surged forward with their spears and tomahawks. After a half hour, Captain Asaph Whittlesey's company was completely outflanked. To counter this encirclement, Denison ordered two companies to turn off at right angles to the main line. The order was misunderstood to mean retreat. Confusion became disorder. The rebel left wing fell back on the right, and what had started as an advance turned into a rout. The outcome of a battle may be determined as much by mass hysteria as by tactical direction. Tories and Indians afterward told a rebel militia captain, John Franklin, who arrived the next day, that "if Cols. Butler and

Denison with their forces had stood their ground one minute longer, they would have gained the victory—that the tories and Indians on the left wing were giving way, and that they would not have stood their ground another fire." In the slaughter, many of the rebels were scalped half-dead. A captured white captain of Indians said afterward, with a wild laugh, "I had worked so hard with my tomahawk and scalping knife that my arms were bloody above the elbows." Every rebel company captain was killed on the field, including Stewart and McKerachan, or if captured reserved for a worse death.

The rebels now thought only of escape, and they headed a mile and a half south to a crossing of the Susquehanna at Monocanock Island. The Indians followed, shooting many in the water and luring others with promises of quarter and then butchering them. Despite the carnage, the two top commanders, Zebulon Butler and Nathan Denison, each rode off on horseback with a handful of men running beside them, managing to fend off pursuing Indians, and reached Forty Fort.

The fate of most of the captives was harrowing. Those not tomahawked suffered prolonged torture. An American survivor stated that he heard Captain James Bidlack pleading and shrieking while he was held with a pitchfork on a burning heap of logs and brush. A Tory captain of Indians saw an officer "bound naked to a tree and flogged with rods for several hours. Pieces of flesh were cut off him at different places, and he remained in this condition for three days, during which the Indians danced continually around this poor fellow among their prisoners of war. Since he was a brave and distinguished soldier, they shouted to him that he should now act like a man at the end of his life."[19]

The rebel fatality list told the one-sided story. Denison reported 302 lost: 1 colonel, 2 majors, 7 captains, 13 lieutenants, 11 ensigns, and 268 privates. John Butler's tally was higher: 376 dead, of whom 227 scalps were taken. He rescued, he said, five prisoners from the Indians with "the greatest difficulty." On the British side, there were only one Indian and one Ranger killed, besides a handful of wounded each.

Forty Fort, with its meager garrison and several hundred women and children, was only a momentary refuge. The day after the battle, John Butler demanded its surrender, along with the remaining forts at Wyoming and Pittstown and several stockades. If Zebulon Butler and his some twenty surviving Continental soldiers fell into the hands of the Indians, they would surely meet the same fate as those taken on the field. Denison, as a militia officer who might be spared, therefore took over the command while Zebulon Butler and his men slipped away. At four o'clock in the afternoon of July 4, John Butler and his Rangers and the Indians headed by "Queen" Esther Montour, a tall, handsome Indian half-blood with soft, black hair, marched into Forty Fort. They flourished a single scalp, Lazarus Stewart's they huzzahed. Butler promised not to harm the inhabitants or their property, and in order to restrain the Indians he had Denison empty the fort's seven barrels of whiskey into the river.

The Indians did not molest the refugees huddled in the forts, but most of them did not wait to find out. They streamed forth, some finding canoes to descend the river, and others, without food or supplies, wading east through the Great Swamp and over the Wilkes-Barre Mountain to the Delaware River, some to perish on the way. Denison reported that five persons were murdered on the road. Lazarus Stewart's widowed wife, Martha, with an infant at the breast and her other six children, the eldest a ten-year-old, boarded two canoes lashed together and floated down the Susquehanna to Bloomsburg, the home of her sister, Mrs. James McClure. After a short stay, still fearful of the Indians, she continued to her old home in Lancaster County.

Butler's pledge to protect property proved empty words. The Indians rampaged through the Wyoming Valley, robbing the inhabitants and plundering and burning their homes and crops. Butler reported the burning of one thousand homes (an exaggeration, since there were not that many in the entire valley) and all the flour mills. One thousand horned cattle and many horses were killed or driven off, as well as flocks of sheep and swine. "Wioming is totally abandoned," reported William Maclay, a delegate from neighboring Northumberland County to the Pennsylvania General Assembly.[20] A mass exodus, "The Great Runaway," began from the whole Susquehanna West Branch Valley.

CHAPTER 4

✦ ✦ ✦ ✦ ✦ ✦ ✦ ✦ ✦ ✦ ✦

"WE DESTROYED MEN, WOMEN, AND CHILDREN"

John Butler considered the no-quarter battlefield slaughter and death torture of prisoners as merely "conformable to Indian custom." The people of the Wyoming Valley considered them a heinous "massacre," and with the sack of the settlements and the attacks on settlers in their fields, the cries redoubled for protection. Connecticut's Governor Jonathan Trumbull urged Washington to send a force of fifteen hundred or two thousand to protect the crops and "pursue the detestable Banditti into their own country." Since Gates had made no move, the Congress turned to the Board of War, and the Board turned to Washington, who until now had been kept in the dark about the expedition.

"I do not find," he reported on August 3, "that any preparations have been made." He conferred with Gates, who blandly "imagined it was laid aside," and with Governor Clinton, who happened to be in camp at White Plains, and both of them counseled against starting so late in the year. He concluded that even if Gates had begun preparations a month earlier, the season would have been too far gone and the available resources of manpower and magazines too limited for an expedition in 1778. A force of not less than three thousand would be required to ensure success. Not more than twelve hundred militia and five hundred Continentals, already on the frontier, were on hand. Further reinforcements could not be spared from

Washington's main army, which was attempting to contain the British in New York and Rhode Island. It would take five months to outfit the expedition, raise the troops, invade the Seneca country, and return. Such a venture, extending more than three hundred miles through wild and unexplored country, would have to contend with the rigors of a north country winter and rivers made shallow at that time of year.

These reservations, however, masked something more fundamental: Washington questioned the advisability of any expedition at all into the Seneca country. He preferred an incursion into Canada, which would "strike at once at the root of the Indian depredations." The proposal against the Seneca "would only lop off a few branches, which would soon spread out anew, nourished and sustained by the remaining trunk," and he went so far as to say that such an attempt would have to await the withdrawal of the British from the northeast. In the meantime, he was willing to spare three hundred Continental troops somewhere near Unadilla to safeguard the frontier. So Washington held an opinion similar to Gates's, except that Gates was attempting a Canadian invasion of his own, without the authorization of Congress or of Washington.

Congress could not dispute Washington's tactical objections, and it agreed that the expedition "be for the present laid aside." But neither did it accept his substitution of an invasion of Canada for an expedition into the Seneca territory. It persisted in its concern for frontier defense and turned over the direction of that operation to him, rather than Gates. Washington had already sent reinforcements of Continentals—Colonel Ichabod Alden's Sixth Massachusetts Regiment to Albany, Colonel Thomas Hartley's Eleventh Pennsylvania Regiment to Sunbury on the Susquehanna River West Branch, and Lieutenant Colonel William Butler's Fourth Pennsylvania Regiment to Fort Schoharie.[1]

Washington might delay, but Brant did not. His raids extended as far to the east as the Hudson Valley, and early in September he burned the settlement of Marbletown, seven miles southwest of Kingston.[2]

With captives and cattle, he returned to Oquaga and Unadilla to assemble a force for an attack along the Mohawk Valley. Colonel Peter Bellinger, the commandant at Fort Dayton, sent out a party of nine scouts to determine his objective, and on September 16, at the head branch of the Unadilla River, they were attacked by a band of Indians headed for German Flatts. Three of the scouts were killed, but the fourth, Adam Helmer, a hardy long-distance runner, escaped. He sped twenty-six miles, keeping ahead of his pursuers, and arrived in the evening, exhausted, at Fort Herkimer. A warning gun also gave the alarm to Fort Dayton, where the inhabitants took refuge. The following morning, the marauders arrived at Fort Dayton—300 Loyalists under Captain William Caldwell and 152 Indians under Brant. The garrison held them off, but it was too small to retaliate. The attackers burned the entire settlement of German Flatts and a ten-mile stretch along the south side of the Mohawk River toward Fort Herkimer, including sixty-three homes and fifty-seven barns stocked with grain and fodder. Hundreds of horses, horned cattle, and sheep were driven away.[3]

Retaliation seemed essential. If not a major expedition, flying raids might still be attempted against focal centers from which the Indians had launched their incursions. Since St. Leger's expedition had come from Oswego, now unoccupied, Colonel Gansevoort at Fort Stanwix dispatched a detachment there under Lieutenant McClellan early in July to destroy the buildings at Fort Ontario and forestall British return. They found only a woman and her children, whom they left in an outbuilding while the other structures were burned.[4]

Since Brant's base of operations had been the two Susquehanna villages of Unadilla and Oquaga, Brigadier General John Stark proposed a raid there in late June. The arrival of Colonel William Butler's force provided the manpower, and Washington considered him "not only a very brave but an experienced Officer, especially for such an expedition."[5] Prisoners reported that the two villages contained, respectively, three hundred and four hundred inhabitants. At the head of 14 officers and 190 enlisted men of the Fourth Pennsylvania Regiment of Continentals, and 20 Rangers from Daniel Morgan's

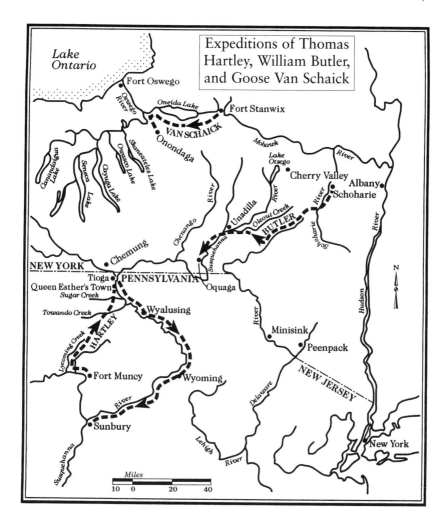

Expeditions of Thomas Hartley, William Butler, and Goose Van Schaick

rifle corps, Butler set out on October 2 from Schoharie, thirty-five miles southwest of Albany.

He started up the Schoharie River, crossed over the mountains in rainy weather along a hazardous, narrow trail to the Delaware, then to the south side of Oleout Creek, and arrived on the morning of October 7 at Unadilla on the Susquehanna. There they learned that Brant had left several days before. He seems not to have known of

Butler's approach and had departed southeastward toward the Delaware Valley, where on October 13 he attacked the little settlement of Peenpack (the present Cuddebackville) on the Neversink River. All the inhabitants there who had not taken refuge in its three blockhouses were killed, including the Swartwout family of a father and four sons.

Butler's force paused long enough for the troops to refresh themselves then continued toward Oquaga, stopping that night in a drenching rain. He waited until the night of October 9 to attack, and after climbing a mile-long, thickly wooded hill, entered the town to find it deserted. Forty houses spread over both sides of the river, constructed of square logs and shingles and equipped with glass windows, stone chimneys, and good floors, "the finest Indian Town I ever saw," he reported. All were burned, along with a large quantity of corn. After another heavy rain, Butler's force turned back, destroying small Indian towns on the way, and stopped at Unadilla to put the entire settlement to the torch. Altogether, they burned four thousand bushels of grain. The expedition returned October 16.[6]

In order to safeguard the return of the settlers of the Wyoming Valley to their desolated homes, early in August Continental Army units arrived to reinforce local militia—a detachment under Zebulon Butler at Wyoming and Hartley's Eleventh Regiment of the Pennsylvania Line at Fort Muncy, near the junction of the Lycoming Creek with the West Branch of the Susquehanna. Nevertheless, attacks by bands of Indians on men in the fields and women and children in their homes were so widespread that there was no safety outside of the forts. Hartley, eager to take the offensive, learned from Pennsylvania's vice president, George Bryan, of William Butler's planned expedition against Oquaga, and he determined to combine with it an attack of his own on Tioga. A thirty-year-old lawyer from York, Pennsylvania, he had served in Canada in 1776 in the engagement at Three Rivers and in 1777 at the battles of Brandywine and Germantown. He saw his raid as part of a comprehensive strategy: "The Expedition from the North and the Expedition to the Westward into the Indian Country will appear about the Beginning of Septr [and] our movement may have a happy effect, I trust these Frontiers will soon be Cleared of the Savages."[7]

For the two-hundred-mile trek through the wilderness, he assembled at Fort Muncy about two hundred rank and file, half the number he had hoped for. With provisions for an estimated twelve days, he started out at four in the morning of September 21, down the roaring torrent of Lycoming Creek. It rained every day, and the men had to wade the creek six or seven times, sometimes breast deep. They had to hack their way through a tangle of wild vines and thick underbrush, climbing steep hills and sloshing through muddy swamps. At Towando Creek, they crossed overland northward to Sugar Creek, where on September 26 an advance guard came upon a party of nineteen Indians. They killed and scalped an Indian chief, and the rest fled. Further along they took two captives, from whom they learned that a deserter from Wyoming had given warning of the expedition.

This made it clear that they had lost the element of surprise, and speed was essential. By nightfall of September 26, they forded the Chemung River at its junction with the Susquehanna and reached an abandoned Indian village at Tioga Point. There they learned from a prisoner that, a few hours earlier, a force of three hundred, mainly Sir John Johnson's Greens, under John Butler's son, Captain Walter N. Butler, who had recently escaped from his Albany jail, had left for Chemung, twelve miles northwestward. They also learned that there had been no sign of the expected American expedition of William Butler from the east. Without such support, and outnumbered by a nearby enemy, Hartley stayed long enough to burn Tioga and the adjacent Indian settlements and regretfully turned back toward Wyoming. "Had we had 500 regular Troops, and 150 Light Troops, with one or two Pieces of artillery," he lamented, "we might have destroyed Chemung, which is now the recepticle of all villainous Indians & Tories from the different Tribes and states."

Injuries had now reduced the rebels to 120 rank and file. On the morning of October 29, at Wyalusing, with whiskey, flour, and prepared rations gone, they had to stop to kill and cook beef. Resuming their march, by two o'clock they reached the deserted plantation of a Loyalist, John De Pui, at the mouth of Tuscarora Creek. Johnson's Greens by then had had time to catch up. With a force of two hundred they attacked the rear troops. "We had no alternative but Conquest or Death," Hartley reported; "they would have murdered us all had they succeeded." He posted his two forward companies on an elevation overlooking the Indians and sent a detachment to circle back behind their rear. Then, with shouts and war whoops, the rebels charged in unison, and the Indians, believing themselves surrounded, fled to the river, leaving ten dead behind them. For the remaining fifty miles to Wyoming, Hartley's men continued unmolested, arriving October 5. They had lost four killed and ten wounded.

Hartley had achieved his immediate objective, but not the larger one of security for the frontier. It might even be said that he had only provoked the Indians. He sent a written message to them at their village at Chemung, threatening to attack with "fire and Sword" if they did not stop the "inhuman Murders" of "helpless Mothers and Infants" and the "barbarous Practice of killing and burning Prisoners." They hotly denied the charges and returned to Wyoming and killed and scalped three men scavenging for potatoes. Hartley was gloomy. "I have given all the Support in my Power to that Post," he wrote to the Continental Congress, "but if Troops are not immediately sent, these Settlements will be destroyed in Detail."[8]

John Butler had "the sincerest satisfaction," he said, that in the destruction of Wyoming "not a single person has been hurt of the inhabitants but such as were in arms; to those indeed the Indians gave no quarter." Oquaga and Tioga changed that. "You Burned our Houses, which makes us and our Brothers the Seneca Indians angrey," declared a deputation of Mohawk chiefs. Among the Senecas, the return of soldiers and settlers to Wyoming and the expedition of Hartley inspired a rumor that a major invasion was in the wings. Four hundred alarmed warriors turned out.[9] The victory at Wyoming had gone for nothing. Butler's restrictions had shackled traditional

Indian-style warfare. In future, no civilians would be spared, neither women nor children.

Ostensibly, Butler was in command of united operations, and his next target was the Mohawk Valley. Crippling rheumatism, however, sidelined him. His son, Walter, would have to take over. Twenty-five years old, he was a lawyer by training, with undistinguished military experience, an inflated opinion of his abilities, and no talent for conciliation. Inheriting his father's disputes, he quickly clashed with Brant, the issue being Butler's claim of authority over the whites serving under Brant. Brant threatened to leave the expedition but was dissuaded by the Indians. Ninety of his men did depart, leaving him with only about thirty followers.

The destruction of Tioga did not prevent a grand council of Tories and Indians from being held there to formulate plans. Butler's force consisted of 321 Indians, mostly Senecas and Cayugas led by Cornplanter, 150 Rangers, and 50 regulars from the Eighth Regiment. The expedition started October 29 from Niagara overland to the Chemung River, on to the Susquehanna, past the ruins at Tioga, Oquaga, and Unadilla. On the night of November 9, an advance party led by Brant and Cornplanter spotted the campfire thoughtlessly lit by a nine-man scouting party sent out from the fort at Cherry Valley. In the early dawn all were taken, and their leader, Sergeant Adam Hunter, a former Loyalist, provided complete information about the defenses of the fort, including the news that two days before, an Oneida Indian had brought word of the coming of the British. He also divulged the location of a house four hundred yards from the fort in which the principal officers were staying.

By November 10, on a cold night under a heavy snow, they reached a wooded hill about six miles from Cherry Valley. Butler wished to move on the fort immediately, but he had only a loose control over the Indians, who would not advance in the snowstorm until the morning. He elicited from them a dubious promise, similar to the one they had given John Butler at Wyoming, not to harm noncombatants.[10]

Cherry Valley, noted for its profuse wild blossoms, had contained some three hundred settlers, most from New Hampshire, at the start of the Revolution. Its Fort Alden, a stockade surrounding the town church, had been constructed by rangers and militia in the spring of 1778 and unpropitiously named for its pigheaded first commander. Ichabod Alden's Sixth Massachusetts Regiment of 250 men had no experience of Indian warfare. On November 8, he received warning of the coming of the British from Gansevoort, the commander at Stanwix—he had heard of it from an Oneida Indian who had brought news of the meeting of the council at Tioga. Brigadier Edward Hand, who had replaced Stark in the northern command at Albany, happened to be at Fort Alden on an inspection trip when the message arrived, and he advised the inhabitants to move their belongings into the fort. After he left, the obtuse Alden, confident that he knew best when it was time to seek shelter, refused admission of personal possessions. Neither did he send an immediate request to Colonel William Butler, at Schoharie, for reinforcement. He sent scouts out to check two incoming roads but neglected an old Indian path, the very one the British were taking. The result proved tragic.

In the morning of November 10, John Butler's entire force advanced to the outskirts of the village and stopped at a swamp, a short distance behind a house where Alden and some of his officers lodged. While the Rangers were examining their rifles and powder for rain damage, shots rang out from two Indians who had surprised two men cutting wood, one of whom, though wounded, managed to reach the fort. A party of Senecas under Chief Little Beard sprang forward to the Wells house, where they were met with fire that wounded three. Infuriated, they rushed into the house. Alden attempted to escape but was tomahawked and scalped. Two captains, two lieutenants, one ensign, and twenty privates were killed. Robert Wells and his mother, wife, brother and sister, three sons, and a daughter were massacred—twelve in all, including three servants. Taken prisoner were Lieutenant Colonel William Stacey, another lieutenant, an ensign, a surgeon's mate, and ten privates. Some of the officers living in other homes managed to escape into the fort, but many were killed or captured. Brant, a friend of Robert Wells, later stated that he had hurried toward his house to protect him but was held up in crossing a large plowed field.

The defenders in the fort were now under the command of Major Daniel Whiting, one of the officers in the outlying houses who had eluded capture. With far fewer men than the attackers, he did not make the mistake of the garrison at Wyoming and did not sally forth to invite destruction. Butler and his Rangers and Indians lacked artillery to penetrate the stockades. After a few hours of musket fire they turned instead to the plunder and destruction of the entire community. Whiting could only sit helplessly by, watching the flames on the horizon, powerless to hinder the pillage and murder. The Indians treated rebel and Tory settlers with equal ferocity. "We Destroyed men, women, and Children," declared their chiefs. All told, the dead included sixteen soldiers and thirty-two inhabitants, chiefly women and children. Butler, while keeping watch on the fort from an overlooking hill in order to prevent Whiting's men from interfering, piously lamented that he could not prevent women and children from "falling unhappy victims to the fury of the savages." He did manage, with the assistance of Brant and another Indian chief, Captain Jacobs, to secure the return of a dozen Tory captives. Altogether, some seventy captives were taken, half of whom were released to return to Cherry Valley and the remainder taken to Indian villages, where they were not unkindly received.[11]

Rebel and Tory both testified to the horror. Captain Benjamin Warren, leaving the fort after the British had gone, was overwhelmed. "Such a shocking sight my eyes never held before of savage and brutal barbarity; to see the husband mourning over his dead wife with four dead children lying by her side, mangled, scalpt, and some their heads, some their legs and arms cut off, some torn the flesh off their bones by their dogs—12 of one family killed and four of them burnt in his house." The Tory Ranger, Captain Richard Cartwright, denounced "such acts of wanton cruelty committed by bloodthirsty savages as humanity would shudder to mention."[12]

*

Governor Clinton became desperate. Cherry Valley, the seventh settlement destroyed during the year, had been considered the most secure, yet had succumbed. He demanded from the Continental Congress "More effective Measures than have hitherto been pursued." Unless help were speedily sent, the Indian attacks would "end in the total Desolation of the most valuable Parts of this state," and with them the grain supply that the Continental Army "depended upon for Bread." Untrained local militia and dispersed detachments of regular troops could not hope to stem the sack of poorly defended settlements. Nothing less than "carrying the War into the Enemy's Country" with a major force would do.[13]

It was not the Congress, however, that Clinton had to persuade, but Washington. Rather than an expedition into the Iroquois heartland, he had preferred an attack on Fort Niagara, the British supply base for the war parties. Did he have the manpower for either venture? Could he now resist Clinton's importunities and the Congress's pressures?

CHAPTER 5

✦ ✦ ✦ ✦ ✦ ✦ ✦ ✦ ✦ ✦ ✦

MISSION
DEVASTATION

In September of 1778, Washington mistakenly believed that Britain was about to withdraw its forces from the United States in order to deploy them against France and Spain in the West Indies. He mistook for total evacuation an amphibious force of five thousand being prepared at New York for an attack on St. Lucia in the Leeward Islands. By October 23, he learned more reliably that the main British army, now under Sir Henry Clinton, who had replaced Howe, was to remain at New York.[1] This meant that American troops could not be spared from the Hudson for an invasion of Canada. If not Canada, could he any longer resist the importunities from the states and from Congress for an expedition against the Iroquois? And if he consented, would he not be contravening his expressed reservations against a halfway measure that could not prevent the raids from springing up again? But the pressures mounted. "The cries of the distressed, of the fatherless and the Widows, come to me from all quarters," he agonized to John Armstrong. They "appeared to leave me no alternative."[2]

There was, in fact, an alternative, proposed by Brigadier General Lachlan McIntosh, who had recently returned from an aborted expedition against the Delawares of the Ohio country. He advocated establishing a network of forts in the heart of the Indian country, cooperating with each other to suppress Indian threats before they could erupt. He had proposed such a system in his native Georgia, and Major General Charles Lee had endorsed it. But Washington had

long opposed such a scheme, which required an extended commitment of troops and an allocation of provisions that he could not
spare.[3] It would not satisfy the public demand for decisive action.

Or did Washington have a deeper motive? In 1929, Alexander C.
Flick, then state historian of New York, advanced a "reinterpreta-
tion": The British had to be deprived of the Six Nations' cornfields,
vegetable gardens, orchards, and herds of cattle as an essential food
source for the British army and navy. Conversely, the American
farms of the Mohawk and Susquehanna valleys had to be protected
as producers of vital crops for the sustenance of Washington's armies.
Most significantly, Washington was looking ahead to the boundaries
America could claim when peace terms were negotiated with Britain.
He wished to establish American claims to western New York and
Pennsylvania as part of a territory reaching to the Mississippi.

Flick published two comprehensive compendiums of documents of
the expedition, but nowhere in them is there corroborative evidence.
The Iroquois economy had not produced the crop surplus or the
distribution technique to provision British armies. ("It is well
known," wrote John Butler, "that they never raise more . . . than will
just suffice for their own subsistence.") American armies did not
depend exclusively on crops of the Mohawk and Susquehanna valleys. Shortages resulted rather from a general economic collapse
caused by soaring prices, constantly inflating currency, and commod-
ity suppliers' speculation. As to Washington's long-term territorial
insights, his surviving 1779 correspondence yields no clues.[4] He had
confessed his motivation to Armstrong—he must satisfy public outrage.

Once his decision was made, he emerged as determined an advocate of revenge as any frontiersman. He would wipe out the Indians'
villages and food stocks. He would provoke them to pitched battle,
and "extirpate them from the Country." They were to call him
"Town Destroyer."[5]

But he still had to contend with the unrelenting demands of the
advocates of a Canadian incursion. Horatio Gates was the prime
promoter. He had an obsession to follow up his victory at Saratoga

with a conquest of Canada, and for the past year he had been pursuing it without consulting Washington. As president of the Board of War, he had maneuvered the appointment of the Marquis de Lafayette to head an invasion army. French Canadians would rally to him, and then Gates could persuade Congress that he himself, not a Frenchman, should assume the command. The scheme had failed. Lafayette had become suspicious, and Congress canceled the invasion. Gates was accused of undercutting Washington as part of a plot, never proved, to supersede him as commander in chief—the "Conway Cabal." He was reassigned to the command at Fishkill on the Hudson, where, as we have seen, he showed no disposition to carry out Congress's directive for an expedition against the Iroquois. In November 1778 he was redeployed to the command at Boston. There he still did not give up the invasion, and this time he was joined as a cohort by Lafayette, who by then had rediscovered a Canadian ambition. On October 13, Lafayette submitted to Congress a bold request to return to France in order to obtain a French naval squadron for an expedition to the St. Lawrence. It would join with major American land forces targeted at Montreal and Niagara.[6]

To Washington's dismay, Congress approved. He rode from his camp at Middlebrook in New Jersey to Philadelphia. Where, he asked Congress, were the 12,600 American troops for such a project, and how were the French to surmount Britain's superior naval power? Would Lafayette not become an entering wedge for French reclamation of Canada? A limited, unilateral American operation against Detroit and Niagara might be attempted, but a move against Montreal should be no more than a feint to divert British attention from the west. The Congress capitulated. On January 1, 1779, they canceled the Canadian invasion. They approved the offensive against Detroit and Niagara.[7]

Gates was bitterly disappointed, and he was furious at what he took to be the substitution of an invasion through the route of the Great Lakes in place of his own by way of the Connecticut River and the St. Lawrence. Casting restraint aside, he wrote John Jay that "Individuals, and not the Public, will be benefitted" by an expedition into Canada "without the Co-operation of the Allied Fleet." In fact, no expedition was actually contemplated. Even the token offensive against Niagara was soon abandoned. When Washington received from Jay a copy of the accusation, he exploded at the "Malevolence" and "little underhand intrigues" with which Gates "eagerly seizes the opportunity of exposing my supposed errors to Congress."[8] Gates was discredited and ignored. The Iroquois expedition had lost its chief impediment.

For the first time in the war, Washington was conceiving a campaign of his own initiation, rather than as a response to a confrontation thrust upon him. Approval from Congress for a revival of the aborted expedition of 1778 came on February 25 — a campaign, said Pennsylvania's President Joseph Reed, "to make the savages, and the more *savage Christians* among them, feel the weight of the American arms."[9] Washington had already begun planning, and his first move was to consult Nathanael Greene, then serving as quartermaster general but retaining his military rank as major general and remaining Washington's most trusted advisor. They were both in Philadelphia on January 5, and Greene sat up until sunrise working out a proposal.

He knew Washington's mind. He did not attempt to contend with objections. The problem of preventing revival of Indian aggression from Canada was shunted to the side. The expedition, he said, must be purely punitive — "to scourge the Indians at the proper season, driving off the Indians and destroying their Grain and as soon as that is completed to return . . ." He proposed a three-pronged sweep of their territory, to begin in June, when their corn crops were about half grown. One division would move from Fort Pitt, a second from Wyoming, and the third along the Mohawk River.[10]

Washington also asked advice from Schuyler, who had long been an advocate of an expedition against the Indians. Like Washington, he had aimed at throttling the raids at their source. His main target had been Fort Niagara, the British refuge and supply center. Washington, however, had already informed him that the need for troops

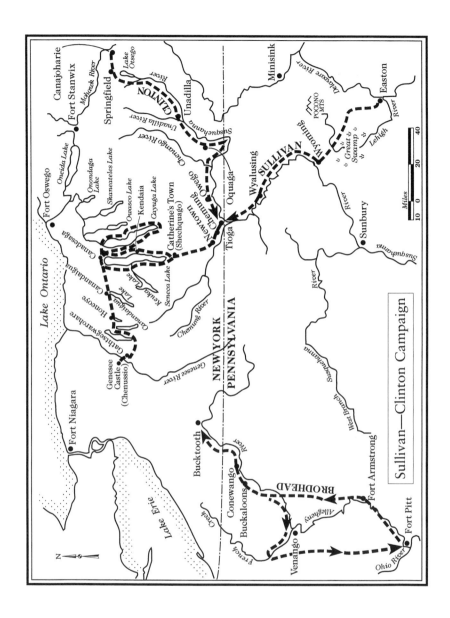

Sullivan—Clinton Campaign

79

to pen Sir Henry Clinton in at New York City had forced cancelation of the Niagara expedition. Schuyler had to devise a new strategy. He proposed a radically different approach—a campaign of surprise attacks on Indian villages for the purpose of capturing old men, women, and children and using them as hostages to bring the chiefs to the bargaining council. "I conceive," he wrote, "that we should then have the means of preventing them thereafter from acting hostily against us." His plan was for a three-thousand-man expedition, moving in two bodies from Albany. The first, eighteen hundred, would proceed to Oswego, leave a garrison of two hundred, and continue to Irondequoit, where an attack could be expected from the whole strength of the Indians, leaving their villages unprotected. Assuming an Indian defeat, two hundred men would be left to secure Irondequoit, and the remainder would march against the defenseless Seneca villages. The second body, of twelve hundred, would move from Albany to Fort Stanwix, attack the Onondaga and Cayuga villages, and then join the first body in a full-scale operation against the Seneca villages. As a diversion, a third force of five hundred would operate from Wyoming to cut off Chemung and prevent the Delawares and the Mingoes from coming to the aid of the Iroquois.[11] Crossing the Indian territory along the north would have the advantage of cutting off the escape route of the noncombatants.

This posed a dilemma for Washington. Greene's plan for the Susquehanna route had all but persuaded him, but Schuyler was senior to Greene, an expert on the New York scene, sensitive to criticism leveled at him for the loss of Ticonderoga, and, as Washington addressed him, a "private friend and a friend of his Country." Washington replied that he was choosing between the Susquehanna and Mohawk routes and needed more information. He enclosed a long list of queries concerning the extent and intentions of enemy forces, the lay of the land, manpower needs, the logistics of supply, and the temper of the Indians.[12]

Schuyler remained convinced that the capture of the Indians' families would be "an almost certain means of bringing the whole confederacy to proper terms." He would alter his plan only to the extent of unifying the two invading bodies from Albany into one, and he labored six days over a detailed prospectus of the operation. That army would move from Albany along the Mohawk to Fort Stanwix, temporarily leaving a garrison of four hundred and continuing to Wood Creek into Oneida Lake, where a stockade for another one hundred men would be left. From there a body of twelve hundred would march south to Onondaga, thence westward to Cayuga, where another stockade would be erected for two hundred men. The troops left behind at Stanwix and Wood Creek would move by water to unite at Cayuga for the concluding invasion of the Seneca territory.[13]

Just as he was concluding his somewhat incoherent schema, a letter of February 16 arrived from Washington asking detailed information about the Susquehanna route and leaving little doubt that he preferred it. Schuyler still would not give up. "A Thought has occurred which I will venture for your Excellency's Consideration," he replied. A force of five hundred might be detached from Fort Stanwix to march fifty miles through open country for an attack on the village of Onondaga. The Onondagas were the "keepers" of the council fire of the Six Nations confederacy, and Onondaga was their "castle." Some of them had come over to the Patriot side, but many had inclined toward the British. All the Iroquois were hard up for food, and the subjugation of the Onondagas could "bring the others to Terms and supercede the Necessity of an Expedition."[14] This proposal was clearly an ill-considered attempt to have things his own way. He was not a well man. "I am torn to pieces and reduced to a Skeleton by the Gout, and disorders still more alarming,"[15] he wrote to James Duane soon afterward, and he may not have been thinking connectedly. As a seasoned negotiator with the Indians, he should have known that an assault on the central symbol of their league would provoke reprisal rather than submission.

For his response, Washington turned again to Greene. In a long position paper, he emphatically disagreed with Schuyler's hopes for a negotiated peace:

The great objective of the expedition should be to give the Indians a severe chastising, anything short of that will not compensate for the trouble and expence in preparing for the expedition. I have no doubt the Indians will be glad to come to term when they see we are about to enter their Country in good earnest; but unless their pride is broke down and they sufficiently humbled Little benefit will result from any Negotiation that may take place. The British will soon spirit them up to commit the same depredations again as they did the last Campaign.

As a palliative to Schuyler, he agreed that an attack on Onondaga was "worth attempting." It fitted into the rest of the program of chastisement. Greene knew nothing about Indian warfare and gave no thought to the hazard of reprisal. "Should it fail," he casually concluded, "I dont apprehend any very bad consequences from it."

Greene's main concern was to promote the Susquehanna route. He had been collecting geographical information from Robert L. Hooper, a deputy quartermaster general more knowledgeable about south central New York than Schuyler, and he was more persuaded than ever that the Susquehanna route was in "every way preferable to that which is recommended by Schuyler. The Stores can be convey'd to the borders of the Indian Country at a much less expence. The approches to the Seneca Country much less difficult and complex, the distance much shorter and the retreat infinitely more secure, in case of a defeat."[16]

These rebuttals Washington embodied in a reply to Schuyler, smoothed somewhat with the hope that the Indians "may neglect in some places to remove the old men women and children and that these will fall into our hands." Failing that, the objective must be to destroy their villages and burn their crops. The campaign would comprise three operations. The main body of three thousand would move northward up the Susquehanna into the Seneca homeland. A second division of one thousand would march westward through the Mohawk Valley. The third of five hundred would attack by way of the Ohio and Allegheny rivers and join up with the first in the Seneca country. As a feint to mislead the British into expecting an invasion of Canada, orders had already been given for a Continental regiment under Colonel Moses Hazen to march northward to Co'os, New Hampshire, on the Connecticut River. Washington did endorse Schuyler's plan for a surprise attack on Onondaga, apparently with no more recognition of the consequences than had Greene.[17]

Having received Washington's approval, Schuyler formulated plans for the attack on Onondaga with Brigadier General James Clinton, the new commander of the Northern Department. They agreed to assign the operation to Colonel Goose Van Schaick.[18] A son of the mayor of Albany, as the head of the First New York Regiment he had served under Montgomery in the 1775 invasion of Canada and in 1777 had been wounded at Ticonderoga. He was a stern, heavy man with graying, coarse hair and piercing eyes and a painful, cancerous gash on his left cheek, where he had been struck with the butt of a French musket. Companies drawn from regiments in the Schoharie and Mohawk valleys rendezvoused at Fort Stanwix on April 16. They totaled 558 officers and men—six New York companies, one each from Pennsylvania and Massachusetts, and one of riflemen—with Lieutenant Colonel Marinus Willett and Major Robert Cochrane second and third in command.

They found assembled there a group of Oneida and Tuscarora Indians, attracted by the preparations, who petitioned to join the expedition. Van Schaick, fearful that through them the Onondagas might be forewarned, denied that anything was afoot, but he sensed that they might be useful as a decoy to discourage any British thought of assistance for Onondaga. On April 18, in falling snow in the early afternoon, he sent northward a party of sixty warriors, led by Lieutenants Thomas McClennan and John L. Hardenbergh, for a raid on a small British garrison at Oswegatchie. It proved unnecessary. Captives taken on the way revealed that Sir John Johnson's regiment of Johnson's Greens at Buck Island was too decimated by disease to constitute a threat. Since Oswegatchie was impregnably garrisoned by two officers and forty men, armed with four cannon, McClennan

and Hardenbergh, after a brief skirmish with a scouting party, returned with several Onondaga and three British prisoners to Stanwix.[19]

That same day, April 18, thirty bateaux of stores arrived at Stanwix from Schenectady. The troops were ordered to draw three days'
provisions and prepare to depart for Onondaga the next morning.
During the night, the boats were conveyed over the Carrying Place
to Wood Creek, to be ready to proceed with eight days' provisions
downstream to meet the troops at Oneida Lake. At sunrise, the snow
still falling, the men started westward down the shore of the creek
and marched twenty-two miles to Oneida Lake, which they reached
by three o'clock. The boats, slowed by trees fallen across the creek,
arrived at ten o'clock. The troops embarked for a rough trip through
the night faced by a high, cold headwind, with two halts for the rear
boats to catch up, thirty-three miles to the foot of the lake. At three
o'clock they disembarked opposite old Fort Brewerton.

Rum was distributed, and the march resumed in two parallel columns one hundred yards apart for Onondaga Lake (then known to
Americans as the Salt Lake). They traveled nine miles protected by
darkness. After a cold night without a fire, the next morning they
reached an arm of the lake, four feet deep, which they had to wade
with their pouches hung on their fixed bayonets. They were now
approaching the creek where Onondaga settlements spread along
both sides for eight miles. Two miles away, the flanking company
came upon an Indian shooting pigeons and took its first prisoner.
Further on, they found a group, from which they caught one woman
and killed another and took two or three children and one white man
captive. Still undiscovered, the Americans surprised the first settlement of fifty-odd houses and then fanned out to encompass the rest
of them, so rapidly that the terrified fugitives fled into the woods,
leaving behind all their possessions.

In an eight-hour sweep of destruction, the Americans plundered
the houses of all the valuables they could carry off, including one
hundred guns and much ammunition. The houses were put to the
torch; chief among them was the eighty-foot longhouse that con-

tained the council fire of the Great League. Five fine horses and a number of hogs were killed, and a large quantity of corn and beans was destroyed. Twelve Indians and "a Negro who was their doctor" were killed. Thirty-four were taken captive, including two sachems, six warriors, twelve women, thirteen children, and one white man. Not a single American was lost. The weather turned fair, and after camping overnight on Seven Mile Island (now Frenchman Island) in Lake Oneida, Van Schaick's men returned to Stanwix by the same route, interrupted only by a small party of Indians, one of whom was killed and the rest beaten off by the riflemen. They had traveled 180 miles in five and a half days.[20]

So Schuyler had his palliation, and to what purpose? If he expected the Onondaga expedition to produce hostages in order to intimidate the Iroquois to negotiation, it proved a delusion. They had no facilities to house the prisoners, and the Oneidas threatened that if some of them were not released, they would join the British.[21] Instead of negotiation, the expedition infuriated the Iroquois to revenge. They recognized that they were experiencing the start of a campaign of merciless chastisement. Paradoxically, Schuyler had supplied the opening gun.

✦ ✦ ✦ ✦ ✦ ✦ ✦ ✦ ✦ ✦ ✦

CHAPTER 6

CRY MASSACRE

The officer appointed to command the expedition, Washington wrote Jay, "has a flattering prospect of acquiring more credit than can be expected by any other this year." Yet in the selection seniority might supersede talent. Charles Lee, at the top, remained under suspension for his conduct at the Battle of Monmouth. Schuyler, the favorite of New York's Governor Clinton, was too often debilitated by poor health even if he could be persuaded to withdraw his resignation. Israel Putnam was judged incompetent. Next in line came Gates, unpalatable though he might be. Reluctantly, Washington offered him the command in a letter that read more like an invitation to refusal than a desire for acceptance. He enclosed a letter to the real candidate, Major General John Sullivan, tendering the appointment to him in the expectation that Gates would decline. Gates could hardly accept, even if he had been so inclined. "The man, who undertakes the Indian service, should enjoy youth and strength; requisites I do not possess. It therefore grieves me," he indignantly replied, "that your Exly. should offer me the only command to which I am entirely unequal." Washington, not too unhappy, wrote Jay that his letter "merited a different answer than the one given to it."[1] In no better health than Gates, Sullivan was also so strapped for funds that he had to borrow money for his journey to Middlebrook, but after a brief hesitation he accepted.[2]

Washington had preferred this man from the beginning. Although he had limited formal schooling, he had received from his father, a schoolmaster, a good basic education and had enlarged it with a wide course of reading. Although he was a New Hampshire lawyer who had obtained his appointment through political prominence rather than military experience, Washington sized him up from their first association during the 1775 siege of Boston as an officer of "enterprising genius." Temperamentally, he was volatile and a hard drinker whose symptoms, as reviewed by a twentieth-century physician, suggested a peptic, bleeding ulcer. His early military engagements were unlucky. At Trois Rivières in Canada, his enterprise translated into imprudence. At Brooklyn Heights in New York he was captured and used by Sir William Howe, as John Adams charged, as a "decoy duck" in promoting negotiations aimed at inveigling the Americans to renounce independence. Exchanged, he redeemed himself in actions at Trenton and Princeton, only to be criticized for failures at Staten Island, Brandywine, and Germantown. Extremely ambitious, he complained to Washington that he had "never yet had a post assigned me where there was Even a probability of Acquiring Honor." This although Washington had urged him not to torment himself with "evils that exist only in the imagination, and with slights, that have no existence at all."[3] He was given an independent command in Rhode Island, where he lashed out intemperately at the Count d'Estaing, commander of a French squadron there, for sailing off to Boston and aborting a combined attack against the British at Newport. He also antagonized Pennsylvanians, whose president, Joseph Reed, when he heard that Sullivan was to command, told Nathanael Greene that he "had no hopes of success." Pennsylvania's General John Armstrong wrote Washington that he preferred Colonel Daniel Brodhead. Pennsylvania congressman Benjamin Rush considered Sullivan "weak—vain—without dignity—fond of scribling—in the field a madman." Washington needed some "madness." And Greene, on whom he relied so heavily for advice, thought that although Sullivan had "not been remarkably fortunate in success," he was "Sensible, Active, Ambitious, brave, and persevering in his temper."[4]

Physically, Sullivan communicated a vigorous image. Broad-shouldered and barrel-chested, he was a solid, if slightly overweight five feet eight inches in height. He had black, curly hair and black, piercing eyes. His features were surprisingly delicate—high, widely spaced cheekbones in a triangular-shaped face, a straight, pointed nose, and pursed lips almost femininely curved. In his impeccably tailored blue uniform, he stood imposingly erect and commanding. His voice was rich and mellow.[5] He sought and achieved popularity with his men.

Sullivan arrived at Middlebrook April 10 to confer with Washington. He studied the proposals of Greene and Schuyler, and he examined the mass of topographical data and maps gathered from knowledge-able officers and local residents. He proved as unpredictable as he was forceful. In a closely reasoned paper on April 16, he argued for Schuyler's plan of a Mohawk route as against Greene's for the Sus-quehanna. Primarily, he wanted a four-thousand-man thrust along the Mohawk as a shield against a British offensive from Canada. The second division, coming up the Susquehanna, should number twenty-five hundred. At first it would serve as a feint to keep the southern Indians away from the Mohawk, and afterward as an offensive into the Seneca country. The next day he reversed himself. A letter arrived from Schuyler to Washington, loyally agreeing to the Susquehanna route and adding that scarcity of flour in New York State could hinder an operation along the Mohawk. Sullivan, deprived of Schuy-ler's support and looking for a face-saving excuse to concede, mag-nified the scarcity of flour into a crucial scarcity of all provisions. Now that the division on the Susquehanna had become the main one, however, he insisted that it should number approximately four thou-sand.[6]

But Washington had had enough of Sullivan's objections. He de-cided that the troops for the expedition would begin on May 12 to rendezvous by the twentieth at Easton, on the eastern side of the Delaware River where it is joined by the Lehigh, and immediately march to Wyoming. He himself would issue orders for the ingather-ing of the units. Sullivan was to leave from his camp at Millstone, New Jersey, to take charge at Easton.[7]

Sullivan arrived May 7 and was so confident that he could meet Washington's timetable of operations that on May 11 he returned to Millstone for a week to clear up unfinished business. Back at Easton, he received formal instructions for his expedition from Washington:

> The immediate objects are the total destruction and devastation of their settlements and the capture of as many prisoners of every age and sex as possible. It will be essential to ruin their crops now in the ground and prevent their planting more. . . . Our future security will be in their inability to injure us[,] the distance to which they are driven[,] and in the terror with which the severity of the chastisement they receive will inspire in them.

Washington seemed hardly to have considered that this ruthless obliteration might rather provoke a fresh rampage of revenge. He even believed it possible that the Indians would sue for peace, that they might deliver up Butler and Brant, that they might join with the Americans to surprise the Niagara garrison and seize British shipping on the Great Lakes. And for such drastic concessions, Sullivan was not empowered to conclude a treaty with the Indians, only to "agree upon the terms of one, letting them know that it must be finally ratified by Congress."[8]

Sullivan still hesitated. What if, he immediately wrote back, the Indians agreed to these terms beforehand? Should the United States not consider whether "greater advantages might not result from having the Command of the Fort and Lakes, which would effectually keep them in awe, than could be derived from the ruin of their country without effecting the other purposes"? Washington did not budge. Sullivan still doubted. Three months later, anxious to protect himself against failure, he wrote Continental Congress President John Jay that "the plan for carrying on the expedition was not agreeable to my mind nor were the number of men destined for it sufficient in my opinion to ensure success."[9]

The instructions specified the composition of Sullivan's command. Two brigades—William Maxwell's and Enoch Poor's, were to assemble at Easton. Sullivan was to march them to Wyoming, where he would meet the third brigade, Edward Hand's, and then proceed to Tioga. The fourth brigade, James Clinton's, was to rendezvous at Canajoharie and either join up with the others on the Susquehanna for a combined incursion, or cooperate for twin advances into the heart of the Indian country, as Sullivan would decide. Speed was essential, Washington emphasized, and he said so again in a second letter five days later.

The focal point of the expedition was at Wyoming, where Hand's brigade was taking shape. He was a native of Leinster, in northern Ireland, and educated as a physician at Dublin's Trinity College. Thirty-two years old, he had emigrated to Philadelphia in 1767 and set up practice in Lancaster. When the Revolution broke out, he served with distinction as a line officer in engagements at Long Island, White Plains, Trenton, and Princeton. As commander of the northern army, he was at Minisink when Washington on April 9 sent him orders for his new assignment at Wyoming.

Zebulon Butler headed the garrison there of one hundred rank and file, two captains, and six subalterns. To reinforce it, Washington ordered out Major Daniel Burchardt's "German Regiment" from Pennsylvania and a one-hundred-man detachment under Major Joseph Prowell from the "New Eleventh Regiment" then at headquarters camp at Middlebrook. From Philadelphia, Colonel Thomas Proctor's Fourth Artillery Regiment was ordered to report to Sullivan at Easton and accompany the troops assembling there on their march to Wyoming, where he would join Hand's brigade. Burchardt brought his unit of three hundred without incident to Wyoming by April 30.

Prowell was not so fortunate. Traveling by way of Easton, along a crude, narrow bridle path, he thought he was out of danger when he was within twelve miles of Wyoming. On the morning of April 23, his unit set out with drums beating and fifes playing for a triumphant arrival. After six miles the vanguard reported sighting several deer browsing, and a hunting detail of seven men hurried forward for the kill. When it neared the crest of Wilkes-Barre Mountain, a band of Indians rushed out from a thickly wooded covert. All seven were slain and scalped. Prowell called for help from Wyoming, and the "German Regiment" marched out to conduct them rest of the way. The dead were buried, and the headboard of their leader, Lieutenant William Jones, was smeared with his blood as a cry for vengeance.[10]

Sullivan arrived at Easton to take charge May 7. Always keen to court popularity, he harangued the few troops as yet assembled there for two hours, promising to consider any of their complaints. A British prisoner reported that "a soldier complain'd of the adjutant— for which as soon as the Genl was gone he was severely beaten."[11]

Early in May, Washington had ordered Maxwell to take his brigade of four New Jersey regiments, totaling 111 officers and 1,294 enlisted men, from their encampment on the coast at Elizabethtown (now Elizabeth) to Easton. Tall, florid-faced, gray-eyed "Scotch Willie" was a native of Tyrone County in northern Ireland who had arrived in America at the age of fourteen and never lost the accent for which he was nicknamed. A hard-drinking, uncouth-looking bachelor, he was a career army commissary officer; he had served under Braddock, Abercromby, and Wolfe in the French and Indian War but had resigned rather than accept assignment to the West Indies. Maxwell, an early Patriot, had been appointed a colonel in one of two New Jersey Continental regiments and had served under Sullivan at Three Rivers and under Washington at Germantown and Monmouth.

Before he could start to Easton, he narrowly avoided a mutiny over inadequacy of pay by the officers of Colonel Matthias Ogden's First New Jersey Regiment. They threatened to leave the service in three days if the Council and General Assembly of New Jersey did not give them immediate redress. They warned also that the common soldiers' pay was so inadequate for their families that large groups were deserting almost every day.[12]

Washington censured the officers' method but acknowledged their grievance. He acknowledged no grievance in the common soldiers' demand for pay increases:

This is a doctrine full of dangerous consequences, and which ought not to be countenanced in any way whatever. Neither is it well founded. All that the common soldiery of any country can expect is food and cloathing. The pay given in other armies is little more than nominal, very low in the first and subject to a variety of deductions that reduce it to nothing. . . . The idea of maintaining the families at home, at public expence, is peculiar to us; and is incompatible with the finances of any government.[13]

The New Jersey legislature conceded enough to avert the crisis of "total dissolution." Bonuses of two hundred pounds were awarded each officer (they had demanded pay in Spanish dollars), and each enlistee received forty dollars. Discontent persisted. Over the next twenty months, mutinies broke out among the troops of Massachusetts, Connecticut, New York, and Pennsylvania.[14]

Ogden's mollified regiment departed Elizabethtown for Easton on May 14, followed by Elias Dayton's on the seventeenth and Oliver Spencer's and Israel Shreve's on the twenty-ninth. Their route took them along the north bank of the Raritan River, skirting the Watchung Mountains, passing through Samptown, a village of six houses, Quibbletown (the present New Market), Bound Brook, and to the fork of the river at its north branch. Here a mutiny nearly broke out in a section of Spencer's brigade. The regiment had just been reconstituted by order of the Continental Congress. Originally a southern New York regiment, it was now broken up and elements consolidated with companies from two Pennsylvania regiments. The New Yorkers objected to "being taken from officers whom they loved"; they petitioned to be reassigned to units from their own state. Washington treated this as rank insubordination. The men's former regimental commander, Colonel William Malcom, resigned, and they gave in and resumed their march west. Passing Readington and Pittstown, they forded the Musconetcong River for the final eight miles through stony country to the Delaware River, where they crossed over to Easton. Lieutenant Samuel Moore Shute, of the Second Regiment, records that he "made very free" with a very good breakfast at a relative's house a mile away. Possibly it was his relative who supplied the fuel for Shute's grating description of Easton as a town of 150 houses "with but three elegant buildings in it and about as many inhabitants that are any ways agreeable. Take them in general they are a very inhospitable set—all High Dutch & Jew."[15]

Enoch Poor had the most outstanding record among the brigadiers. At forty-three years old, he was a third-generation Massachusetts farmer and cabinetmaker with little schooling who had moved to Exeter, New Hampshire, and emerged as a trader and shipbuilder, a veteran of the French and Indian War, and a former member of the New Hampshire provincial congress. He had participated as a colonel in actions in Canada and at Ticonderoga, Trenton, and Princeton. The troops he commanded as brigadier at the two battles of Saratoga had earned a major share in the victory and had suffered heavy losses. Since then he had served at Valley Forge and Monmouth.[16]

When Washington issued orders for him to repair to Easton, he was at home on leave, and his three New Hampshire regiments were on temporary assignment to Major General Alexander McDougall, who had replaced Gates in command of the Hudson Highlands. On May 9, Joseph Cilley's First Regiment started out toward Easton from its camp at Soldier's Fortune, about six miles north of Peekskill, New York. They were followed eight days later by George Reid's Second and Henry Dearborn's Third, which crossed the Hudson at Fishkill and were met at Newburgh on the opposite shore by Poor, returning from New Hampshire. They marched through New Windsor, Chester, Warwick, and Hardiston, where rain forced them to remain two nights. The next morning, after a loud dispute between some officers and the obstreperous Tory landlord of the town tavern, the troops marched off, this time under a hot sun, crossing into New Jersey, through Sussex Court House and the Moravian village of Oxford, and arriving at Easton on the morning of May 26. Captain Daniel Livermore, of the Third Regiment, saw the community differently from Shute—a "pleasant town," chiefly Low, not High Dutch, with Jews as the principal merchants.[17]

*

Washington had methodically collected a vast array of geographical data on the territory the expedition would traverse, and his first consideration was for the sixty-five-mile route Sullivan would take from Easton to Wyoming. A road would have to be cut through the uninhabited wilderness of about the last thirty miles, and two regiments were assigned—Spencer's and Colonel Philip Van Cortlandt's Second New York Continentals, then quartered at Wawarsing in New York's Ulster County.

Van Cortlandt was an experienced surveyor on his own extensive lands. He started out May 4, reaching the Delaware by way of the Neversink River at the present Port Jervis and arriving at Fort Penn (the present Stroudsburg) on May 11. Five days later, his unit was joined by Spencer's regiment at Learn's Tavern (the present Tannersville), twenty-eight and a half miles northwest of Easton. This was the last settlement out of Easton, and as far as the wear of the traffic along the old "Lower Road to the Delaware" had rendered the path passable for the army's wagons and artillery. More than half of the way ahead lay over the steep and rocky Pocono Mountains. The rest of the road wound along the Pocono Plateau, densely forested with heavy timber and thick laurel and containing large numbers of deer, bear, and rattlesnakes, across frequent intersecting streams and three soggy marshes—the "Great Swamp," the "Shades of Death," and the "Bear Swamp." Three of Van Cortlandt's men, quailing at the prospect, deserted and were caught and court-martialed. Oliver Arnold was sentenced to be shot, Edward Taylor to run the gauntlet of three regiments "with a Centinel at his breast to regulate his pace," and John Stephen to receive one hundred lashes.

Two local guides, Andrew Montanye and Stephen Hadsall, reported constant signs of lurking Indians, to whom the expedition was obviously no secret. As the work progressed, successive supply camps were established. Engineers, spade men, and axmen labored through days of fog and rain, and on May 31 Cilley's First New Hampshire Regiment arrived to help out. Log fillings had to be embedded in swampy areas, boulders removed from rocky stretches and stacked on adjacent ridges, and bridges built over streams too deep to be waded. "The number of Sloughs & Creeks are almost Incredible," Sullivan found. Discipline was strict, and for stealing rum from the commissary John Curry received seventy-five lashes and Michael Sellers fifty.

Meanwhile, a second work crew at Wyoming, under Colonel Zebulon Butler, composed of settlers idled by the Indian raids, had begun a road eastward to join the approaching force from Easton. They hacked their way to Wilkes-Barre Mountain, two and a half miles east of Wyoming, where the two groups met on June 13. Five hundred men had built what they now called the "Sullivan Road" (the present Pennsylvania Route 115) in remarkable time.[18]

At Easton, Sullivan delayed. He might have started his troops toward Wyoming while the road was building, but he heard from Hand and from President Joseph Reed of Pennsylvania that the boats that were to have been shipped to Wyoming from Sunbury had not arrived and that supplies at Wyoming were so deficient that the troops arriving from Easton would only consume scarce provisions. Nor was he satisfied with the numbers of tents, packhorses, and wagons supplied by Colonel Robert L. Hooper, Jr., the resident deputy to Quartermaster General Nathanael Greene. This was the beginning of a long tangle of wrangles with quartermasters, commissaries, and the Pennsylvania Executive Council that continued throughout the campaign. Charges flew back and forth, and they confirmed Sullivan's previous reputation as a complainer who would never be satisfied.

Meanwhile, the inactive troops became restive. Several men painted themselves as Indians and threatened two officers. One of the men caught received one hundred lashes, and another was forced to run the gauntlet through three regiments. Stealing, extortion from civilians, and desertion were continuing problems; and deserters, when caught, received punishment of fifty or one hundred lashes on the bare back. Three soldiers of the Eleventh Pennsylvania Regiment were hanged for the murder of an inhabitant who had refused to sell them liquor. The severest punishment was reserved for two Sussex County, New Jersey, civilians, Lawrence Miller and Michael Rosebury, whom Sullivan took it upon himself to court-martial. They were sentenced to the gallows for enticing soldiers to desert and were kept in suspense four weeks until the execution. Rosebury, unrepentant, was hanged. Miller, scheduled next, showed contrition. He was allowed to suffer for fifteen minutes with the halter around his neck while his crimes were recounted, and then, almost fainting, he was pardoned. Anti-Indian resentment flared up against four Stockbridge guides who had joined the expedition, and Sullivan warned that agitators would be treated as "the most inveterate Tory." As a saving respite, on June 14 Martha Washington stopped at Easton on her way to Virginia. She was escorted the next morning by Sullivan, Poor, Maxwell, and a party of twenty officers as far as Bethlehem.[19]

By June 16, word arrived that the road to Wyoming was ready, and Sullivan was, as he put it, "asham'd" to delay any longer. Then a storm held them up for two days. They started out with caution, alert to ambush from the tangled trees and looming boulders of the "Shades of Death." An advance guard of Maxwell's brigade led the way. Next came Proctor's artillery—four brass three-pounders, two six-pounders, two 5½-inch howitzers, and one coehorn. Then, in order, were the main body of troops, the baggage train, and a rear guard of one hundred picked men from Poor's brigade. They marched at daybreak, halted at seven for breakfast, continued until eleven, and camped for the day to refresh and avoid the heat. Even with the newly made road, the trip was fatiguing, and extended rests were sometimes necessary. "The whole country from Eastown to wyoming is very poor & Barren and I think as never will Be Settled," noted Sergeant Moses Fellows of the Third New Hampshire Regiment. In the swamps trees grew so thick that the men could not see the sun at noon. Visibility was no more than ten feet, and wolves howled from the darkness while the men groped their way forward. Three wagons and the carriages of two fieldpieces broke down. When the men emerged at last, from the heights they could see the Blue Ridge Mountains ahead, and on the east the Delaware Water Gap. On June 23, from a hill two miles away, the beautiful valley of

Wyoming lay revealed below, and Hand's men were waiting to welcome them.[20]

Almost a year had passed since the slaughter of the Battle of Wyoming, but the field at Wintermoot bore mute evidence of the carnage. Bones of the unburied corpses spread over the ground for nearly two miles, and some skulls, noted Lieutenant Samuel Moore Shute of the Second New Jersey Regiment, had "part of their hair on—the other part taken off with the Scalps—Others with bullet holes in, or the Scull Split with the tomahawk." A guide pointed out a mass grave containing seventy-three skeletons. A large stone was designated "Bloody Rock," where fifteen prisoners, promised mercy at surrender, had been seated in a circle and then clubbed one by one by the crazed "Queen" Esther Montour, whose son had been slain the day before the battle. A death maul, the execution instrument, was exhibited—a hard maple knot the size of a three-pound cannonball. Two of the captives had broken away to report the ordeal.[21]

Searing memory was already at work magnifying the horror. The battle was mourned as a "massacre." The killings at "Bloody Rock" were charged to "Queen" Esther Montour, singing and dancing in her fury as she butchered her victims. Accounts abounded of the wanton slayings, torture of captives, and sufferings of exposed women and children fleeing through the swamps. The most shocking testimony came from two escaping American soldiers, concealed in the bushes, who said they saw a comrade, Henry Pencel, discovered by a pursuing Loyalist who turned out to be his younger brother, John, Jr. "You won't kill your brother, will you?" Henry implored. John cursed him for a "damned rebel," shot him, tomahawked him, and scalped him.[22]

If Sullivan had any lingering reservations about the policy of chastisement, the desolation at Wyoming resolved them. He had earlier been a declared atheist and then a deist. Now he was a devout Christian, searching the Scriptures for the message of divine retribution, and he spent a day composing a thirty-page dissertation to prove the truth of Scripture and the divinity of Jesus. He read it to the approving Chaplain Kirkland during the better part of an evening and morning, and Kirkland pronounced the devastation that the expedition planned "a just & speedy retaliation for British & savage barbarity" and "a necessary link in the grand chain of events, to bring about the enjoyment and establishment of the liberties and privileges of this land."[23]

Independence Day fell on Sunday, so the army waited until July 5 to celebrate. For a banquet for Poor's and Hand's officers, an eighty-foot spruce-and-hemlock arbor was erected with a marquee at each end. Eighty-seven officers and guests assembled. The feast was bountiful, and the toasts began—the Fourth of July, 1776; General Washington and the army; the king and queen of France; General Lincoln and the southern army; General Sullivan and the western army. Then came the summons everyone was waiting for. Two skulls were held up. The toast rang out: "Civilization or death to all American savages!"[24] Eighty-seven hands raised their glasses fiercely aloft.

June 29, thirty-six boats had arrived from Sunbury, convoyed by Spencer's Fifth New Jersey Regiment. Each boat carried two to three tons of stores and provisions, and it seemed that Sullivan's needs might be satisfied. But word came from Estherton that of the 186 barrels of salt beef waiting to be sent from there, more than one-third were tainted. Sullivan had requested 1,000 head of cattle, but only 200 had been delivered, and 150 too poor to walk had been left behind at Sunbury. For transport, there were far too few boats and a deficiency of packsaddles for horses.

The Pennsylvania Executive Council had promised 720 rangers and riflemen, but none had arrived—the council could not compete with the higher wages offered by the Continental Army. Boatmen, packhorsemen, and cattle drivers were in such short supply that more than 1,000 men had to be drafted to fill in from line units. Deducting also garrison troops and officers, Sullivan calculated that only 938 effective rank and file remained available at Wyoming. The total of these plus those expected from Clinton would amount to no more than 1,500.

Sullivan communicated his resentment to his troops by having read to them on July 21 a letter from Washington himself, declaring that "had the Board of War complied with his request, and their own engagements respecting clothing, the numerous brave and virtuous soldiers at this post would not be suffering through want of any article in that way."[25]

Washington received Sullivan's complaints with growing apprehension of his excessive cautiousness. His alarm came to a head when he learned that Sullivan had instructed James Clinton, in his preparations for the journey to join forces at Tioga, to accumulate boats, stores, and provisions sufficient for three months. The expedition would be bogged down, and secrecy and surprise would be sacrificed. His concern, he sternly wrote Sullivan, was "inexpressible," and he urged that Clinton send back to Canajoharie provisions and stores in excess of those necessary to sustain him until his arrival at Tioga. As for Sullivan's supply complaints: Supplies of clothing sent were in greater proportion than those for the other armies. Salt meat and hard bread must be expected to spoil and should not be depended on as a principal resource. One hundred head of cattle were on their way to replace the spoilage. With regard to manpower: It may not have been as great as Sullivan had requested, but it should be equal to the size authorized. Sullivan's estimate of one thousand men to be withheld for garrisons and escorts was "far more considerable" than necessary—less than one-third of that number would be sufficient.[26]

Sullivan would not be silenced. "Notwithstanding the flattering Accounts given by those Employed by Quarter Masters & Commissaries. . . . when near your person," he replied, he could not hope to subsist his army without the provisions Clinton would bring. He not only stood by his manpower projections but appealed for justification to President John Jay of the Continental Congress. "I call upon the members of Congress," he wrote, "to witness to the world that I early foresaw & foretold the danger & used ev'ry means in my power, to procure a force sufficient to ensure success but failed to obtain it."[27]

Washington might well have disciplined Sullivan for going over his head. Not seriously concerned that his supporters in Congress might censure him in favor of Sullivan's well-known contentiousness, and not wishing to lose the services of a competent general, he waited almost four weeks before sending Congress a lengthy, documented history of the evolution of the plans for the expedition and in essence repeating his replies to Sullivan.

He also showed Sullivan's letter to Greene, who took until September 19 to gather the evidence for his defense. It could not be expected, he declared, to have all supplies available at the outset of the expedition. There was to be a network of depots from which sufficient deliveries would be made in stages, and had Sullivan "consulted his real wants instead of grasping at every thing he could get, he must have been sensible of it." Despite Sullivan's complaints, the means of transportation were more than adequate. Orders for construction of 150 two-ton flat-bottomed bateaux had to be revised for larger boats with keels and round futtocks capable of navigating the rock-strewn rapids, and even then most of them were completed within a few days of Sullivan's arrival at Wyoming. Of the 2,200 packsaddles Sullivan had requisitioned, such surplus was provided that 240 were left behind at Wyoming and another 300 at Easton. Of bateau men, between two and three hundred were enlisted (not Sullivan's figure of one hundred), and of pack-horsemen there were between sixty and seventy.

Neither did the Board of War allow Sullivan's vitriolic charge against it in the general order to his troops to go unanswered. It requested investigation by a congressional committee, which reported that shoes, shirts, overalls, and hunting shirts had been issued in plentiful supply in the face of Sullivan's excessive and imprecise requisitions.[28]

When the troops were not occupied with drills, inspections, or convoying supply boats from Sunbury and wagon trains from Easton, hunters found the woods full of deer and wild turkeys and the river flowing with fish, including one catch of a twenty-seven-pound, two-foot-nine-inch rock fish. When some of the men straggled from camp and plundered inhabitants, orders required roll calls at noon as well as morning and evening. Among the German troops there was discontent, and July 13 at night, maintaining that their term of enlistment had expired, thirty-three men stole out of camp. An Indian tracker guided a fifty-man pursuit team that brought them back. They were court-martialed, five of them sentenced to be shot and the rest to be reduced to the ranks and run the gauntlet of three regiments. On the day of execution, Sullivan pardoned them all.[29] He could not afford to lose fighting men.

Despite his complaints, his situation had begun to improve. On July 9, 43 loaded boats arrived, escorted by Lieutenant Colonel Adam Hubley with his Eleventh Pennsylvania Regiment of 291 enlisted men. The rise of the Susquehanna speeded up river transportation, and fifteen days later, Hand arrived from Sunbury with a flotilla of 112 boats loaded with stores and provisions and was greeted on shore with the firing of thirteen cannon, which he answered with thirteen on the boats. Seventy-eight loaded wagons were due in a few days from Estherton. Lacking yet were supplies of one thousand blankets and five thousand shirts that Sullivan urgently requested from the Board of War. Still, if he waited any longer he might find himself once again "ashamed." On July 24, he issued orders to prepare to march on the twenty-eighth. He left behind, to garrison Wyoming, a 108-man force under Zebulon Butler of those least likely to endure an arduous march. And he dispatched orders to Clinton to start out from Canajoharie on August 9 for a union of the two forces at Tioga.[30]

Continual rain held up departure for several days, and while the army waited there was a somber evocation of the expedition's mission. The two officers of the men tomahawked on the road to Wyoming, Captain Joseph Davis and Lieutenant William Jones, had been Freemasons of Military Lodge No. 19, and the brotherhood determined to give them a ceremonial burial. Sullivan was a member and Proctor was Master of the Lodge. The bodies were disinterred and carried to the Wyoming town graveyard. Twenty-four musketeers with reversed arms escorted the coffins, to the beat of a dirge played by a band of muffled drums and fifes that was followed by officials, 150 brethren in Masonic attire, the Eleventh Pennsylvania Regiment, and local townspeople. The downpour was so heavy that Chaplain William Rogers, also a Mason, delivered a short prayer instead of a eulogy; he postponed the eulogy for a later observance. The musketeers fired three volleys. The red gravestone proclaimed that the slain men had been "massacred by the savages on their march to the relief of the distressed inhabitants of Wyoming."[31]

CHAPTER 7

✦ ✦ ✦ ✦ ✦ ✦ ✦ ✦ ✦ ✦ ✦

"A SOIL WORTH CONTENDING FOR"

At noon on July 31, rain still falling, a cannon at Fort Wyoming boomed the signal for troops to start for Tioga along the Susquehanna's east bank. Flags flew, drums throbbed, fifes whistled. Serving as guides were two Wyoming militiamen, Captain John Franklin and Lieutenant John Jenkins, and two Indians, Captain Jehoiakim, a Stockbridge, and Hanyost, an Oneida. Hand's light corps constituted the advance guard, moving in three columns, preceded by a probe detail of twenty-four men. A mile behind followed the main body of Maxwell's and Poor's brigades under Sullivan's immediate command. Next came twelve hundred packhorses and a drove of some seven hundred beef cattle. On the first day, the rear guard consisted of Ogden's First New Jersey Regiment. On successive days, it would be a regiment taken alternately from Poor's and Maxwell's brigades. On the river, Proctor, aboard his flagship, "The Adventure," commanded the fleet of 214 boats carrying his artillery and the army's baggage. They were manned by 250 soldiers drawn from other regiments and propelled by 450 boatmen wielding setting poles against the current. The army of 3,200 to 3,400 often marched Indian file, strung out along two miles. For cover, a flanking party of sixty-five men under Captain William B. Gifford, of the Third New Jersey Regiment, kept watch on the west side of the river, and four light boats kept abreast of them to carry them across if necessary.[1]

The mood of the men was upbeat. Sullivan was "the friend of a

Soldier altho it may be a tax upon the Citizen," wrote Greene. He recognized this as his last chance to make his mark, and he would not permit even his own bleeding ulcer, "a violent bilious disorder" that continued during the entire expedition, to dim his determination. Nor would he be sidetracked by calls for help from Sunbury, which was threatened by a raiding party of one hundred British regulars and two hundred Indians who on July 28 had captured nearby Fort Freeland and killed thirteen defenders. "As Pennsylvania has neglected to furnish me with the Troops promised for this Expedition," he acidly advised, "she Certainly will be enabled to defend her Frontiers without much inconvenience."[2]

At first the army traveled through country far different from the Easton-Wyoming road's barren gloom. Nights and mornings were generally foggy and often rainy, with sunshine late in the day. In the rich farmland of the Wyoming Valley, within a mile of the river, they saw remains of the homes and barns destroyed the year before. Luxuriant grass and lush vegetation covered large stretches. The route of the fleet was not so smooth. It had to navigate "Wyoming Falls," where two boats were lost; their cargoes were salvaged, though.

Ten miles above Wyoming, across the junction with the Lackawanna River, the Susquehanna entered a series of ridges, sometimes two to three hundred feet high. One of them, marveled Major James Norris of the Third New Hampshire Regiment, "seemed to over look the World." The "Warrior Path" that the army followed led through a rocky defile above the beautiful, one-hundred-foot-high "Falling Spring," where many poorly tied packs of flour slipped and scattered and several horses gave out and fell to their deaths. To shorten the distance at frequent bends of the winding river, the path led across mountains and swamps infested with rattlesnakes and wolves.[3]

On August 4, Sullivan informed his troops that he had received information that they could expect an enemy attack within a day, and he ordered a flank division of two hundred to cover the army on the right and a second to protect the packhorses. The following day, fifty miles from Wyoming, as the army approached Wyalusing, the scene of the attack the year before on Hartley's expedition, they found fresh Indian tracks, camping places, and one of their canoes and a raft. "An engagement was expected throughout the day," wrote Chaplain William Rogers, "but granting that the enemy had a fair view of us, of which we had not the least doubt, they suffered us to pass unmolested." Rumor circulated that 450 British troops and a large number of Indians under Brant were gathering to oppose the Americans. Scouting parties found tracks but had no sight of the enemy.[4]

August 9, the fleet arrived at the mouth of Sugar Creek on the Susquehanna's west bank. Captain Gifford reported finding a recently established Indian village, Newtychanning, on the far side of the creek. Its twenty-eight log houses had been hastily evacuated. Proctor dispatched a detail on shore that burned the entire town to the ground. This was the first destruction of the expedition. Because of the fear of retaliation, Van Cortlandt's and Cilley's regiments were sent over to reinforce Gifford.[5]

August 10, the army was about three miles from Tioga, where the Chemung River empties into the Susquehanna. The previous night they had seen a fire on a mountain on the west side of the Susquehanna. It might be an Indian encampment, a sign of an impending ambush. Sullivan only a day before had felt so ill that he could not sit a horse; he had turned the command over to Maxwell while he traveled aboard Proctor's boat. He was back now and unsparing of himself. Although the weather was stormy, rather than risk disaster he rode with his brigadiers at the head of three regiments, one from each brigade, to check out a safe spot for the army to ford the river. At the place they selected, about a mile and a half below the junction of the two rivers, his aide-de-camp, Adam Hoops, with a detail of four men, swam across and discovered only a cow supposedly left by the Indians in their haste.[6]

At 7:30 the next morning, Hand's light corps moved first, as cover for the main body. At the fording place, opposite the present Milan, where the Susquehanna was 330 yards wide, the water was deep and the current strong. Hand led the way, dismounting from his horse, and plunged in up to his armpits with his men. They took off their clothes and tied them around their necks, hung their cartridge boxes on their bayonets, and waded in platoon formation, grasping each other for support. By nine o'clock the advance party had crossed and formed a line of cover a hundred yards from the shore. The fleet, meanwhile, had come up, and Lieutenant Colonel Thomas Forrest landed several six-pounders on the west shore and fired a few shots across to the woods on the east to warn off hidden attackers. The main body then arrived at the ford and breasted the current. Some of the men fell down and seized horses' tails or were helped by strong hands. One of the fallen began floating downstream and was saved by Lieutenant Colonel Francis Barber, the adjutant general, who almost drowned himself in the effort. Chaplain Hunter, from astride his horse, dragged a man across the river by his cane. All had safely crossed by ten o'clock.[7]

The army was elated. With flags furled and the band playing, the men marched a mile northward, past the ruins of Queen Esther's Castle that Hartley had burned the year before, to the junction of the Chemung River with the Susquehanna, and crossed over, this time at a narrower ford, to Tioga, at the peninsula between the two rivers. Tioga, with its lush meadows and stunning vistas, was the gateway to the magnificent domain of the Six Nations. An Indian town had existed there in years past, and at the site was a burying ground of some one hundred graves, each beneath a mound four to six feet high. Scoffing soldiers dug up several of them for meager mementoes of a pipe, a tomahawk, or beads. The farm boys from Connecticut, Massachusetts, and New Hampshire had small concern for the culture of a forest people. Neither did they consider the "most fatal disorders" from decomposing bodies, against which it became necessary to warn them in general orders. Accustomed at home to the backbreaking tillage of their little rocky plots, they looked longingly at the rich potential of this inviting land. Chaplain Rogers was their faithful spokesman, dutifully echoing Sullivan's exhortation to smite the enemy who had committed "savage barbarity to our fellow citizens" and never uttering a word of regret at the hardships to Indian civilians. "Surely," he marveled, "a soil like this is worth contending for."[8]

Only one of the arrivals at Tioga, Dr. Jabez Campfield, surgeon in Spencer's Fifth New Jersey Regiment, expressed disquiet at the prospect: "I very heartily wish these rusticks may be reduced to reason by the approach of this army, without their suffering the extremes of war," he wrote in his diary; "there is something so cruel, in destroying the habitations of any people, (however mean they may be, being their all) that I may say the prospect hurts my feelings."[9]

The army was now twelve miles away from their first significant resistance at the Indian village of Chemung. A scouting party was sent out under Captain John N. Cummings of the Second New Jersey Regiment. One of its members, Lieutenant Moses Van Campen, a hardened Pennsylvania frontier fighter whose father, brother, and uncle had been killed and scalped by the Indians, was sent to reconnoiter the village. He and a companion, both disguised in painted Indian dress of breechcloth, leggings, moccasin, and feathered cap, circled the outskirts and, by counting the fires and estimating the number of Indians at each, brought back a report that the community contained between six hundred and seven hundred.[10]

Sullivan promptly issued orders for a massive attack at daybreak of August 14. Maxwell had fallen ill and remained in camp with a small force to guard the tents and baggage. The troops started at nine o'clock on the evening of August 13, marching all night through a thick swamp, dark, tangled woods, and precipitous defiles. The path was so unfamiliar and difficult that the army arrived late and could not see the village in a dense fog. Hand was to attack from the north and Poor from the east, while Sullivan, with some New Jersey troops, would approach at the front. Across the river, Lieutenant Colonel George Reid, with two New Jersey regiments, would guard that escape route. When the fog lifted at the sunrise of a hot day, the carefully positioned troops beheld only one or two Indians fleeing the deserted town of thirty-nine houses. Cowbells could be heard of cattle driven off into the woods.[11]

Hand volunteered to pursue the Indians with Hubley's regiment and two companies of Wyoming militia. A mile northward, on the east side of the Chemung, they ran into an ambush of twenty Delawares under Roland Montour, a son of Queen Esther, concealed behind a narrow ridge, Hogback Hill. Hand dislodged them with a bayonet charge, but not before six of his men were killed and seven wounded, including Captain John Franklin, who was disabled with a shot in the shoulder. Second Lieutenant John Shreve, seventeen-year-old son of Israel, narrowly escaped the fate of the man killed at his side: "He touched me when he fell." The Indians carried away their wounded and one dead. At this point, Sullivan caught up with Hand's force and ordered it back to Chemung. He was not happy with what in the twentieth century has come to be called "friendly fire." There had been, he found, "a wanton discharge of all the muskets . . . without any kind of aim, meaning or order and leveled at no object, but endangering those officers who are endeavoring to restore them to order, and spreading carnage among themselves."[12]

The houses put to the torch at Chemung were sturdily built of split and hewn timber covered with bark. They had no chimneys or floors, and there was little inside them other than baskets, buckets, and deer and bear skins. Two large buildings apparently were public houses, one containing what appeared to be a religious idol. A "glorious Bonfire," Major James Norris of the Third New Hampshire Regiment observed. They found more than a hundred acres of corn "in the milk" and gardens of cucumbers, watermelons, pumpkins, squash, and beans. Forty acres were reserved for the army's future needs and the rest, estimated to yield a potential thousand bushels, cut down. While Israel Shreve's New Jersey troops did their work in the fields, they were fired upon by Indians concealed in the nearby woods. One man was killed and six wounded.[13]

The army returned to Tioga to await the arrival of the brigade from the Mohawk. In order to safeguard the stores, boats, invalids, and women and children left at Tioga, a fortification enclosing four strong blockhouses was erected between the two rivers. The soldiers named it "Fort Sullivan." A garrison of 250 would man it under the command of Israel Shreve, who, weighing 320 pounds, would have

LEFT: *Sir William Johnson*, c. 1772, mogul of the Mohawk Valley. Painting attributed to Matthew Pratt. Johnson Hall State Historic Site, New York State Office of Parks, Recreation and Historic Preservation.

RIGHT: *Sir John Johnson*, c. 1795, son of Sir William and Loyalist Lieutenant Colonel of regiment of "Royal Greens." Unattributed painting. Johnson Hall State Historic Site, New York Office of Parks, Recreation and Historic Preservation.

Joseph Brant, 1786, eminent Loyalist Mohawk chief. Painting by Gilbert Stuart. New York State Historical Association, Cooperstown, New York.

Cornplanter, n.d., Loyalist chief of the western Senecas. Painting by F. Bartoli. Collection of the New-York Historical Society, New York City.

LEFT: *"Good Peter,"* 1792, patriot chief of the Oneidas. Painting by John Trumbull, Trumbull Collection, Yale University Art Gallery.

RIGHT: *Samuel Kirkland,* n.d., Congregational minister to the Oneidas and guide to the Sullivan expedition. Unattributed painting. Hamilton College, Clinton, New York.

RIGHT: *Sir Frederick Haldimand,* n.d., British Commander in Chief of Canada. Unattributed painting. National Archives of Canada, C-003221.

LEFT: *Christian Daniel Claus,* n.d., Loyalist Colonel and agent to the Mohawks. Unattributed painting. National Archives of Canada, C083514.

Peter Gansevoort, c. 1794, Colonel, Third New York Continental Regiment and commander of Fort Stanwix. Painting by Gilbert Stuart. Munson-Williams-Proctor Institute Museum of Art.

RIGHT: *Philip Van Cortlandt,* n.d., Colonel, Second New York Continental Regiment. Pastel attributed to James Sharples. Independence National Historical Park Collection.

LEFT: Benedict Arnold, tentatively identified, n.d., Major General of force that relieved Fort Stanwix of British siege. Painting attributed to Cassidy. Frick Art Reference Library.

Marinus Willett, n.d., Lieutenant Colonel, Third New York
Continental Regiment. Painting by Ralph Earl. The Metropoli-
tan Museum of Art, Bequest of George Willett Van Ness, 1917.
[17.87.1]

Massacre of Wyoming, 1858. Painting by Alonzo Chappel. Chicago Historical Society. Although the artist entitled his painting a massacre, the engagement was in fact a battle in which the men killed were militiamen.

George Washington, 1787, Commander-in-Chief, planner of
the Sullivan campaign. Painting by James Peale. Independence
National Historical Park Collection.

John Sullivan, c. 1786, Major General, commander of the campaign against the Iroquois. Copy of painting by R. M. Staige. Independence National Historical Park Collection.

ABOVE: *Mohawk Village in Central New York*, c. 1780. Engraving. William Cullen Bryant & Sydney Howard Gay, *A Popular History of the United States* (New York, Charles Scribner's Sons, 1881), 4:1.

RIGHT: *Daniel Brodhead*, n.d., Colonel, Fourth Pennsylvania Continental Regiment. Unattributed painting. State Historical Society of Wisconsin.

LEFT: *James Clinton*, c. 1795–1800, Brigadier General, commander, Fourth Brigade of the campaign against the Iroquois. Independence National Historical Park Collection. RIGHT: *Enoch Poor*, 1873, Brigadier General, commander, Second Brigade of the campaign against the Iroquois. Painting by U. D. Tenney after Thaddeus Kosciusko. Collections of the State of New Hampshire, Division of Historical Resources.

Clinton's Brigade at Canajoharie, n.d. Painting by Edward P. Buyck. Canajoharie Library and Art Gallery.

LEFT: *Henry Dearborn*, c. 1796–1797, Lieutenant Colonel, Third New Hampshire Continental Regiment. Independence National Historical Park Collection. RIGHT: *Joseph Cilley*, 1872, Colonel, First New Hampshire Continental Regiment. Painting by U. D. Tenney after Jonathan Trumbull. Collections of the State of New Hampshire, Division of Historical Resources.

Arthur Lee, c. 1785, Congressional commissioner at the 1784 Treaty of Fort Stanwix negotiation. Painting by Charles Willson Peale. Independence National Historical Park Collection.

had hard going through the rough country the expedition faced. Sullivan now felt sublimely confident. "No Force they can send against me after a Junction is form'd with Genl Clinton can possibly prevent my effecting the Purpose of my Destination," he wrote Congress. On August 16, Poor and Hand set out with a picked force of 900 to meet and provide protection for Clinton.[14]

James Clinton, elder brother of Governor George Clinton, was a "plain, blunt soldier" from New York's Ulster County on the west side of the Hudson, then still a frontier locality. In the French and Indian War, he had served as a militia captain under John Bradstreet at the taking of Fort Frontenac in 1757. As a Continental brigadier general, he escaped with a bayonet wound at the loss of forts Clinton and Montgomery in the Hudson Highlands in 1777. In civilian life, he was an engineer and surveyor, skills that would stand him in good stead in this campaign. He made his will. He prepared to set out.[15]

Since May, from his headquarters at Albany, he had been issuing directives for the collecting of supplies at Canajoharie. Two hundred boats were transported by land from Albany to Schenectady. There, under the direction of the division quartermaster general, Henry Glen, they were loaded with three months' provisions and shipped up the Mohawk to Canajoharie under the escort of Colonel Peter Gansevoort's Third New York Regiment from Albany and Lieutenant Colonel William Butler's Fourth Pennsylvania Regiment, summoned from the Middle Schoharie Fort (the present Middleburgh). Five hundred horses and cattle were also gathered there.[16]

Clinton himself arrived at Canajoharie June 17. He established his headquarters at Roof's Tavern, where he took charge of the troops he was assembling. The New York regiments, in addition to Van Cortlandt's Second, of 281 men, included Gansevoort's Third, of 458 men, Lieutenant Colonel Frederick Weissenfels's Fourth, of 367 men, coming from Albany, and Colonel Lewis Dubois's Fifth, of 383 men, coming from Fort Plain on the Mohawk. Major Daniel Whiting brought the Sixth Massachusetts Regiment of 313 men from Fort Alden. Also arrived were William Butler's regiment of 174, a detachment of 100 of Daniel Morgan's Riflemen, and a 31-man detachment of Colonel John Lamb's Second New York Artillery Regiment. This brought Clinton's total force to 2,107. In addition there was Colonel John Harper's unnumbered company of Schenectady and Tryon County militia volunteers.[17]

From Canajoharie, men and supplies had to transfer across the uphill, twenty-mile carrying place to Springfield Landing (the present Hyde Bay) at the north end of Otsego Lake, the origin of the Susquehanna. Between June 19 and 24, five hundred loaded wagons, many driven by local civilians, "going steady," creaked back and forth over steep hills along three rough roads. It took six to eight teams to haul a wagon carrying a flat-bottomed boat thirty-five to forty feet long, six feet wide, with a fifteen-hundred-pound capacity.[18]

The boats were floated down the lake to the southern end and moored at the outlet creek, which was almost dry with summer drought. The water level there was too low to allow passage of such heavily laden boats. Here Clinton called upon his expertise as an engineer for a bold construction feat. He dispatched two companies of the Sixth Massachusetts Regiment under Captain Benjamin Warren to dam the outlet at the southern end of the eight-mile lake so as to raise the water level more than two feet. At the same time he sent one hundred riflemen under Major James Parr to clear out the outlet creek. Clinton established his headquarters at the south end of Otsego Lake (the present Cooperstown) on July 2 and awaited orders from Sullivan to march.[19]

Six weeks passed. The lake was beautiful, but the weather was sometimes warm and at other times unseasonably cool and often rainy, and many of the men came down with dysentery. "Both officers and privates," wrote Chaplain John Gano, "grew extremely impatient of remaining so inactive, fearing the campaign would fall through." Regimental commanders were instructed to keep their troops busy with drills twice a day.

In later years, a veteran, James Williamson, recalled one drill conducted by Lieutenant Colonel Pierre Regnier, commander of the Fourth New York Battalion, that showed his demeaning attitude toward blacks. When a light-skinned recruit was slow to execute a command, Regnier, a native Frenchman, bellowed, "Halloo! you plack son of a bitch wid a wite face!—why you no mind you beezness!" and joined in general laughter.[20]

Neither were the men in any mood to welcome a group of thirty-five Oneida warriors, who arrived on July 4, the day after a group of Indians had been driven off by sentries during the night. The officers were busy celebrating Independence at a grog party thrown by Regnier, and Clinton had to issue a general order warning the men "not to insult the Indians who are in Camp, nor crowd around them." Eventually, all but two of the Oneidas departed.

Tensions also arose among officers. A dispute in the Sixth Massachusetts Regiment was disruptive enough to produce a court-martial, though it acquitted Captain Daniel Lane of "vexatious and malicious" charges of character assassination. In the Third New York Regiment, in an eruption of a long-standing dispute, Captain Cornelius T. Jansen was arrested for publicly calling Colonel Dubois a rascal and a liar. An officers' court of inquiry persuaded Dubois that Jansen had been provoked by "Envious and Designed Persons to stain My Reputation."[21]

At last, orders arrived from Sullivan to start for Tioga on August 9, a Monday. Clinton asked Chaplain Gano not to mention the move in his sermon on Sunday, but worshipers were told to be "ready to depart on the morrow" anyway. When Gano concluded, Clinton rose and ordered each captain to appoint men to draw the loaded boats from the lake into the outlet below, string them in line, and ready them to start the following morning. At six o'clock in the evening, the sluiceway was broken up and the water poured out into the dry outlet. At nine in the morning, the boats, with three men in each, were unmoored and the current carried them over the shoals and flats that were previously impassable. In the second boat, with a cannon, rode Clinton. Second from the rear was another cannon. On land, Butler's light infantry and rifle corps led the way as advance guard on the river's west side. Behind came the flanks, with the horses and cattle between columns, followed by the rear guard. Drum signals and cannon shots were to warn of danger from front or rear. Clinton was euphoric. "The troops have advanced thus far without the least accident, in perfect health and high spirits—the most difficult parts of the river are passed," he wrote his brother.[22]

The Susquehanna was a winding river, with many sharp twists and turns, twenty yards wide and one and a half to five feet deep at the start. Twenty miles southward, it quickened to rapids and widened to forty yards, spawning island clusters as it passed through a ridge of mountains. Mornings were heavy with dew and fog, occasionally followed by an afternoon shower. The land at one side was sometimes dense with butternut, elm, ash, maple, birch, and beech, and barren on the other side, and the marching troops waded back and forth, on the way disposing of rattlesnakes flushed out of their lairs by the flooding waters. The river's rise had frightened the Indians, and the only signs of them were abandoned settlements and hastily evacuated campsites.

The expedition reached Unadilla August 12, where it picked up the westward route taken by William Butler's party the year before. Butler had left standing the homes of three settlers thought to be Patriots, but it was now learned that they had gone off to the British. The buildings were promptly burned. By the afternoon of August 14, they arrived at the burned-out town of Oquaga, in a pleasant mile-wide valley between high hills. "We arrived in Six days from lake Otsago to this place, which is by land computed to be eighty miles and 140 by water, in consequence of the crookedness of the river," wrote Charles Macarthur, surgeon of the Fourth Pennsylvania Regiment, in his diary, "and what is very remarkable Since the body has been together . . . tho' the men have thro' almost unsurmountable fatigues and difficulties have lost but one man who expired on the 14 inst. with a putrid fever."[23]

They rested two days while they waited for two hundred New York militia under Lieutenant Colonel Albert Pawling, due from Warwasing. When a detachment could detect no sign of them, Clinton resumed his advance. (Pawling arrived at Oquaga two days later and, finding Clinton gone, returned and never joined the expedition.) Four miles below Oquaga lay a Tuscarora town of ten houses, Shawhiangto, which the men burned, and ten or twelve miles further another Tuscarora town of five or six houses, Ingaren (near the present Great Bend, Pennsylvania), and a field of corn and potatoes, which they also burned. With these, and burnings of other isolated houses as they went, Clinton's program of destruction had begun. When the army reached the Chenango River, almost as wide as the Susquehanna but not so deep (at the site of the present Binghamton), a force of one hundred riflemen under Major James Parr was dispatched four miles upstream to level Chenango, a town of twenty houses, but they found that the Indians themselves had destroyed it the previous winter.

In the evening of August 18, two messengers, Asa Chapman and Justus Gaylord, arrived from Poor with the news that he was eight miles away, having marched twenty-five miles by land and sixteen by water from Tioga. A signal gun was fired, and it was heard at Poor's camp on the Susquehanna, at the mouth of Chocunut Creek. Clinton's men marched at seven o'clock the following morning to meet him, burning nine houses on the way. They found that he had been busy destroying Chocunut, an Indian settlement of twenty houses east of the Susquehanna, near the present Vestal, and seven houses three miles to the east, all that remained of a previously burned larger town of fifty. No time was lost, despite an afternoon shower. With Clinton's men in front and Poor's at the rear, the combined force covered sixteen miles and at sundown reached the mouth of Owego Creek, where an all-day rain kept them through August 20. While they waited, a party was sent a mile further to burn Owego, an Indian town of twenty houses, "to Grace our Meeting," wrote Lieutenant John L. Hardenbergh of Van Cortlandt's Second New York Regiment. The next morning opened very pleasant, and the march resumed southward for the final leg of the journey, but six miles from Sullivan's camp it was delayed by swift rapids. Fourteen boxes, containing twenty-seven thousand cartridges, and three barrels of gunpowder were lost when two boats overturned. At one o'clock on

August 22, the Clinton-Poor troops joined Sullivan at his camp on the west side of the Susquehanna and were greeted with the discharge of thirteen cannon and a dinner Sullivan hosted for all officers.[24]

With the united army poised to begin the invasion of the Indian country proper, the destiny of that magnificent domain was already on the minds of the invaders. It remained uncertain whether Pennsylvania or New York had jurisdiction, but on August 25 six of Sullivan's principal officers banded together to lay claim to the land of the Senecas. Hand, Van Cortlandt, Major Nicholas Fish of Van Cortlandt's regiment, Ogden, Barber, and Lieutenant Benjamin Lodge, the expedition's surveyor, each invested ten thousand dollars in an association to purchase from whichever state was the possessor a huge tract west of the Susquehanna between the forty-second and forty-fifth degrees latitude.[25] It would constitute the western third of the present New York State, reaching up to Canada. It would be their bonanza in the surge of civilization.

✦ ✦ ✦ ✦ ✦ ✦ ✦ ✦ ✦ ✦ ✦

RESISTANCE

While Sullivan waited, the expedition to the west had already begun. Washington had appointed Colonel Daniel Brodhead, commander of the Western Department, to lead an invasion from Fort Pitt up the Allegheny River, through the country of the western Senecas and the Munseys (a hostile faction of the Delawares), eventually to unite with Sullivan's army. By April 21, however, he decided that Brodhead should not leave the Ohio territory too long unguarded. He was to aid Sullivan only as a diversion, after which he would withdraw to prepare for an attack on Detroit.[1]

Washington had reservations about Brodhead, an unpopular forty-two-year-old Pennsylvanian with a history as an intriguer, but he turned out to be an efficient devastator. He started out August 11 with a force of 605, his own Eighth Pennsylvania Regiment of Continentals as the nucleus. A month's provisions were transported sixty miles upriver by a one-hundred-man work crew as far as Mahoning (the present Templeton), where the cargoes were unloaded to packhorses. From there the expedition traveled overland forty miles to meet the Allegheny again at Cushcushing (the present Tionesta). Twenty-five miles further, at Conewango (the present Warren), an advance guard of fifteen whites under Lieutenant John Hardin and eight Delawares under Captain Sam Brady encountered a party of thirty or forty Senecas and Munseys under the Seneca chief Gu-ya-soh-doh paddling down the river in seven canoes. The warriors landed to fight. Overwhelmed, they fled, carrying with them their wounded and leaving behind five dead and their canoes, equipment, provisions, and eight guns. Three of the Americans were slightly wounded—the famous scout Jonathan Zane; an interpreter, Joseph Nicolson; and a Delaware, Nanoland.

Brodhead's way was now unopposed. Crossing to the west bank of the Allegheny, where for six miles his men had to wade into the river in order to pass precipitous hills, he followed an old Indian path for another twenty miles and arrived at a network of eight Indian towns centered around Bucktooth (the present Salamanca). The inhabitants had fled at the invaders' approach, in their panic leaving behind several packs of deerskins. There were 130 homes built of square and round logs, some spacious enough to house four families. In the fields were five hundred acres of high-quality corn and vegetables. Brodhead's men took three days to destroy everything. Returning down the Susquehanna, they found a cluster of three towns twenty miles above French Creek—Conewango, Buckaloons, and Maghinquechahocking—and burned all their thirty-five houses, some new or under construction. The expedition returned by way of Venango (the present Franklin) to Fort Pitt September 14, many of the men now barefoot and scantily clothed. They had compensation. Not a man had been killed or taken prisoner. Plunder in the amount of three thousand dollars was sold and distributed among the troops.[2]

Why, demanded Six Nations chief Teaquanda at a council in Montreal on June 19, as he angrily threw a wampum belt on the table, did not the government build a fort at Oswego as a bastion and supply depot against the threatening rebels? The Iroquois League had forsaken its neutrality and sundered its unity, but "The Great King their Father did not assist them in the Time of their Distress," declared another deputation a month later at Fort Niagara.[3]

The agent of the king who might supply this assistance was Lieutenant General Frederick Haldimand, Carleton's replacement as governor of Canada. He was a sixty-one-year-old, French-speaking Swiss career soldier who had served under the Dutch in Europe and with distinction under the British in the American colonial wars. For the defense of all of Canada, his command consisted of sixty-five hundred regular troops, fourteen hundred Loyalists, and an uncertain number of unreliable English and French militia. His store of provisions was critically low. Detroit had some produce grown by the remains of the small French colony, but Niagara had none, and the supply of salted rations available from Quebec was severely limited. From his headquarters in Quebec City, Haldimand had to decide where he should allocate his limited resources—Detroit, Niagara, or Montreal.

At first, the danger in the east seemed the most immediate. Moses Hazen was building a road to Montreal that was a clear rebel preparation for invasion. The recently concluded French-American alliance posed the threat of a naval attack up the St. Lawrence. And the wavering allegiance of the French Canadians weakened the power to resist. On March 15, however, General Sir Henry Clinton wrote from New York that this threat was no more than a feint. That switched Haldimand's emphasis to the west, where the Americans under George Rogers Clark had captured Vincennes and might move against Detroit. Haldimand dispatched an aide-de-camp, Captain Dederick Brehm, who had served six years there, to investigate, and his report confirmed Detroit as the likely rebel target.[4]

In his concentration on safeguarding the gateways to Canada, Haldimand had not fathomed Washington's design of a campaign to destroy the settlements of the Iroquois. His principal source of information on rebel activities in the territory of the Six Nations was the reports of John Butler, relayed through his superior, Lieutenant Colonel Mason Bolton, commander of Fort Niagara. In late April 1779, Butler wrote that a spy had brought word that "the Rebels intended to send three thousand men this Summer against the five nations." On May 13, Butler wrote that a prisoner had disclosed that Edward Hand would lead three thousand men up the Susquehanna and that another force of two regiments and a large contingent of militia would move up the Allegheny River. Butler's son, Walter, wrote directly to Haldimand that the Susquehanna force would be supported by another from Fort Stanwix. And on July 3, John Butler announced that the campaign was indeed under way:

> It seems now beyond a Doubt that the Rebels are coming up the Susquehanna. A Deserter came in this morning who left Wioming eleven days ago; He says that a General Hand was already there with six hundred men and two small pieces of Cannon, and that the Generals Sullivan & Maxwell were daily expected with nine Regiments and as many pieces of Cannon; he says, it was talk'd of amongst them that another army was to come from the Northward, and a third across from Fort Pitt or Fort George, and that their Designs is to cut off the Indians as they came along, and then join their Forces to attack Niagara.[5]

Four days later, Butler sent Haldimand the most accurate report of all: A Caughnawaga Indian had come from Oneida with word that the rebels were at Lake Otsego and would march to Tioga to meet a second force coming from Wyoming, together to "trample under foot the Six nations and then reduce Niagara."[6]

But while these messages poured in, Sir John Johnson was in Quebec, having earlier assured Haldimand that according to his sources the report of a rebel expedition against the Six Nations was "groundless." Butler, he now warned, could not be trusted, for he "would remain where he was or thereabouts till he could join the army from New York with safety, or till it was too late to do anything." Haldimand believed Johnson before Butler. "It is impossible the Rebels can be in such force, as has been represented by the Deserters to Major Butler, upon the Susquehannah," he wrote Bolton. "I am convinced that Detroit is the object, and that they show themselves, and spread reports of expeditions in your neighborhood merely to divert the Rangers and Indians from their main purpose."[7]

At Niagara, however, the Indians' alarm about the destruction of Onondaga had made action imperative. To reassure the Senecas, Bolton on May 2 sent John Butler to Canadesaga, their "castle," with three hundred Rangers and a few Indians. Yet Bolton viewed the assault on Onondaga as a ruse to draw attention away from Wyoming and Fort Pitt, where a body of American riflemen had recently been ambushed. At Canadesaga, the troops soon found themselves subsisting on stale salt meat imported from Ireland. The Indians were worse off, some reduced to scrounging for roots and leaves. Food became so scarce that by June 19 Butler considered sending his men to the Genessee River falls, five miles below Irondequoit, where they might feed on fish and receive boats bringing the few provisions available from Niagara.

Then came the conclusive news that the Americans were massing at Wyoming and Otsego. Without waiting for further orders, Butler dispatched an expedition to each locality, both to distract the American offensive and to seize cattle for his critically low larder.[8]

Brant led a party of sixty Indians and twenty-seven white men southwest to Minisink (the present Greenville, east of Port Jervis), ten miles west of Goshen. Passing through Chemung on July 8, they arrived at Minisink in the middle of the day on July 20, only to find most of the cattle dispersed in the woods. The settlement was undefended, and Brant remained until the following morning, burning ten houses and eleven barns, a gristmill, and a church. He was guided by a local Loyalist, Anthony Westbrook. Four scalps were taken, including that of the schoolmaster, Jeremiah Van Auken, who sacrificed his own life in attempting to shield his pupils. The children were saved, nevertheless. Brant painted on the little girls' clothes his distinctive mark, which protected them from harm by his own men, and the girls spread their aprons over their brothers to include them as well. In fact, he kept his men from killing any women or children and even permitted one woman to save two feather beds and bedding from the flames.

Meanwhile, the militia appeared. Under the command of Colonel John Hathorn, 120 of them came from Goshen, and caught up with the departing raiders as they were crossing the mouth of the Lackawaxen River. Brant and forty of his men, however, ambushed the American rear. After prolonged firing, the Americans ran out of ammunition and were completely routed. The Indians took more than forty scalps, including that of Hathorn. Brant did not spare combatants, but he thought he saw one of them, Captain John Wood, give the sign of a Master Mason. A proud Mason himself, Brant returned the signal with the Masonic handshake and gave him his blanket for the night. The next day, to Brant's outrage, Wood admitted that he was not a Mason, but he was allowed to survive as a prisoner. Brant's losses totaled three killed and ten wounded.[9]

On July 9, Captain John Macdonnel, with 50 Rangers and some Eighth Regiment regulars, set out for the West Branch of the Susquehanna. He was joined on the way by Cornplanter, at the head of 120 Senecas and Cayugas. Traveling through heavily wooded, mountainous country, they reached the Muncy Valley of the West Branch of the Susquehanna on the evening of July 27. They continued all night and arrived in the morning at Fort Freeland, about ten miles below Fort Muncy and four and a half miles east of the West Branch. It was a stockaded, two-story log house belonging to Jacob Freeland. Within were thirty-three defenders (thirteen Continentals and twenty militia) and fifty-two women and children. A farmer, James Watt, looking for his sheep near the fort, was tomahawked, but not before his cries produced a rifle shot from the fort that struck the attacker. The garrison held out until nine o'clock in the morning, when Captain John Lytle, accompanied by a town elder, John Vincent, agreed to surrender all the able-bodied men on condition that the women and children be allowed to go free. They departed unmolested, including four aged men and a slight young man, William Kirk, whose mother dressed him as a girl.

Meanwhile, word of the attack reached a group at the stockaded home of Hawkins Boon four miles to the south. He led an impromptu force of thirty-four to the rescue. At eleven o'clock the following morning, they surprised the British and killed two dozen. But the far superior British recovered and began encircling the Americans. Boon and eleven others were killed, and the rest fled. The British then plundered and burned every house and barn in a thirty-mile stretch of the valley. Although they took away 116 cattle, the Indians helped themselves to half of them, leaving 62 for Macdonnel to bring back.[10]

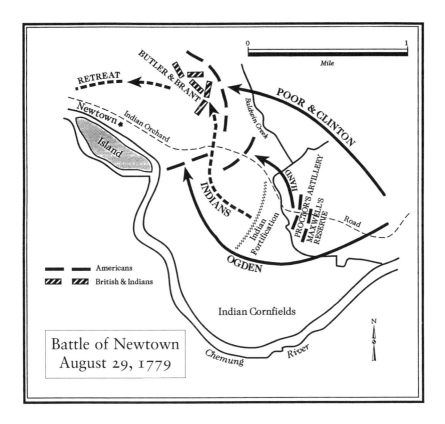

Battle of Newtown
August 29, 1779

At Canadesaga, John Macdonnel brought reports from prisoners that made it clear to John Butler that he faced "some of the best of the Continental Troops commanded by the most active of the Rebel Generals, and not a Regiment of Militia among the whole." He sent runners to Bolton, urgently requesting that "every Indian about Niagara may immediately sett off to this Place, Messessagoes as well as the rest, and march Night and Day, till they join me," and to his son, Walter, instructing him to "march immediately upon Receipt of this with every man you have fit for Duty, and use all Convenient Speed till you reach this Place." By August 15, between four hundred and five hundred had arrived. Considering the size of the army they were opposing, the Indians did not flock to protect their homeland. Some had already fled, and others were concerned only with the safety of their own villages; even the Delawares of the imperiled Chemung-Susquehanna area sent fewer than thirty warriors. Butler wished to start on August 16, but the Senecas would not move without their traditional feast and war dance. They set out the next day to meet Brant and his party at Chucknut, a mile from the Delaware village of Newtown, five miles below the present Elmira.

There, four days later, the combined force totaled approximately 700. The greatest part were Indians. The whites numbered 180 Rangers, a small detachment of 14 Eighth Regiment regulars, and 30 of Brant's Volunteers. Brant, recovering from a slight buckshot wound in his foot, received in a recent encounter with rebel militia at Little Falls, worried about the low numbers: "I am a little afraid we shall have hard work to drive the enemy back, for our Friends are too slow in joining us." Butler was worried, too. He believed that if 500 men had joined the Rangers, at least 1,000 warriors would have turned out. He felt so doubtful of the prospect that he proposed to the Indian chiefs that a tactic of harassment, rather than direct confrontation, was the most viable plan, but they refused.[11]

They were fourteen miles from Sullivan's camp at Tioga. The Delawares, in order to protect Newtown, had selected a position for ambush a mile to the east, which Butler thought too exposed. With the approval of a few of the chiefs, on August 27 he moved the camp a few miles higher up. The following morning, another group of chiefs, led by the English-speaking Delaware Hoch-ha-dunk, in defense of his home territory, demanded to return to the first location. Brant strongly supported Butler, but Old Smoke and Cornplanter deferred to Hoch-ha-dunk. "I of course was obliged to comply," Butler lamented.

The place chosen for a stand was a half-mile-long ridge (in popular terminology a "hogback") facing the road Sullivan would take. The ridge fronted Baldwin Creek, a northwesterly tributary of the Chemung, with a steep mountain to the left and, to the right, a narrow pass leading from a plain in a bend of the Chemung. A three-foot-high breastwork, made of logs from some nearby dismantled buildings, was thrown up behind a skillful concealment of propped-up, cut pine trees and shrub oaks. At the center, with John Butler, were the main body of his Rangers under Walter Butler, the few men of the Eighth Regiment detachment, and some Indians. At the foot of the mountain was the main body of the Indians. At the right were McDonnel with sixty Rangers and Brant with his Indians and Volunteers. The trail that Sullivan's unsuspecting army would be following, after crossing the creek, turned to the right, and his left flank would be exposed to withering fire from the breastwork. While he was thus engaged, Indian reserves would attack his right flank, stampeding the packhorses and completing the demoralization.

In the burning August sun, the men awaited the rebels. Butler had sent off his supplies and baggage, and his men had no blankets to shelter them. Each man received only seven ears of corn a day. Indian-white tensions increased, and when a false alarm from two Delawares shooting deer on the mountain inspired a temporary retreat for fear of encirclement, the Indians hooted derision. On the morning of August 29, Butler discovered that "some officious fellow among the Indians" had altered the line at the left so as to leave a passage for a flank attack. The chiefs, reported Butler's military secretary, Richard Cartwright, "thro' mere sulkiness," would not oppose him.[12]

At Tioga, the Americans' united army, now numbering five thousand, readied itself to sally forth against the seven-hundred-man foe. Was Sullivan's buildup that essential after all? Hand did not think so. With a supply of only twenty-seven days' provisions, he confided to his uncle, Judge Jasper Yeates, "our force or rather number of mouths is almost double what it should be." The men grumbled that the labor of hauling nine pieces of artillery and their appendages across New York State to the Genessee River was "as impracticable and absurd as an attempt to level the Alleghany mountains." Hand hoped the Indians would "fight us early (if at all) that only can prevent our being laught at."[13]

Sullivan issued orders to march August 25. He reassigned several regiments to the brigades of their states. Van Cortlandt's Second New

York Regiment was transferred from Hand to Clinton in exchange for William Butler's Fourth Pennsylvania Regiment and Parr's rifle corps. Alden's Sixth Massachusetts Regiment (Whiting commanding) moved from Clinton's to Poor's brigade. When Sullivan discovered that they did not have enough containers for flour, he issued orders for "all the Taylors, Sail makers, and such others as can wield a Needle" to cut up tents for flour sacks. When a shortage of horses to carry provisions and ammunition developed, all officers below the field level were required to turn over their mounts as pack carriers.[14]

On the appointed day, rain began at eight o'clock in the morning, continuing until evening; this delayed departure until eleven in the morning of the twenty-sixth. Ahead, Parr's dispersed rifle corps reconnoitered the way. A mile behind came Hand's advance corps in six columns, followed by Proctor's artillery, with the black cattle and three columns of packhorses on each side. Maxwell's brigade marched as a column at the left, flanked by two hundred chosen men under Ogden. Poor's brigade marched as a column at the right, flanked by two hundred under Dubois. Clinton's brigade brought up the rear, and on the river, boat crews poled twenty supply craft upstream. The Reverend Rogers, left behind as garrison chaplain, watched the procession with misgivings: "The great parade and regularity which is observed, must unavoidably in the end, letting alone all other obstacles, greatly defeat the purpose of the expedition, considering the coyness and subtilty of the Indians."[15]

The army traveled northwestward through level country (the present Route 17), but the going was slow, and after four miles, at five o'clock they reached a fording place beside a five-hundred-acre grassy plain. They found, however, that the river, swollen with the recent rains, had risen three feet, and they encamped for the night. The next morning the river remained too high to attempt a crossing, and the army marched along the east bank through heavily wooded country, the road no more than a footpath. They reached a mountain (probably Glory Hill, northwest of the present Waverly), which Poor's brigade climbed, but the artillery and baggage wagons had to snake along a narrow, three-fourths-mile defile overlooking a twenty-foot-high perpendicular bank. Wagons overturned, several broke up, and three packhorses with their flour sacks and baggage fell into the river and drowned. It took one hundred men seven hours of cutting, digging, hauling with drag ropes, and cursing against the artillery to break through. Two streams also caused delays, and Clinton, slowed at the rear, had to camp at one of them. The rest of the army, having progressed six miles, stopped for the night at a plain two miles from Old Chemung, which two weeks earlier they had burned. They found eighty acres of ripe beans, squash, pumpkins, potatoes, cucumbers, watermelons, and corn whose stalks measured fifteen feet. The men sat up until one o'clock in the morning gorging themselves—Lieutenant Shute recorded that he consumed ten ears of corn, a quart of beans, and seven squashes. The troops were instructed to gather enough corn to use the next day in place of the scarce flour. They torched the remaining crops, including corn that would have filled five thousand bushels.[16]

The morning of August 28 was taken up with repairing broken ammunition wagons, and the march resumed at two o'clock. A mile along the way they found a mountain so high and precipitous that the defile at the water's edge, the "Narrows," could not be sufficiently widened. Hand's, Poor's, and Clinton's brigades struggled over the top, finding a view twenty miles around, but the artillery and packhorses, escorted by Maxwell's brigade, had to cross and recross the river in order to bypass the mountain. At the first ford, Lieutenant William Barton observed, the water was "crotch deep," but at the second, a half mile further, it was waist high, and the swift current carried away men and animals. Three horses drowned, and the men barely managed to escape by holding hands. Chaplain Hunter once more carried one man and dragged another across. By evening, having covered three miles, they encamped at New Chemung.[17]

That afternoon a small scouting party that had been sent out the previous evening returned with a report that four miles ahead they had seen a great number of campfires spread over an area so extensive as to leave no doubt that it was occupied by a formidable force preparing to give battle. Clearly, an engagement could be expected the next day.

In the early morning, the camp was startled awake by the firing of some guns, which turned out to be the riflemen clearing out their arms as they prepared to lead the day's advance. At nine o'clock the army crept cautiously forward, the riflemen spread out at the front, followed by Hand's light corps. After two miles of rough, hilly country, the main body halted to allow the artillery and baggage to scale a difficult height, while the advance troops continued ahead. The riflemen passed the ridge where Hand's engagement of August 14 had occurred, and a mile further, at a low, marshy ground, encountered several Indians who fired and fled. Parr here sent a climber up a tall tree, and there he discovered Indians in war paint crouching behind the camouflaged half-mile-long breastwork. The secret of the ambush was out. Parr immediately relayed the discovery to Hand, and he ordered the light corps to form three hundred yards before the Indian line, while the riflemen moved up to the bank of Baldwin Creek, within one hundred yards of the breastwork. The Indians several times emerged, fired, and retired, attempting without success to lure the Americans into the trap.[18]

Sullivan called a council of war, which laid out a plan to surround the enemy and bring them into an open action rather than allow them to withdraw. Poor and Clinton would ascend the mountain at the enemy's left, while Ogden's 250-man First New Jersey Regiment would flank the right. At the front, Hand's infantry and rifle corps would divert the enemy's attention. Allowing one hour for Poor to reach the mountain, Proctor's artillery would commence the attack with a heavy bombardment, supported in reserve by Maxwell's brigade. Behind the breastwork, John Butler sensed this design. Supported by Brant and Fish Carrier, the Cayuga chief, he urged the Senecas and Delawares to retire to the mountain to avoid entrapment. They refused.[19]

Poor started out at three o'clock, but he encountered a swamp so thick with bushes for a mile that he had only reached Baldwin Creek by the time Proctor began his cannonade. For two hours the British and Indians were subjected to a rain of shells, grapeshot, and spikes from six three-pounders, two 5½-inch howitzers, and a coehorn. Shells bursting behind their lines frightened the Indians into thinking they were surrounded. After a half hour the greater part of them fled. Butler with the remaining Indians and his Rangers retreated to the mountain where Poor was on his way up.

Poor's men pressed forward up the half-mile steep incline, bayonets drawn and not returning a shot in the face of the fire which "poured on them like hail," dashing from tree to tree. Dearborn's Third New Hampshire Regiment reached the top first. Lieutenant Jonathan Cass of that regiment, coming upon a wounded warrior, snatched his tomahawk from him and clubbed him with it. The brunt of the fire was borne on Poor's extreme left by Lieutenant Colonel George Reid's Second New Hampshire Regiment, nearly a gunshot away from the main body, which found itself almost surrounded. Corporal Hunter and two privates were killed. Major Benjamin Titcomb was shot in his torso and both arms, Captain Elijah Clayes received a ball in the torso, and Lieutenant Nathaniel McCauley suffered a shattered knee. Two sergeants and thirty-one rank and file were also wounded. McCauley's leg was amputated that night, while Chaplain Hunter watched, "a scene more distressing than that in the day." McCauley died the next morning.

Dearborn, ahead and to the right of Reid, at the top of the hill, became aware of his plight. Too far from Poor to check for permission, Dearborn on his own initiative took his troops down the hill to relieve Reid. He found Reid about to attempt a desperate bayonet push to extricate himself from an imminent encirclement at his right. Dearborn's men attacked with a heavy volley and drove the Indians back. By this time Clinton's brigade had reached the hill, and in charging up without a stop many men dropped and almost fainted in the severe heat. The Indians could resist no longer, and the retreat halloo sent them running, some astride baggage horses, every man to save himself. Littered behind them were packs, blankets, gun covers, and even kettles with corn boiling over the fire. In violation of their usual practice, they abandoned their twelve dead, including one squaw, whom the Americans immediately scalped. One of them, from his appearance and garments, appeared to be a Seneca chief; that was confirmed a week later by an American who had just escaped from long imprisonment among them. A white man, found among the Indian fallen, feigned death and was stripped, but a suspicious officer examined him and found him alive. Some men wanted to shoot him; others wanted to tomahawk him. The officer slapped him and told him to get up. The pretender rose to his feet, begging for mercy, and remained a prisoner. After a total engagement of six hours, most of the Indians made good their escape. John Butler believed that they would have been "cut to pieces, . . . had the rebels acted with any spirit."[20] This might have been possible if Sullivan had not mistakenly allowed only one hour for Poor to make his way through the swamp that obstructed his way.

The failure of the Americans to close the trap allowed the British and Indians to escape with limited casualties. Detachments pursued them for two miles, killing eight Indians and taking a black Loyalist soldier prisoner. No Indians were taken prisoner. In all, John Butler reported ten men killed and nine wounded, but the Americans found at least twenty bodies. The Americans lost eight dead, including four wounded who died within two weeks after the action—Abner Dearborn, a sixteen-year-old nephew of Henry Dearborn, Sergeant Demeret, Joshua Mitchell, and Sylvester Wilkins. Thirty-three others were wounded.[21]

The Americans gave no quarter, and they could be barbaric. Major Daniel Piatt, of Ogden's First New Jersey Regiment, sent out a party to hunt for bodies of dead Indians. They found several beside a path, covered with leaves. They "skinned two of them from their hips down for boot legs," wrote Lieutenant William Barton, "one pair for the Major the other for myself."[22]

When pursuing Americans arrived at Catherine's Town, they found hiding in the woods a white-haired old Cayuga woman, too infirm to leave. She had been tended by a young woman who promptly fled. A soldier spotted her and felled her with a rifle shot. Another man ran forward and killed her with a bayonet thrust through her back. The terrified abandoned woman sat speechless as an officer took up his gun to shoot her. One of the guides, Thompson Maxwell, intervened: "I told him if he did I would shoot him next." Here Sullivan appeared, Maxwell later reported, "approved of what I have done,—treated her kindly,—gave her everything she stood in want of, even to rum," and had a small hut built for her.[23]

Following their victory, the Americans put Newtown and the orchards and fields of crops to the torch and the ax. Newtown was a village of about twenty houses, so like those of the settlers that they were thought to have been built by Tories. Situated on the left bank of the Chemung River, it faced a beautiful falls on the opposite side. The fields of corn, beans, peas, potatoes, and squash were of "so great a quantity," wrote an American soldier, "that it can scarcely be credited." A cluster of uninhabited structures straddling Baldwin Creek appeared to have been intended as the principal military food magazine. It took two days to destroy everything the Americans could not eat.[24]

The fleeing Indians and British stopped on the evening after the battle at Nanticoke, a village of eight houses on the east bank of the Chemung. The next day they moved to Catherine's Town (the present Montour Falls), a village of about thirty houses near the south end of Seneca Lake. Two runners had arrived there from Newtown, proclaiming the "death halloo" of defeat, and the women of the village, faced with losing their homes and their autumn harvest, wished to surrender and make peace. But the preservation of Catherine's Town was not Butler's prime concern. He warned that they would only be used as hostages, and urged that they seek refuge at Niagara, where they would be provided with food and clothing. Meanwhile, Walter Butler arrived with a fresh group of Rangers and Indians who threatened to scalp any fainthearted woman. They proposed to return and fight, but John Butler was not ready for that step either. He intended to keep his decimated force at a safe distance from the rebels and regroup for a later encounter.[25]

CHAPTER 9

✦ ✦ ✦ ✦ ✦ ✦ ✦ ✦ ✦ ✦ ✦

SHORTFALL

Sullivan's overwhelming victory at Newtown presented him with an unforeseen option. The weak turnout of warriors signaled an open road for the march of the invaders. Washington had not directed him to attempt the capture of Niagara, but might he not extend his campaign, living off the harvests of vacated fields, perhaps not even pausing to destroy the deserted villages, and crown his expedition with the conquest of the bastion of the north? For he was "too remote from Congress & from the Commander in Chief to Receive the necessary Instructions & therefore was obliged to follow those Steps which my own Judgment Dictated." The strain told on him, and one of his officers noted that "The old smile was there but the General's face looks thin and his complexion sallow. I fear he is not in good heart over what is expected of the Campaign."[1]

Sullivan did not know how poorly located and designed Niagara was. Canadian Lieutenant Governor John Graves Simcoe declared that it was "not defensible with its present fortifications or Garrison, or if reinforced to double its numbers." The fort's commandant, Lieutenant Colonel Mason Bolton, reported that his garrison was inadequate to man works of eleven hundred yards in circumference. Neither did Sullivan know how little he had to fear from Haldimand's belated efforts to stop him. On September 2, Haldimand had received word from Bolton that the rebels had reached Tioga. Bolton warned that the Indians' chiefs would desert the Crown unless they received significant reinforcements, and his message was backed up by another from David, a noted Mohawk chief.[2]

Haldimand concluded that the Iroquois villages appeared to be lost, but that Fort Niagara might be saved if the Indians could be persuaded to remain loyal. He sent orders to Sir John Johnson, then with his Greens at Lachine, to proceed with 380 picked men to the relief of John Butler and to take charge of the combined force.[3] Shortage of provisions prohibited a larger reinforcement, but a show of support was essential. Yet even that gesture encountered an immediate obstacle when Johnson asked for an order to force Butler and Brant to return recruits whom they had lured away from his Greens. Haldimand sharply admonished him that he might be held to account if he did not resolve their differences. Admittedly, Major Butler was "deficient in Education and liberal sentiments" and his son, Walter, "conceited and petulant," but the father had great influence over the Indians, and "a little attention wins his Heart."[4]

In any case, Johnson was far away from Sullivan's army, his troops were lacking in equipment, and his transportation up the St. Lawrence was slow. He did not arrive at Sodus Bay, his designated rendezvous with Butler on the southern coast of Lake Ontario, until October 13. He planned to join Butler and Brant for an attack on an Oneida village, but the Canadian Indians who had accompanied him adamantly refused to fight their brethren. He decided that the season was too advanced for further action, and he returned to Canada.[5]

Sullivan considered his choices and turned cautious. He elected to play it safe, justifying himself with his usual complaint of lack of supplies. He declared that he did not have provisions for the additional fifteen days that the campaign would require. He did not even have packhorses to carry them if he was to complete his assignment of inflicting total ruin upon all the Seneca, Cayuga, and Mohawk settlements. By his best calculation, he said, he had on hand only twenty-two pounds of flour and sixteen pounds of beef per man, and these were subject to losses from accidents on the road and on water.[6]

He dramatized his magnified plight with a flamboyant appeal to his troops. At dusk, the day after the Newtown battle, they were called out in formation and an address was read to them. Not for the first time, Sullivan bared to the men his charges of the "inattention of those whose business it was to make the necessary provision." Would they agree, he asked, to accept half rations of half a pound of flour and half a pound of meat per day in those areas where vegetables were available to make up for the other half? They would be paid in money for the withheld rations. If willing, they were to respond to the signal "Recover arms." The men knew well enough that there was plenty of food in the fields, and they were quite willing to trade their own pickings for extra pay. (The Congress authorized ten dollars monthly subsistence in lieu of food not supplied.) With one exception, all muskets were raised, and three cheers resounded down the line. A longtime Irish veteran observed that he had "never heard soldiers cry huzza! for half allowance before; however, as they all had, he would."

Enthusiasm was not, however, as universal as it seemed. The next morning, every colonel gave those of his men who felt that they could not endure the hardship the permission to return to the garrison at Tioga. A few braved ridicule to accept. Cilley even tried to persuade a fifteen-year-old recruit in his regiment, Richard Drout, to return, but he tearfully insisted on remaining.[7]

Nathan Davis, a private in the First New Hampshire Regiment, described the men's subsistence. The daily half ration of a half pound of meat was "rather an apology for beef," since the cattle had been worn scrawny with the constant driving. The Indians' corn and beans made good succotash at harvest time. But when the corn became too mature, it had to be ground into meal resembling hominy, in old tin kettles found in the Indian settlements. Every fourth man not on guard duty had to sit up all night grating the corn. They mixed the meal with boiled squash or pumpkin, kneaded it, and baked it into cakes. The result was "relished well."[8]

On August 31, the army started up the Chemung River into the Iroquois heartland. Sullivan sent the heavy artillery, along with the wounded and the wagons, back to Tioga, retaining only four brass three-pounders and a small howitzer. The morning was cool and clear after an all-night heavy storm. The troops labored through six miles of "hideous mountains" and thirty-feet-deep ravines and then turned north at Newtown to "a most beautiful piece of country remarkably level." Scattered houses on the way were burned, including two so well-constructed as to inspire speculation that Tories had built them. At Kanawaholla, a "very pritty" town (at the present site of Elmira), all twenty houses containing featherbeds, buried furniture chests, and household goods, was burned, and the nearby crops were cut down. Several boats were spotted escaping upstream, and Dayton's Third New Jersey Regiment, together with a company of Parr's riflemen, was sent after them. The pursuit was fruitless, but Dayton burned a small town, Runonvea (the present Big Flats), and several large cornfields before overtaking the main army the following day. The army had turned up the western shore of Newtown Creek and stopped for the night on a plain of high grass at the site of the present Horseheads.

The next morning, the army continued along the path of the present Route 14, snaked through a narrow defile between a mountain and a marsh, and a mile further, by eleven o'clock came to a thick, miry, nine-mile-long swamp. It was bordered on both sides by high hills, "uneven as a sea in a tempest," over which the right flank marched. The main body plunged straight ahead, into a dense tangle of spruce, pine, hemlock, and shrubs. A mile into the swamp, a halt was called for an hour to clear the way for the artillery. Over the next five miles, the terrain sloped downward to Catherine Creek, which flowed northward into Seneca Lake. In order to overcome bogs, ravines, and tree windfalls, the troops had to cross and recross the twisting creek at least fifteen times. About sunset, they emerged into a short stretch of clear land, but by dark they entered another, more difficult section of the swamp.

The men sank up to their knees in mud and mire, and the night was so black that each could find his way ahead only by holding onto the man ahead. Fires lit at intervals provided only momentary relief. The horses intermingled with the artillery, churning the morass still deeper. Two broke their necks, several fell into ditches and were killed, and two drowned in the creek. Sacks of flour and baggage, men, horses, and cattle were strewn along four miles of misery, and all the while everyone feared that the Indians might at any time pounce from the impenetrable darkness. "In a word," wrote Chaplain Andrew Hunter, "the whole army was a perfect chaos." Poor's and Hand's brigades reached the end of the swamp by midnight, but Clinton's, at the rear, together with many of the horses and cattle, spent the entire night in the quagmire before struggling out in the morning. "Had the savages availed themselves of this opportunity," noted Lieutenant Barton, "it could have proved very fatal to us, for they might with ease have destroyed a great part of our provisions, with a party very inconsiderable."[9]

A half mile beyond the swamp, straddling both sides of Newtown Creek, was Catherine's Town, named after a sister of Queen Esther. Sounds of howling dogs gave warning that the enemy might be offering battle, and some riflemen were sent to reconnoiter. The infantry, with fixed bayonets, formed two columns, ready to rush forward. The riflemen returned to report that Indians had just abandoned the town, leaving kettles of corn over fires still burning. Apparently, they had been caught by surprise, not having imagined that the army would attempt the swamp during the night. The weary troops, many without blankets and baggage (lost in the swamp), camped by the fires, which they fed with bark torn from the houses. One structure, a gambrel-roofed house thirty feet long and eighteen wide, they thought was Queen Catherine's palace.

The next day they burned the entire town and destroyed the crops. They found hiding in the woods a white-haired old squaw, a Cayuga or a Tuscarora, too infirm to leave. She had been tended by a young squaw, who promptly fled. A soldier spotted the young one in hiding and felled her with a rifle shot. Another man ran forward and killed her with a bayonet thrust through her back. She was afterward found stripped naked. Meanwhile, the terrified, abandoned old woman sat speechless as an officer took up his gun to shoot her. One of the guides, Thompson Maxwell, intervened: "I told him if he did I would shoot him next." Here Sullivan appeared and supported Maxwell.

The squaw still would not talk to Indian interpreters, until one of them drew his knife and threatened to scalp her. She found her speech and told of how the town's women had wished to make peace and how John Butler had resisted the demands of the newly arrived party of warriors to return and fight. Sullivan ordered Blue Back, one of the Oneidas, to build a bark hut for her, stored with a precious keg of pork, a supply of biscuit, and even some rum.[10]

Up Catherine Creek and along the east side of Seneca Lake, Sullivan's army swept onward. September 4 the village of Condawhaw, north of the present Hector, was burned. September 5 they destroyed Kendaia's twenty houses, a warriors' burial ground with painted boxes mounted over the graves, large adjacent cornfields, and an orchard of eighty trees. They found hiding there an escaped captive of the Indians, Luke Swetland of Wyoming, who had been taken a year earlier and adopted by an Indian family. He informed that although the Indians were dejected by the defeat at Newtown, Butler and Brant had assembled a force of one thousand and planned to make a stand at Canadesaga. After Onondaga's destruction, Canadesaga, home of Old Smoke, became the new fireplace of the Confederacy. It was the symbolic location to attempt resurgence.

Forewarned by Swetland's information, Sullivan advanced to Canadesaga with great care. By the afternoon of September 7, his army reached the Seneca River, the outlet at the lake's northeast tip. Crossing to the west, on the great trail from Albany to Niagara, the troops struggled along a narrow defile between the lake and several morasses until they came to a field of pumpkins and other vegetables three miles from the town. Here Sullivan made his disposition for an encirclement. Maxwell's brigade would move to the right, Hand's to the left, and Sullivan with Clinton's and Poor's would be at the center. When Sullivan arrived at his station, he was astounded to find that his troops, instead of readying for a rapid assault, had loaded themselves down with vegetables, each man decorating his bayonet with three pumpkins. "You damned unmilitary set of rascals!" he stormed, "what, are you going to storm a town with pompions [pumpkins]!" Shirts were unbuttoned, and squashes, melons, and mandrakes rolled out.

But it developed that Canadesaga was deserted. Only a three-year-old, half-starved, begrimed white boy remained behind, who could say only that "his mamy was gone." Canadesaga Creek flowed through the town, the largest the expedition had yet encountered, containing about sixty closely spaced houses, some made of hewn timbers and others of logs or bark. At the center were the ruins of a stockaded fort and blockhouse that Sir William Johnson had built in 1756. In a small log house they found an empty keg, marked "Spirits for Col. Butler." Nearby grew extensive fruit orchards and corn and vegetable fields. They girdled the trees and cut down and burned the crops. Until the child could be put up for adoption, artillery captain Thomas Machin took over his care.[11]

The disregard for order and caution that had so disturbed Sullivan suggested a larger morale problem. How convinced were the rank and file of the value of their expedition? Had they truly beaten Indians whom they could not confront? Would starving bring them to heel if, as Major Jeremiah Fogg, Poor's aide-de-camp, despaired, "they feed on air and drink the morning dew"? Sullivan needed to demonstrate support from the troops, and he decided once more to sound them out. "Pimps and tale bearers were brought from every brigade," wrote Fogg. A war council examined the reports. Sullivan declared that they showed the men prepared to endure the final sixty miles of the expedition.[12]

Still, it remained clear that they must quickly wrap up the expedition's mission. In order to achieve greater mobility, the sick and the lame and the disabled horses were sent back to Tioga under escort by a detachment of fifty men under Captain John Reed of the Sixth Massachusetts Regiment.[13]

CHAPTER 10

✦ ✦ ✦ ✦ ✦ ✦ ✦ ✦ ✦ ✦ ✦

AMBUSH

Stillness met the oncoming invaders. "It is difficult to account for the conduct of the Indians, who quit their towns, & suffer us to destroy them, their corn, their only certain stock of provisions, without offering to interrupt us," mused Dr. Campfield.[1]

One village, Scawyace (near the present Waterloo), on the trail between the north ends of Seneca and Cayuga lakes, was so totally abandoned that Sullivan left its destruction to a mere scouting party of four militiamen under Colonel John Harper. At some locations, there were extensive orchards and ripe vegetable fields. Major Parr took 140 riflemen to destroy Gothseunquean, on Kershong Creek, on the west side of Seneca Lake, seven miles south of the present Geneva. He still had to call for more men to help in the labor of girdling, cutting, and burning, a task that took two days. "Several officers thought it a degradation of the army to be employed in destroying apple and peach trees, when the very Indians in their excursions spared them, and wished the general to retract his orders for it," reported the Reverend William Gordon. Sullivan nonetheless replied that he was determined "to destroy everything that contributed to their support." (Hand and Dearborn looked the other way.) Gordon later gathered information from participants for a history of the Revolution.[2]

Following a delay caused by a heavy rain, the army left the flattened Canadesaga at noon of September 9, and after traversing eighteen miles through swampy land and large, formerly cultivated fields, arrived the next morning at the twenty-yard-wide outlet to Canandaigua Lake. The only fordable place was an opening through dense thorn bushes on both sides, an ideal location for an ambush. Cilley's First New Hampshire Regiment, normally in the advance, stood sulkily on guard until sunset, with complaints and curses, while the rest of the men waded across shoulder-deep, their cartridge boxes mounted atop their knapsacks. Cattle and the baggage train followed.

A half mile ahead lay the town of Canandaigua. Without waiting, Sullivan ordered Hand to attack with four infantry regiments. Hand hesitated. He would obey, he said, but it would be dark by the time he reached the town, when the invisible enemy could inflict a useless waste of lives. Nearby sat the fretting Cilley on his horse. "Give me leave and I will take the town, with my regiment alone," he called to Sullivan. Permission promptly granted, he led his troops forward, each grasping the garment of the man ahead as they groped their way along an Indian footpath. They encountered, reported Private Nathan Davis, no worse enemy than the darkness, "and a thousand musketoes to each man." At the army's approach, the Seneca women and children had fled to a hiding place on Squaw Island near the foot of the lake, leaving cooking fires still burning. Three Seneca men remained in the village and were taken prisoner. Canandaigua was a town of twenty-three houses, two miles from the lake, on a rise of land beside a rivulet. Some of the structures were as large as thirty or forty feet long by ten feet wide, with chimneys instead of the usual hole in the roof of Indian custom. Under the bark floor of one of the houses, Cilley's men dug up fourteen silver dollars. They found a dog hanging by its neck, a wampum belt tied around its middle; the Indians intended it as a war sacrifice and would have made the skin into a pouch filled with tobacco and set afire.[3] Once again, the town and the crops were reduced to ashes.

The prisoners informed Sullivan that forty-one miles to the west was Chenussio (also known as Little Beard's Town and Genesee Castle), "the grand capital of the Indian country," where the Indians and the Rangers had raised large crops to maintain their raids on the

American frontier. "This information determined me at all events to reach that settlement," wrote Sullivan, "tho' the state of my provisions, much reduced by unavoidable accidents, almost forbade the attempt. My flour had been much reduced by the failure of the packhorses & in the passage of creeks & defiles, and twenty seven of the cattle had been unavoidably lost." Indeed, Chaplain John Gano reported that the men were "amazing weak and emaciated by their half allowance and green corn."[4]

From Canandaigua, after traversing still another swamp, the army climbed several high hills, from whose tops they could see to the west a wide stretch of flat land covered with forests and fields of tall grass. A march of thirteen more miles brought them to the foot of Honeoye Lake and, a half-mile to the north, the Seneca village of Hanneyaye (the present Honeoye), on the east side of the lake's outlet. They were now twenty-five miles from Chenussio, and Sullivan reduced his army for a rapid strike. There were still 250 incapacitated soldiers, and he left these men behind, along with the spent horses, cattle, and baggage, in the care of a cadre of fifty under Captain Cummings. They spared one of the village's twelve houses from the flames to serve as a blockhouse. They buttressed it with kegs and bags of flour and pierced it for portholes in its sides for the two three-pounders also left with Cummings; they surrounded it with a barricade of branches from axed apple trees.[5]

After a heavy rain, the lightened army, carrying only half-rations, deemed adequate for the remaining thirty miles, resumed its march on September 12, climbing steep hills and threading narrow defiles to the outlet of Hemlock Lake. Beyond was a tableland "Eaqual to any we have seen," wrote one of the expedition's surveyors, Thomas Grant. The soil so impressed one of the men, Lemuel Richardson, that he returned after the war and cleared a farm there. By nightfall, having covered eleven miles, the strung-out troops made camp along a three-quarter-mile stretch two miles east of Kanaghsaws, a hastily abandoned town of eighteen houses on the east side of the inlet near the head of Conesus Lake. One of the houses was the residence of Chief Big Tree, a Seneca who had advocated neutrality until the

American invasion, when pressures of his tribesmen had forced him to side with the British. Another house belonged to Captain Sunfish, a prosperous escaped slave. All were destroyed.[6]

For the territory ahead, Sullivan had no reliable guide. Available maps, he said, "serve not to enlighten but to perplex." They did not show that since 1771 Chenussio had removed from the east side of the Genesee River, at the mouth of Canaseraga Creek, to the west side, two miles to the north. He therefore called in Lieutenant Thomas Boyd, one of Parr's men, and ordered him to take three or four riflemen, a guide, and an Oneida chief to reconnoiter Chenussio and explore whether it might be open to a surprise attack. Boyd, a twenty-two-year-old native of Northumberland County in Pennsylvania, was a handsome, brash officer who had been stationed with his unit at Schoharie in the autumn of 1778. He had gotten a local girl, Cornelia Becker, pregnant, but had shrugged off her entreaties to marry her. As he departed, she hung on his neck, but he only threatened her with his sword. She cried after him that she "hoped he would be cut to pieces by the Indians."

He took it upon himself to interpret Sullivan's instructions to include a foray as well as scouting party, and recruited twenty-six volunteers.[7]

At Canawaugus (the present Avon), ten miles north of Chenussio, the invaders' approach to the Senecas' capital at last moved the chiefs to attempt a final stand. "The Indians seem in better spirits & more determined than I have seen them since they left Chuchnut," reported John Butler. Old Smoke and Brant had resolved their differences, and "they concur with each other on every occasion." They were heartened by Bolton's dispatch from Niagara of a light infantry company of the Thirty-fourth Regiment, with ammunition and provisions. Those reinforcements, however, were still on the way, and the most that Butler could muster was a combined force of 400 Indians and Rangers.[8]

It might seem quixotic for such a small force to challenge Sullivan's overwhelming numbers, but Butler and the chiefs planned an

ambush in terrain remarkably similar to that in which Edward Braddock's hapless army had been cut to pieces by Indians at the Battle
of the Monongahela during the French and Indian War in 1755.
Butler and the Indians left Canawaugus in the afternoon of September 12, and early the next morning they positioned themselves at the
site they intended for the attack. The trail the Americans were to
follow led westward across an inlet of Conesus Lake at a gap between an impassable marsh to the north and an impenetrable underbrush swamp to the south. Butler had destroyed a bridge there, and
the Americans had to stop to rebuild it. Beyond the bridge, the path
ascended a steep hill along a half-mile-wide space between two ravines. In these ravines, and at the crest of the hill, three-quarters of a
mile west of the bridge, the British and Indians waited in concealment
to spring upon the advancing troops.[9]

Accident uncovered their design.

Boyd's party, with the Oneida chief, Honyose Thaosagwat, and
the Stockbridge, Captain Jehoiakim Mtohksin, as guides, set out at
eleven o'clock on the night of September 12, passed through Kanaghsaws, crossed the inlet, climbed the hill, and headed westward toward
Chenussio. The two forces remained unaware of each other. In the
dark, Boyd's men passed Butler's right flank, without being discovered. Early in the morning, they arrived before Gathtsegwarohare,
two miles below Chenussio, near the present Hampton Corners. Taking one of his men with him, Boyd went forward to reconnoiter and
found the town abandoned. He rejoined his party, and while remaining concealed in the woods to await daybreak, sent two men back to
report to Sullivan. At sunrise, seeing four mounted Indians entering
the town, Boyd made an incomprehensible decision. Heedless of being discovered, he sent a detachment to attack them. One of the
detachment was Timothy Murphy, short, swarthy, and pugnacious,
a famous scout and marksman. He killed one Indian, but the others
escaped, one wounded. Too late, Boyd realized his serious danger,
and he turned back toward the army. Halfway, he paused to await
Sullivan's coming and dispatched two additional men with news of
his location. The men ran into five Indians and returned to Boyd for

protection. Against Honyose's advice, Boyd's full force pursued the Indians, who shrewdly perceived an opportunity to trap the Americans. They retreated out of range, luring Boyd's men toward the left of Butler's camp.

Meanwhile, another group of Indians, concealed on a hill up closer to the American army, had spotted an unarmed surveying party led by Captain Lodge coming up the hill, and began firing on them. Corporal Calhoun was mortally wounded, and Lodge, dropping his compass, fled from an Indian brandishing his tomahawk. A nearby American camp sentinel shot the pursuer in the nick of time.

Butler, hearing firing from two directions, feared that he was being surrounded. He sent his entire force to the scene, and Boyd's men found themselves completely surrounded. They took refuge in a small grove of trees, where they made a desperate stand. At first, they inflicted heavy casualties, until the Indians charged them, firing so close at point-blank that powder marks were found on the dead men's flesh. Boyd was wounded.

Eleven men on the flanks, including Murphy, escaped, one wounded in the hand. Two of them, running along the lakeshore, were attacked by three dogs but killed them. They were joined by Jehoiakim Mtohksin, and the three made their way back to the army. Thirteen were killed in combat, including seven riflemen, five members of William Butler's Fourth Pennsylvania Regiment, and a volunteer. Boyd, Sergeant Michael Parker, and Chief Honyose were taken prisoner. Boyd and Parker were placed under the protection of Brant as his personal captives. Not so Honyose. His elder brother, Gah-ne-gi-e-song (the lemonade), fighting for the British, recognized him, carrying a Indian scalp tied to his belt. He loudly reminded him how he had tried to persuade him to join the side of the Crown and denounced him now as deserving death. He would not himself kill him, but "the Senecas might do as they pleased." Chief Little Beard dispatched him with one blow of his tomahawk.[10]

Three-quarters of a mile away, Parr and a scouting party of riflemen heard the firing and hastened forward. The Indians detected them and fled, leaving behind one of their dead and a wagonload of packs, clothing, and weapons. When the escaping men from Boyd's detachment and Lodge's returning surveyors arrived in the American camp, Sullivan immediately sent Hand with his advance troops to the rescue. They also arrived too late. In the grove where they had fallen lay the corpses of six of Boyd's men, tomahawked and scalped. Other bodies were scattered in the surrounding woods.[11] Their sacrifice had thwarted the larger entrapment that John Butler and his chiefs had planned for the main American army.

That same day, September 13, the bridge completed, the army crossed the inlet on its southwestward way to the Genessee. Nine miles beyond the scene of the slaughter, as the troops neared Gathtsegwarohare, to the east of Canaseraga Creek, the advance party reported that the enemy had drawn up in battle array, apparently intending a last stand. Sullivan prepared to attack, with Maxwell's brigade at the left, Poor's at the right, Hand's in the center, and Clinton's in reserve. But by sundown, when the army arrived at the town, the Tories and Indians had fled across the creek.[12] Gathtsegwarohare contained twenty-five recently built houses, with adjacent corn and vegetable fields.

At 3:30 the next morning, still wary of surprise, the men were awakened by a signal gun and kept on the alert until sunrise. By six o'clock, the enemy nowhere in evidence, two thousand men set to work throwing some of the crops in the creek and burning the rest with the buildings, a task that took six hours. By noon, the army laboriously began crossing the muddy creek, and after two hours entered a half mile of timbered bottomland. On emerging, they beheld a waving stretch of prairie, novel to natives of the eastern seaboard. The Genessee Flats, a plain extending twelve to fourteen miles along the Genessee River and several miles inland, was covered with bluegrass and timothy, five to eight feet high and so dense that officers on horseback could see only the guns of the marching men. "Not a rise of ten feet through the whole, not a stump on it. A few acres of timber which stands in small groves make it appear much more beautiful," wrote awestruck Major John Burrowes.

The open expanse exposed at a view the sight of the troops parading in precise procession, with a horn trumpeting the progress of the light artillery, and even the packhorses maintaining orderly formation. Within two miles, they reached the Genessee River at a forty-yard-wide fording place almost a mile from the present Mount Morris. The current was strong, and the men crossed in platoons with locked arms. On the far side, next to a hill of white oak, stood two houses, which they soon burned. Beyond came a swamp, and after another hill and swamp, their northward march brought them to a seven-mile grass plain, as beautiful as the one on the other side, through which flowed the winding river with its rocky cataracts. Here, at five o'clock, between the river's west bank and the present town of Cuylerville, they found the capital of the Seneca country.[13]

Of a sudden, horror replaced the beauty. Paul Sanborn, a private in a detachment on the extreme right of Clinton's brigade, which was approaching the village, came upon the mutilated and partly dog-eaten bodies and severed heads of two American soldiers. Even disfigured, one was recognizably Boyd's. The second, from a scar and broken front teeth, was identified as Parker. Their condition showed that they had been beaten and speared in countless places. Their fingernails and toenails had been pulled out, their tongues cut out at the root, their noses and ears cut off, their eyes gouged out. The skin had been cut off Boyd's penis and scrotum. Strips of flesh had been cut from Parker's back, where a knife had been left protruding. A stark lesson, wrote Colonel Henry Dearborn, "from which we are taught the necessity of fighting those more than divels to the last momemt rather than fall into their hands alive."

We can piece together the torment which these men had suffered from recollections a half century later of John Butler's military secretary, Richard Cartwright, and a Seneca warrior, Bucktooth, who was present but claimed not to have participated. Brant had decided to spare the captives in order to bring them to Butler for questioning. Boyd disclosed to Butler that Sullivan had five thousand troops under Hand, Poor, and Clinton and four pieces of artillery, yet only enough provisions to take them to Genessee. Butler supplied a guard of Rangers to protect the prisoners, but when they reached Chenussio, young warriors, furious at the destruction of their homes, could not be restrained.

An oft-repeated account of what happened then comes from the recollection many years later of Mary Jemison, a white captive of the Senecas. As she described it, Little Beard had Boyd stripped and tied to a sapling. A hole was cut in his abdomen through which his intestine was drawn out and tied to the sapling. He was then unbound and driven around the pole until he had extracted the whole of his intestines before he was at last beheaded.

But she, although married to a Seneca chief, did not herself witness the torture. The warrior Bucktooth states that he was personally present, and his version is different. Boyd and Parker, he says, were stripped and made to run the gauntlet between two lines of warriors, each allowed one blow of the fist. Then the two men were knocked down and beaten to death. Only afterward, apparently, were they butchered to the condition in which they were found.[14]

Chenussio was the largest of the Seneca towns, situated on an elevated plain in a bow of the river, with a brook running through it. It contained 128 well-built houses untidily scattered in no particular pattern. Most of them were large, with multifamily, two-tier berths lining both sides. They had only a hole in the roof to let out smoke. "The rubage of one of their houses, is enough to stink a whole country," wrote Dr. Jabez Campfield. The town's main structure was a two-story council house of peeled logs, with the gable ends painted vermillion. The panicky inhabitants had fled, leaving large quantities of husked corn, and fires still burning in some of the dwellings.[15]

For Sullivan's men it was a day of both sadness and joy. They buried Boyd and Parker with full military honors under a clump of wild plum trees. Then, knowing that they would go no further, they relaxed rationing and enjoyed a meal of beefsteak and potatoes.

The next morning, Sullivan announced to the troops that "the immediate Object of this expedition is accomplished," and that he would "not fail to inform America at Large how much they stand indebted to them." From six o'clock until two in the afternoon, he put them to work in the surrounding two hundred acres of vegetable gardens and cornfields, gathering the tall corn and piling it on torn-down houses to fuel huge fires. They demolished the entire town, with an estimated fifteen thousand bushels of corn.[16]

All the while, though, they faced potential peril; a hint of it came from a white woman who had escaped from captivity by Indians and who was carrying her two-year-old son. She had been taken at Wyoming on November 5 of the previous year, and her husband, Edward Lester, and another child had been killed. She reported Indian discontent with Butler, who had decided that he had no alternative but to withdraw to Niagara. According to the later reminiscences of the Seneca Bucktooth, the Indians reorganized for an action of their own. They expected the Americans to continue on to Niagara, and they planned an ambush, with parties concealed on both sides of the Genessee. Sullivan might indeed have marched on to another town, Canaqwaugus, filled with refugees, below Chenussio on the same side of the Genesee; but his scouts had not discovered it. Instead, he turned his expedition back toward Tioga, and the Indians abandoned their ambush.[17] They attempted no further resistance to the march of the army of destruction.

CHAPTER 11

✦ ✦ ✦ ✦ ✦ ✦ ✦ ✦ ✦ ✦

"To Extirpate Us
from the Earth"

Sullivan was given to bombast.
Yes, his troops had turned back to Tioga, but despite his proclamation of congratulation to them, his mission was not yet completed.
Thus far they had destroyed the habitations of the Senecas. Still
almost untouched were the Cayuga villages; they became the target
of his return march.

The army left for Tioga on September 16, and Captain William
Henderson's sixty-man advance patrol that day found in their path
fourteen bodies of Boyd's party, "in a most terrible mangled Condition," shuddered Lieutenant Erkuries Beatty. They were buried with
the honors of war.

Mornings turned very cold, with hard frost. At Hanneyaye, on
September 17, they were relieved to find Cummings's cadre safe.
Here they slew many of the spent horses, rather than allow them to
fall into enemy hands. When they were about to set out the next day,
they found that so many of the surviving horses had strayed beyond
recall that the officers, including Sullivan himself, had to dismount
and use their steeds for pack carriers.[1]

On the way to Canadesaga, the army met the Oneida Bluebeck
(Oneiga) and two of his tribesmen, arriving with an urgent message
for Sullivan. The leader was a flamboyant young sachem, bearing
rich belts of wampum and adorned "in the most gorgeous manner"
with silver rings. Some hung within a lock of hair dangling from his
forehead. He wore three in his nose and one hung from each ear; six

large rings surrounded his neck, and bracelets encircled both arms. He brought a message from an Oneida war council, a plea to spare the villages of the Cayuga. A Cayuga party, headed by Chief Tegatleronwane, wished to make peace with the Americans and had demonstrated this by the release of some prisoners. The Oneidas therefore requested that Sullivan not destroy the Cayuga cornfields, "as we cannot furnish them with provisions should we be able to find them and bring them to our town, having already so many of the Onondagas to support."[2]

Was this an opportunity to divide the Cayugas from the Senecas and promote an eventual peaceful settlement? Indeed, as early as April, an American agent, James Dean, who lived with the Oneidas, had reported that the Cayugas were ready to sue for peace. Too far from Congress to seek guidance, Sullivan had only Washington's instructions. He was "not by any means" to "listen to any overture of peace before the total ruin of their settlements is effected," a determination that he repeated three and a half months later, to make the extermination "so final and complete, as to put it out of their power to derive the smallest succor from them, in case they should attempt to return this season." Afterward, Washington allowed, Sullivan might negotiate "the terms" of a treaty, "letting them know that it must be ratified by Congress." Following these guidelines, Sullivan sent Dean with his reply to the Oneidas. With an outpouring of scorn, he stated that he proposed to proceed with the destruction of the Cayuga villages, allowing only that "these Cayugas, who wish to be thought friendly, may come in with their families & submit themselves to the direction of Congress."[3]

And he promptly ordered two detachments to scour the Cayuga territory. Colonel William Butler, with Parr's riflemen, five hundred men of his own regiment, and the Oneida braves, was to destroy the towns on the east side of Cayuga Lake. The Oneidas were to attempt to persuade the Cayugas, with whom they had intermarried, to surrender, failing which their homes would be leveled. Colonel Henry Dearborn, with two hundred men, was to sweep the west side of the lake.[4]

*

Dearborn set out at eight o'clock in the morning of September 21 and marched sixteen miles along the Cayuga's west shore, encountering two small towns and two larger ones—one, "very prety," about a mile and a half from the present Canoga, containing ten houses, and another, a mile below, containing nine houses. Wherever they found corn and vegetable fields, the crops were gathered into the houses and sent up in flames. They made slow progress through the trackless forest, the terrain "so horredly rough & bushey that it was hardly possible for us to advance." They met no resistance, and the only Indians found, on September 22, were three women and a young cripple cowering in a wigwam. Dearborn took two of the squaws, forty years old, captive. The third was too old and the cripple too infirm to travel. Afterward, when Dearborn had rejoined the main army, there was a shocking report, later recorded only by Lieutenant William Barton of Ogden's First New Jersey Regiment. As Barton, a careful diarist, tells it, Dearborn had left one house for the two to remain in, with orders to his men not to molest them. When the troops had marched some distance, however, two soldiers sneaked back, locked the door, and set the house on fire. Efforts to save the trapped squaw and the cripple inside were futile.[5]

Dearborn had been informed of a large village, Coreorgonel, near the end of the lake. He found it on the morning of September 24 on the west side of the Cayuga inlet, two miles south of the present Ithaca. It contained twenty-five houses, and the troops labored until sunset to destroy them. Here Dearborn was to have met Butler, who had not yet arrived. The following morning, anxious to rejoin the main army, he waited no longer and marched eighteen miles westward to Catherine's Town. Not finding Sullivan there, he continued six miles to the Bear Swamp, where he camped for the night, and the next day at noon he joined Sullivan at Kanawaholla (a head on a pole, the present Elmira). There, at the junction of the Chemung River and Newtown Creek, Fort Reed had two weeks earlier been established as a palisaded supply depot, manned by a garrison of two hundred men armed with a three-pound cannon and stocked with one hundred head of cattle and stores of flour and liquor.

Dearborn and his men arrived a day late for a "feu de joie," which

men in the fort had staged to celebrate news of Spain's declaration
of war against Britain. Thirteen discharges of cannon were fired,
followed by a running fire of three rounds per man through the single
file of the assembled infantry from right to left. Sullivan, not satisfied
with the volume, demanded it repeated while he himself rode,
whipped and spurred at full gallop, down the line, each man firing as
he came opposite. He ordered distributed to each brigade a fat ox
and five gallons of spirits. Hand had by now established himself as
the army's liveliest celebrant. In the evening his men constructed a
large bower, illuminated by thirteen pine-knot fires. With himself at
one end and Colonel Proctor at the other, the officers squatted on
the ground for the feast to the accompaniment of thirteen toasts. In
recognition of Hand's Irish nativity, and indeed the ancestry of many
of the other officers, they proposed that "the kingdom of Ireland
merit a stripe in our standard," and they concluded with the appeal
that "the enemies of America be metamorphasized and in pack horses
and be sent on a westward expedition." Then followed two Indian
dances, led by the prancing Hand himself.[6]

Butler's detachment left Canadesaga at three o'clock on September
20, and after eight miles they came to Scawyace (the present Waterloo), on the north bank of the Seneca River. When Colonel Harper's
four scouts had hurriedly torched it twelve days earlier, they had left
eighteen houses standing and eight acres of corn still in the ground.
Also, on the rocky bed of a quiet section of the stream were several
stone-walled fish ponds thirty to forty feet in diameter. Early the next
morning, a detail of two hundred men under Major William Scott,
of Cilly's First New Hampshire Regiment, was assigned to destroy
the corn. The expedition's diarists say nothing about liberation of the
fish.

Butler's main force continued along the lakeshore, seven miles
through barren country and four miles through a fertile, wooded
swamp, destroying scattered houses and cornfields on the way, and
on the morning of September 22 they reached Cayuga Castle (Goio-
gouen), the tribe's capital, on the north bank of Great Gully Brook
(a mile and a half from the present Union Springs), where Scott's

detail caught up with them. Cayuga Castle contained fifty large, square, well-built log houses, in which the troops found a supply of salt and several muskets branded "United States." The town was the hub of two more communities. Two miles east of the Castle were the thirteen houses of East Cayuga, and on the south bank of Great Gully Brook was Upper Cayuga, with fourteen houses. Together they had 110 acres of corn, a peach orchard, and fields of potatoes, turnips, onions, pumpkins, and squash. It took the troops until three o'clock in the afternoon of September 23 to burn the houses and destroy the crops. That day, five miles southward, Butler's force completed its mission of destruction at the town of Chonodote (the present Aurora). They put its fourteen old houses to the torch, cut its cornfields to the ground, and girdled fifteen hundred peach trees. On September 25, after marching over mountains with eighty-foot and fifty-foot falls and through thickly wooded swamps, the troops arrived at Coreorgonel, still smoking from the fires set the previous day by Dearborn's men. Following in Dearborn's tracks, Butler joined Sullivan and the main army at Kanawlohalla on September 28.[7]

Sullivan's mission of destruction was now almost complete. Only the settlements on the Chemung River north of Kanawlohalla remained. He detached a body of five hundred men upstream in thirty boats commanded by Captain John Livermore. Navigating between mountains closing to the river's edge on both sides, the fleet reached a few houses and some large cornfields. There the detachment was divided in two, one wing under Colonel Van Cortlandt to take the right shore, the other under Colonel Dayton to take the left. They loaded the boats with corn and vegetables and returned to Fort Reed. Van Cortlandt and Dayton denuded the settlements and fields along both shores and returned within two days. On the morning of September 29 the main army demolished Fort Reed and set out for Tioga.[8]

One act of forbearance somewhat mitigates this draconian tide of desolation. Reports had reached Sullivan that a nucleus of six or seven Mohawk families still residing at their lower castle at Fort Hunter was serving as a spy nest, funneling intelligence to the British on American plans and movements. The upper castle, at Canajoharie, was now inhabited by the Oriskas, friendly to the rebels. On the same day that Butler was dispatched on his mission, Sullivan ordered Colonel Peter Gansevoort to proceed with one hundred picked men to Fort Hunter and destroy it and "captivate" the Indians living there. Gansevoort marched to the Mohawk River, stopping at Fort Stanwix, and on September 29 surprised and captured all the Indians he found in the settlement's four houses. He found the houses well provisioned with household utensils and plentiful livestock and grain, "much better," he noted, "than most of the Mohawk River farmers." He was about to demolish them when a delegation of local white inhabitants, driven from their homes by the Indians, petitioned to be permitted to occupy the vacated Mohawk houses until they should establish their own accommodations. Contrary to his orders, Butler consented, first taking an inventory of all the possessions to prevent looting. When he arrived with his prisoners at Albany, he found Schuyler there. Schuyler was at this time head of the Northern Department Indian Commission, and he interceded for the Indians. They had been permitted to remain at Fort Hunter on condition of peaceable demeanor, a "Contract they have not violated," he protested, and asked that Sullivan place them in protective custody until Washington should release them. Washington did so by letters of October 12 and 25.[9]

The army reached Fort Sullivan at Tioga, the supply center of the expedition, on the afternoon of September 30. A celebration of self-congratulation began. Orders were issued for every man to shave his face, powder his hair, and wear a twig in his hat. "Not a negro or mulatto could escape the honor," wrote Private Nathan Davis, and at the sight of nearly three thousand whitened men, "in rags and tatters, nearly naked, with the remaining parts of their garments hanging in streamers behind them . . . even our Chaplain forgot his gravity." Marching to the fort in formation, they entered and were greeted by the garrison with a thirteen-gun salute, which they returned in kind. Colonel Shreve hosted the general and the field officers to a sumptuous meal, while the fifes and drums of Colonel Proctor's regimental band provided continuous music. Two days later, Sullivan in his turn played host. The climax came with an Indian dance led off by a young Oneida sachem and several of his warriors, singing to the clash of a rattle, a knife, and a pipe. Followed by the officers wearing face masks, all joined together at the end of each dance with a rousing Indian war whoop.[10]

The enlisted men had no formal dinner. As in all eighteenth-century armies, they cooked their own individual meals, but rations of beef and flour were liberally increased, including a gill of whiskey per man. (Officers received half a pint of rum.)

On October 3, a five-hundred-man fatigue party set to work demolishing Fort Sullivan. The pickets were pulled up and cast in the river, and the abatis was burned. The next morning the sick, the lame, and the men without shoes were placed on boats in the shallow river. The rest of the army marched fourteen miles to where the water deepened and the following day got into boats for the final sixty-five miles. At Wyoming, October 7, Colonel Zebulon Butler greeted the arrivals with a thirteen-gun salute and hosted the officers to a another victory feast.[11]

Orders came from Washington on October 9 for Sullivan to take his army immediately to headquarters at West Point in order to prepare to cooperate with the expected arrival of Count d'Estaing's fleet northward from Georgia.[12]

Sullivan still smarted from the strictures he had received early in the campaign. Determined to win approbation, he sent a lengthy report of his achievements not only to Washington but in duplicate to Congress President Jay. He had, he wrote, leveled forty Indian towns and destroyed 160,000 bushels of corn (as determined by a committee Sullivan appointed) and a vast quantity of vegetables and fruit trees. (In fact, a tally assembled from the surviving reports and diaries yields thirty-two towns. "If a few old houses which had been deserted for several years, were met with and burnt," wrote the Reverend Gordon, "they were put down for a town.") Only forty men had been lost, including those from sickness and accident. "Except one Town situated near the Allegany about 50 miles from Chinesee there is not a single Town left in the Country of the five nations," he asserted. (There were, in fact, three, including Canawaugus, only a few miles from Chenussio.)[13]

This braggadocio did not sit well with Washington, who had complained to Congress of Sullivan's dilatory reports—he had received no returns of Sullivan's troops since mid-July and no word from Sullivan himself since the August 29 Battle of Newtown. Sullivan's letter, reported Gordon, "made him the laugh of the officers in the army remaining under gen. Washington; one declared it was a little mischievous to print the whole account." Washington congratulated Sullivan in a single bare sentence and forwarded the report to Congress with another brief testimonial, although, in a proclamation to the army, he lauded Sullivan "for his great perserverence and activity, for his order of march and attack, and the whole of his dispositions." And the Congress, after adopting a motion of thanks to Washington, Sullivan, and the officers and soldiers, set aside the second Thursday in December as a national day of thanksgiving.[14]

But Sullivan was mortified by the cold reception he received from the officers when he arrived at headquarters. On November 6, he sent Washington a request to retire on the ground of ill health. Washington did him the courtesy of a personal visit to dissuade him, but it was clearly a formality. Three days later Sullivan submitted his request to Congress. His friends there attempted to accept it only conditionally, as long as necessary to regain his health, but only New Hampshire, Massachusetts, and North Carolina would agree. Congress approved the resignation.[15]

If Sullivan's assignment was to eradicate the villages and sustenance of the Iroquois, he had succeeded. But if his mission was to eliminate the Iroquois threat to the European occupation of the Six Nations heartland, he had achieved only a momentary respite.

His supercautious insistence on overwhelming numbers of men and correspondingly plentiful supply had caused delay in starting his expedition, which lost for him the element of surprise. The noncombatants had ample warning of his approach, and he did not capture one populated village. He therefore had no opportunity to seize hostages that might produce negotiations.

His was a hollow victory at the Battle of Newtown, for he failed to block the enemy's escape. If he had sent a sufficient force along the east shore of the Chemung River to cooperate with Poor's and Clinton's brigades at the right, he might have enveloped and made prisoner the entire enemy.

His about-face without an attack on Niagara revealed a deficiency of enterprise. Such an undaunted leader as Benedict Arnold, who had forged ahead to Montreal two years earlier under far more trying conditions, would never have turned back eighty miles from his objective.

Finally, Sullivan's abandonment of the forts he had erected at Hanneyaye and Tioga left the entire territory from the Delaware at the east to the Allegheny at the west, and from the Susquehanna at the south to the Mohawk at the north, defended only by Fort Stanwix against the hazard of a revenging army advancing from Niagara.

For the Iroquois were driven to desperation. "Had Sullivan acted with more prudence and less severity," wrote Bolton, "I am satisfied we should not have had one-third of the Six Nations in our interest at the present time." The merciless march of the Continentals left no alternative. The rebels, declared Old Smoke, "wish for nothing more, than to extirpate us from the Earth, that they may possess our Lands, the Desire of attaining which we are convinced is the Cause of the present War between the King and his disobedient Children."[16]

"Extirpate" was the very word Washington had used July 4 in a letter to Lafayette.[17]

✦ ✦ ✦ ✦ ✦ ✦ ✦ ✦ ✦ ✦ ✦

CHAPTER 12

"BETWEEN
TWO HELLS"

The refugees streamed to Niag-
ara, 2,628 of them by a count on November 11, 1779, and increasing
to 5,000 by the end of the year. Arrivals of Senecas, Cayugas, Delawares, Chugnuts, and Onondagas joined Oquagas, Mohawks, Tuscaroras, Oneidas, a scattering of Loyalists, and the western Indians
already there. Providing for their necessities presented a mammoth
problem for ailing Major Mason Bolton, suffering from rheumatism.
Detailed supply lists show that chiefs received scarlet-laced coats and
leggings and gold-laced feathered hats, while women received petti-
coats and leggings with ferreting, horn combs, spring knives, vermil-
ion dye, thread, and needles. The garrison of fewer than four hundred
fluctuated in number as they were parceled out to reinforce outlying
areas.[1]

The fort stood sentinel on a twenty-foot-high triangular rise on the
east bank of the turbulent Niagara River, where it empties into Lake
Ontario at its southern rim. The enclosure of eight acres was protected on the land side by sod-covered outworks surrounded by a
ditch and on the water side only by a stockade. At each of the north
and south bastions was a massive stone blockhouse, guarding between them the two-and-a-half-storied 48-by-96-foot granite rectan-
gular chateau built by the French in 1727 and christened "The House
of Peace" as a bulwark against the Iroquois. Above its four-foot-
thick walls was a nine-dormered garret that provided shelter for a
raking battery of guns. Twenty-five other structures crowded the

remaining space of the enclosure: a stone chapel, a powder magazine, a bakehouse, a provision storeroom, log houses for officers' quarters, and barracks for the enlisted men.[2]

Although Haldimand had strengthened the defenses with additional heavy artillery, as a bulwark against the Americans the location and design of the fort were far from adequate. Its deficiencies, stated engineer Gother Mann, could not be corrected "without breaking new ground and going into the labour and expense of a new system."[3]

Across the river from the fort stood wooden barracks built for Butler's Rangers, and half a mile upstream were the wharf and buildings of Navy Hall, which housed the Provincial Marine. Beyond, stretching for seven miles below the fort, as far south as Lewiston, came the continuous miserable encampments of the Indians, living in tents, flimsy huts, and dugouts. The winter of 1779–80 proved the most severe anyone could remember. The snow fell five feet deep, and the cold became so intense that deer died in droves, leaving the Indians dependent on uncertain supplies of food from the British.[4]

With shipments from overseas unreliable, local suppliers became the main source, and profit-hungry merchants stood ready to reap large rewards. Since John Butler, as acting superintendent of Indian affairs, could assign the contracts, he formed an alliance with the Niagara merchant Edward Pollard and later with another merchant, Thomas Robinson. In October 1779, however, Guy Johnson arrived at Niagara to resume his duties as superintendent. He replaced Butler's associates with his own alliance with the firm of William Taylor and George Forsyth. In 1781, exposure of their shady practices of inflated prices and fictional deliveries led to Johnson's disgrace and replacement by his brother-in-law, Sir John Johnson.[5]

The exiles clung to the hope of return, and their sufferings stoked their determination for revenge. Old Smoke told Guy Johnson on December 16 that "although we have received a severe blow, our Hearts are still good & strong, and our Arms are not feeble, neither are we at all discouraged. We lost our Country it is true, but this was

to secure our Women & Children; and we do not look upon ourselves as overcome."[6]

To American overtures, initiated by Philip Schuyler, they remained
impervious. He sent Johnson a proposal for exchange of prisoners
and with it an appeal to the Six Nations from the Continental Congress to lay down their arms and return to neutrality without penalty
of reprisal. A four-man volunteer Indian deputation carried the message: two Oneida chiefs—seventy-three-year-old Skenandon, their
premier war leader, and Good Peter (Agorondajats), and two Fort
Hunter Mohawk chiefs—Little Abraham and White Hans (Una-
quandahoojie). The emissaries arrived at Niagara on February 13,
under a guard sent out to meet them. They delivered Schuyler's letter
and then requested a general meeting with the Indians. Johnson first
permitted separate interviews with Old Smoke and the Mohawk,
Aaron Hill (Kanonraron). Old Smoke angrily charged the Oneidas
with inviting the Americans to invade the Iroquois homeland and
declared of the Americans that the Indians "had experienced their
Perfidy so often that he would pay no Regard to any Thing they
could say, nor would he ever submit to the Rebels."

This did not deter Little Abraham from conveying a message from
the Continental Congress that "if the Six Nations would return &
live in Peace at their Old Homes they should have Nothing further
to fear from them, but might remain quiet & undisturbed, that this
was now the last offer that should be made, which if they rejected,
they had nothing further to expect, as no Terms would afterwards be
granted them." On February 17, the four "rebel" Indians were allowed to meet with an assembly of Johnson and his officers and the
Six Nations chiefs. Little Abraham and Good Peter, bringing several
wampum belts, appealed not only to the chiefs, but also to the
powerful women. At a meeting the next day, they received their
answer. "You have the Assurance," thundered Aaron Hill, "to come,
while the hatchet you employed against us, is yet in Your Hands,
and tell us that you have a great Regard for our Peace and Welfare.
Deceitful Set!" and with that he returned the belts. The four rebels
were not permitted to return home. They were thrown into an un-

heated and unlighted stone cell, so freezing that Little Abraham ultimately died there.[7]

Before Schuyler's message had arrived, the Indians' campaign of
revenge had begun, but not now under John Butler. The Cayugas
and the Delawares blamed him for the destruction of their villages
and had once threatened to turn him over to the Americans. With
Haldimand in power, he would now be subservient for military operations to Sir John Johnson, who had set up headquarters at Sorel.
At Niagara he would take orders for Indian operations from Guy
Johnson. Although the Iroquois remained under the nominal leadership of aged Old Smoke, Brant emerged as field chief, even though
Guy Johnson thought his importance exaggerated. "He is very Zealous," observed Haldimand, "and has been very attentive and useful
in Striking Small Strokes at different Places, destroying Grain &ca
which have partially distressed the Enemy, but the Reports of his
having effected any thing of Material Consequence are Totally without foundation."[8]

As early as February 1780, in the face of the continuing bitter
cold, through the snow-covered woods Indian war parties set out
from Niagara. Brant (now commissioned a captain) gathered a force
of about three hundred Indians—Cayugas, Tutelos, Mohawks, Senecas, Delawares, Onondagas, and five whites under Henry Nelles, a
captain in the Indian Department. At their war dance, Johnson presented them with wampum belts, and when they departed on February 11, four guns from the fort saluted them.[9]

The further Brant's party penetrated into the Seneca country, the
more apparent became the total barrenness that Sullivan had left
behind him. There were no huts for surcease from the icy wind and
no food stores to make up for the meager provisions carried from
Niagara. They had to pause and tend to the sick. Several died. They
needed, Brant decided, to fan out in small groups, each to target a
different objective, and to forage for smaller quantities of food. The
largest division headed for Oswego, as a protective measure to forestall any rebel attempt at that strategic location. The other divisions
remained together until Tioga, where one headed for the Delaware

River and Minisink and the other turned east toward a nest of three forts at Schoharie. Brant himself took charge of the latter, a mixed group of nineteen Indians and five whites.[10]

On April 7, on his way to Schoharie, Brant, at the head of his raiders, came upon a group of fourteen syrup gatherers outside of Harpersfield, near the headwaters of the Delaware. The spring had come late, and the snow had just fallen, but there was nevertheless enough of a thaw for syrup-making to commence. Brant's men appeared so silently that not a shot was fired in defense. Three of the settlers were shot down, and twelve surrendered. Their leader was Captain Alexander Harper, a schoolmate of Brant.

Fifty years later, Freegift Patchin, one of the captives, described what happened. Brant himself raised his tomahawk over Harper's head but paused to ask how many troops were at Schoharie. Harper had the presence of mind to pretend that three hundred Continentals had arrived three days before. This made an attack by the small party of Indians unthinkable, and Brant held an all-night conference to formulate new plans. Harper could understand much of the dialect, and he heard demands to put the captives to death. But Brant prevailed with a decision to take them to Niagara. The captors remained suspicious, and they questioned Harper again at a council the next morning. With no alteration of countenance, he stood steadfastly by his deception. Before leaving, Brant's men burned Harpersfield and took the remaining townsmen prisoner, releasing three women. One of the prisoners, Walter Elliott, was sent home three days later with a letter from Brant, proclaiming the humanitarian treatment of captives but threatening to destroy them "without distinction" if the rebels did not treat their prisoners with equal consideration. Elliott also brought a letter from Harper to his wife, stating that Brant had "used me, and all them that is taken with me extremely well," but asking futilely for prisoner exchange.[11]

For the captives, the three-week trek though the snow, without snowshoes and forced to carry heavy loads of plunder on their backs, nearly became a death march. They survived only because Brant, ill with ague, had to rest every other day. Captives who could not keep up with the Indians could expect to be tomahawked, and this was the fate of an elderly man, taken at Harpersfield with his two grand-sons. An Indian with his face painted black as the mark of an executioner took the man to the rear and soon returned, dangling the bald scalp in the faces of the grandsons. Those who kept up, however, in accord with Indian custom, received food rations equal to those of their captors. Some corn, obtained from a grudging Loyalist on the Delaware River who admonished Brant to take "more scalps and less prisoners," was impartially distributed, two handfuls a day. When the Indians had finished their cooking, they turned their kettles over to the prisoners for their own cooking.

Brant took his starving company down the Delaware and across to the Susquehanna, where they floated on rough rafts to the mouth of the Chemung. Near the ruins of Newtown, wolf tracks led to the half-devoured carcass of a horse in the snow. They cooked and hungrily consumed its frozen underside. Passing from the Chemung to the Genesee, they met a group of Indians from whom they bought a horse, which they roasted with groundnuts and gobbled up, intestines and all, using white ashes for salt. As they left the Genesee for the march to Niagara, Brant killed a snake that he found sunning itself on a bare hillside sunspot and cooked it for hot soup, which cured his ague.[12]

Approaching Niagara, the captives faced the harrowing prospect of running the gauntlet among a throng of vengeful Indians. Brant, who gave no quarter in battle, showed himself enough of a Christian to prevent such mass murder. He knew that a niece of Harper's, Jane Moore, had been taken a prisoner at Cherry Valley and brought to Niagara, where she married a British officer, Captain John Powell. He therefore sent a message to Powell, requesting that he arrange to assign many of the warriors down Lake Ontario, so as to absent them from the gauntlet. Powell obtained permission from Butler and sent the Indians off, out of harm's way, with a liberal quantity of rum. When Brant's party arrived at Niagara, about May 1, the gauntlet through which the captives ran consisted mainly of old women and children. Even so, Freegift Patchin suffered two blows on the head from a squaw and a boy.[13]

Brant's raids were a sample of the havoc being wrought on settlements along the Mohawk, Delaware, and Susquehanna river valleys. John Butler reported that between February 3 and September 3, 1780, of 59 war parties sent out from Niagara, 43, totaling 1,403 men, had returned and 16, with 892 men, were still out. As a result of the raids, 142 rebels had been killed and 161 taken captive; 81 women and children were released. The war parties had seized 247 horses and 922 cattle and had destroyed 2 churches, 157 houses, and 150 granaries.[14]

No less than the Indians, the Loyalists thirsted for revenge, and Sir John Johnson's regiment of Royal Greens became the vehicle of their spleen. Upon his return from his aborted expedition of October 1779, the regiment had been scattered for the winter among installations at Sorel, Carleton Island, and Coteau de Lac. Johnson himself, after failing to obtain passage on a boat to England in order to petition for the establishment of the regiment in the regular army, had settled in Montreal for the winter.

With the coming of spring, he proposed to Haldimand, in letters of March 27 and April 3, 1780, that he put together a major force to invade the Mohawk Valley, not only for "destroying and laying waste everything before us," but for securing Loyalist recruits for his regiment from the valley. With Haldimand's approval, he assembled 539 men at Lachine: the regiment's 200; 108 under Captain Thomas Scott from the Fifty-third, the Twenty-ninth light infantry, and the Thirty-fourth regiments; 21 from Lieutenant Colonel Baron de Creutzbourg's Hanau Regiment; 130 Mohawks; and 80 Lake of Two Mountains Canadian Indians.[15]

Sir John Johnson's expedition set out in boats of the Provincial Marine up Lake Champlain on May 3, preceded by the Canadian Indians as scouts. Hindered by contrary winds, it disembarked at Split Rock, near Crown Point, on May 12. By then the manpower had declined to 528, owing mainly to some falling sick and, one suspects, to desertion. Secrecy was essential, and Haldimand had instructed Johnson to offer Indians rewards to hunt down and scalp deserters. Nevertheless, reports of the expedition reached Goose Van Schaick in Albany by May 17.[16]

At Crown Point, the troops transferred to land and turned westward, reaching Schroon on May 16 and, proceeding southward, arrived at Johnstown on the evening of May 21. The plan had been to send a detachment of two hundred whites on a surprise night march to Stone Arabia, nine miles west of the Johnson estate and "the most plentiful Grain District in the Country." The rest of the force, including the Indians, would attack Caughnawaga, four miles south of Johnstown. Johnson divided his force accordingly, but when he assembled the Indians to give them their instructions, they adamantly insisted on a united attack on Caughnawaga. He had no choice but to agree. Following the Indians' plan, therefore, the two divisions united at Caughnawaga, at the house of Dow Fonda, burning and pillaging everything in their path. From there they set out up the river for Stone Arabia, but within a mile of Anthony's Nose, most of the troops were too exhausted to proceed further. Again, the Indians took over the direction of the expedition. Even after a brief rest, surfeited with plunder, they refused to continue to Stone Arabia, maintaining that the inhabitants had fled with their effects to the opposite shore, leaving their houses empty and taking with them the boats, without which their pursuers could not cross the river. Disregarding Johnson, they turned back to Montreal, and he could do nothing but follow them.[17]

The rebels in Johnson's pathway had been powerless. Because their one appreciable American installation, at Fort Stanwix, was undermanned and unprovided and for nine months the garrison had gone without pay, thirty-one men had mutinied. Governor Clinton had directed Van Schaick to assemble a resistance force, but he had too few regulars available, and the militia of Tryon County, he replied, "as good as refused to turn out." The force that he did collect was too late, and with only two days' provisions had to retire.[18]

In terms of Johnson's objectives, his expedition had succeeded. He had burned 120 houses, barns, and mills, containing "vast quantities" of flour, bread, Indian corn, and other provisions, and a considerable store of arms. He had slaughtered many cattle and had seized seventy horses. The Indians had killed 11 men (fewer than Johnson had expected). He had captured 27 prisoners, 14 of whom, too old or too young, he had released. He had rescued 143 male Loyalists (most of whom enlisted with Johnson) and a number of their women and children. He had taken 30 male and female black slaves, 17 of whom belonged to Johnson, Claus, and Guy Johnson; whether by force or consent it was not reported.

Although on July 2, 294 formerly rebel Onondagas, Tuscaroras, and Oneidas had cast their lot with the refugees at Niagara, a hard core in the Mohawk Valley remained loyal to the rebels. These apostates, as the pro-British Iroquois saw them, now became targets of Brant's next foray. He assembled a war party of 314, including Skenandon and Good Peter, who had been released as a reward for the accession of the newly converted arrivals at Niagara and in expectation that they could persuade the remaining Oneidas in the Mohawk Valley to join their pro-British brethren. Twelve white volunteers and Lieutenant Joseph Clement of the Indian Department also served in the force. They set out on July 11 and two weeks later arrived at the Oneidas' chief village, Kanowalohale, to find its houses deserted. All were burned, including Kirkland's church and a small fort. The village's residents had fled to Fort Stanwix for shelter, and Brant, pursuing them, arrived July 26. Four hundred six of them, however, reached the fort's confines. Brant paraded his men before the fort, but the fort's artillery answered their rifle fire; they had to leave lest rebel militia show up at their rear.

Next, Brant divided his force into two parties, one to attack the white settlement at Canajoharie and a second to attack nearby Fort Plank. Between them they laid waste a six-mile stretch along the river, four miles wide. Many of the settlers were warned soon enough to escape into the fort with its two guns, but Colonel Abraham Wemple reported passing "dead bodies of Men & Children most cruelly murdered," and Guy Johnson reported twenty-nine people killed and forty captured, but some women and children were released.

After this, most of Brant's men returned to Niagara, but small parties under Brant, Cornplanter, Blacksnake, the Tuscarora Sagwarithra, and the Cayuga Fish Carrier continued to rampage through the Mohawk and Delaware valleys. One of the captives was later recognized as Cornplanter's white father, the trader John Abeel, whose house was among the many burned. Cornplanter offered to provide for him in his own home, but the old man elected to return to his white family.[19] Other raiding parties, to the west, scourged the Susquehanna, Juniata, and Allegheny valleys. After a raid on a settlement near the Raystown Branch of the Juniata, one of the captives made to run the gauntlet, a Mrs. Elder, managed to hang onto her long-handled frying pan. When a warrior, in stooping to strike her, dropped his loincloth, she doubled him with a blow to his genitals. The onlooking chiefs laughed loudly and let her alone.[20]

Despite these attacks, 1780 had produced a bumper crop of grain, harvested and ready to supply rebel troops. Sir John Johnson determined to prevent the grain from serving that purpose. No sooner had he returned from his first invasion of Tryon County than he began planning a second. On August 24, Haldimand approved, with the added objective of punishing the remaining Oneida rebels. As a diversion, he authorized a simultaneous expedition across lakes Champlain and George under Major Christopher Carleton.[21]

Johnson's assembled army departed from Oswego on October 2. It totaled 780—280 regulars, 150 of Johnson's Greens, 200 of Butler's Rangers, and 150 Indians under Brant. The artillery and baggage were shipped up the Oswego and Oneida rivers while the troops marched to meet them at the east bank of Chittenango Creek, where the boats and a quantity of provisions were concealed. The artillery was placed on sleds hastily put together, and the expedition passed Oneida Lake and then crossed over to the Susquehanna, foraging on the way to replenish dwindling provisions, and heading for Schoharie. By October 13, with reports from scouts and spies warning of rebels gathering a force of two thousand to oppose them, the Indians voiced reluctance to venture so deep into rebel territory. Twenty Cayugas turned off toward German Flatts, and Johnson barely managed to dissuade the rest from following them.

By October 17, the expedition reached the uppermost of the three Schoharie forts (the present Fultonham), a single-story building enclosed by a stockade and breastwork. The inhabitants had fled to the forts, whose combined garrisons totaled 225. The Americans had indeed been warned, and a signal gun from the upper fort notified the other two of the enemy's approach. Johnson attempted to bombard the upper fort with a small mortar and a brass three-pounder but found them unable to breach the defense. He then sent out Ranger Captain Andrew Thompson and two men with a white flag to demand surrender, but three times their advances were met with rifle shots. The countryside, nevertheless, lay unprotected, and Johnson sent his men to destroy farms and kill animals within fifty yards of each of the forts. A cold northwest wind served to fan and spread the flames.

At three o'clock in the afternoon, Johnson turned northward along the west bank of the Schoharie River toward the Mohawk, a path so muddy that he had to bury the mortar in a swamp. Halfway, he detached a party of 150 Rangers and Indians under Captains Thompson and Brant to destroy the settlement of Fort Hunter on the other side of the Schoharie. This accomplished, the army continued its march of devastation up the south bank of the Mohawk, and a detachment under Captain Richard Duncan was sent across to the north bank to finish off what had escaped the notice of Johnson's first expedition. Johnson's goal was Stone Arabia, the target the Indians had forced him to forgo in May.[22]

Only by October 13 had the Americans officially responded to their peril. Militia Brigadier General Robert Van Rennselaer, Schuyler's brother-in-law, upon receiving a report of the invasion from a deserter, ordered out his Claverak, Albany, and Schenectady militia brigade of six or seven hundred to assemble at Schenectady on October 18. With the news of the burning of the Schoharie settlements, Governor Clinton ordered him to depart in pursuit of the British, and he himself would follow with additional troops. Van Rennselaer sent instructions to Colonel John Brown at Stone Arabia and Colonel

Lewis Dubois at Fort Plain to hold off the enemy until he arrived to launch a combined attack.

Johnson's army arrived at Fort Paris, three miles north of the Mohawk, at the present Palatine Bridge, on October 18. Colonel Brown, in command of a force of 130, received information from two deserters from the enemy that the only British force on the river's north side was Duncan's weak detachment. He therefore decided not to await Van Rensselaer but to attack on the morning of October 19. Captain Casselman remonstrated, but the bespectacled, Yale-educated Brown would not listen. Johnson, in the meantime, crossed over under cover of an early thick fog, and the rebels now faced an overwhelming force. Johnson discovered them on the heights above Stone Arabia, behind a fence in a wooded area. He sent Brant and the Indians to flank them on their right and Captain Macdonell's Rangers to flank their left, while he himself attacked with the regulars at the front, across a thirty-yard open field. The heavily outnumbered Americans were routed. Brown and thirty-nine of his men were slain, and two were captured. Johnson lost four of his troopers killed, one wounded, forty-one missing, and three deserted. Five Indians were killed, and Brant received a wound in the sole of a foot.[23]

Van Rensselaer's brigade, which had grown to nine hundred, including fifty Oneidas, arrived an hour after the battle, too late to rescue Brown but not too late to engage Johnson's troops. He wasted precious time, however, in choosing a site to cross to the north side of the river. An officer of the Oneidas, Lieutenant Colonel Louis Atayataroughta, became so furious that he brandished his sword at Van Rensselaer and called him a Tory. When the troops did finally cross, they came up to the British near nightfall at a stockaded blockhouse near St. Johnsville, known as Fort Klock. After a smart exchange, Johnson's men escaped to a peninsula in the river. But Van Rensselaer's undisciplined men, fallen into disorder, were in danger of firing on each other. They clamored, nevertheless, to pursue, yet he drew back a mile to await the dawn. By then the British had departed, and he had the river once again to recross. His outraged men charged that he had permitted Johnson to escape because they were related by marriage. At a court-martial the following year, Colonel John Harper accused Van Rennselaer of "want of energy." His acquittal, it was said, depended on family connections.[24]

Johnson might still not have escaped if a party sent from Fort Stanwix had succeeded in destroying the getaway boats concealed at Chittenango Creek. Acting on information from an undercover Loyalist, Johnson's force surprised the party without a fight; four men were killed and fifty-six captured. Johnson returned without further incident to Canada.

He reported his mission a success, in the face of a constant scarcity of provisions so extreme that the officers' horses had to be slaughtered for food, even including the mount of Old Smoke. Johnson had lost only nine killed, two wounded, and fifty-two missing. He had, he said, destroyed one thousand houses, one thousand barns containing 600,000 bushels of grain, thirteen grist mills, and unnumbered sawmills. Governor Clinton, however, estimated only two hundred dwellings burned and 150,000 bushels destroyed.[25]

Carleton's 778-man diversionary expedition started from St. Johns on Lake Champlain and, landing at South Bay on October 10, appeared at Fort Ann, whose commander, Captain Adiel Sherwood, promptly surrendered his garrison of seventy-five. The fort, a rude blockhouse enclosed in a stockade, was burned, as were the nearby settlements of Kingsbury, Queensbury, and Fort Edward. Next, Carleton moved against Fort George, at the foot of Lake George, and its commander, Captain John Chipman, with a token resistance, surrendered his garrison of fifty.

Previously, on October 7, a detachment of 134 and some Mohawk Indians under Major John Munro had set out from Crown Point overland to the southwest, coming on October 16 to within ten miles of the fort at Ballston. A guide disclosed that there were 150 men in the fort, with 100 more expected. Munro decided to avoid the fort, but to attack the residence of its commander, Colonel James Gordon. Along roads "the worst I ever traveled," at one o'clock in the morning he found the colonel at home. Lieutenant Patrick Langan, with the Rangers and Indians, rushed in, while the rest of the men stood in line outside with shouldered arms and fixed bayonets. Gordon and his family were all captured. That was as far as Munro ventured. Though he had orders to join Sir John Johnson at Saratoga, he judged the journey too hazardous and turned back to rejoin Carleton at Crown Point on October 23. He had lost two killed, three wounded, and two deserted. Two Indians had been killed and one wounded. He had shown compassion. When four prisoners had proved unable to travel, he left them at a spot hidden from the vengeful Indians.[26]

Passion for revenge had fueled the Indian and Loyalist incursions, and this had increased their usefulness to Haldimand. But by 1781 he was faced with more pressing concerns. Captured papers of Continental Congress president Henry Laurens indicated plans for an invasion of Canada in the spring, involving a squadron of the French navy. The invaders could expect support from the French population and from largely Catholic Canadian Indians. Aside from the garrisons at indispensable posts, Haldimand informed Germain, he could not assemble more than twenty-five hundred men capable of taking the field. He now concentrated on a more strategic goal—the attempt to win over Ethan and Ira Allen's Green Mountain Boys to the British side. During the diversionary expedition of the previous year, Christopher Carleton had established contact with Ethan Allen through a Vermont Loyalist, Justus Sherwood. Lengthy negotiations with Haldimand followed. To demonstrate to Vermonters the protection British arms could provide, he planned a third expedition to the Mohawk Valley. As before, he still aimed to devastate the settlements, but the Americans had learned to shelter their families, grain, and cattle in fortified houses—twenty-four of them in the sixty-three miles between Schenectady and German Flatts.[27]

In the absence of Sir John Johnson, who was granted leave to sail to England on family business, the command was given to Major John Ross, head of the Royal Greens' second battalion and a veteran of the French and Indian War. A detachment under Colonel Barry St. Leger was to occupy Crown Point. Ross's force, assembled at Oswego, totaled 734 men, including 234 Greens, 112 regulars, 12 German *Jäger*, 167 of Butler's Rangers, and 209 Indians. On October 10, the expedition's vessels moved up the Oswego River to Oneida Lake and left the boats at Canasarago on Oneida Creek. Thence it marched eight days through very bad weather to the vicinity south of the Mohawk between the Schoharie and the Hudson, which had not previously been devastated in Sir John Johnson's two invasions. Passing through Argusville, Currytown, Glen, and Auriesville, Ross forded the Schoharie at its mouth and headed for Warren's Bush, equidistant from Fort Hunter, Schoharie, and Schenectady.

No resistance as yet appeared, for St. Leger's advance had caused troops to be assembled at Saratoga and Albany. But now alarm guns alerted the entire area, particularly a force of 416 at Canajoharie under Marinus Willett. Ross, however, learned that Willett had mustered 2,000 men, and he concluded that he must accomplish his destruction immediately. Traveling fourteen miles at night through a driving rain on miserable roads, he reached Warren's Bush by morning. He assigned Captain Gilbert Tice, at the head of the Indians, to level the community, and by ten o'clock, Ross reported, "the whole settlement for seven miles was in flames." They had destroyed 22 houses, 28 barns, 1 grist mill, 5,411 bushels of grain and peas, 109 tons of hay, 172 head of cattle, and 33 horses. Despite Ross's boast, he had hardly dented the year's rich harvest. "And what they did destroy," Willett observed, "was much the Greatest part of it the Property of Disaffected persons." With Willett on his heels, Ross could accomplish nothing more before heading precipitately home. At one o'clock, he crossed the Mohawk to Johnstown.[28]

Willett had learned from a captive the strength of his foe. He raced through the raining night, crossed the Mohawk at Front Hunter with some difficulty, and caught up with Ross at four o'clock in the afternoon of October 25. There he divided his force into two sections. Sixty Massachusetts troops and 150 Tryon County militia under Major Aaron Rowley circled through the woods behind Ross's rear, and Willett with his militia and levies faced up to Ross's front. Ross, unable to escape, turned and advanced. Willett's men seemed to be winning, but unaccountable panic seized them and the battle became a rout. They left behind their only fieldpiece. At last, Willett rallied them, and with Rowley's threat to Ross's rear and the coming of night, the British withdrew six miles. Willett took fifty prisoners.[29]

Now Ross thought only of returning safely to Canada. Rather than take the route by which he had come, now known to the Americans, he struck out northward toward Carleton Island. Snow fell, and visibility became so poor that he could not locate the path until October 29. At this point, the Indians from Canada declared that they intended to return home rather than to Carleton Island. They left the following day and narrowly escaped Willett's advance force, which now made its appearance. Willett had withdrawn to nearby Fort Dayton until he could determine the direction Ross would take. His force had grown to about five hundred with the arrival of one hundred more Tryon County militia, but he had been slow to follow Ross. Ross headed westward to Garoga Creek and reached West Canada Creek at two o'clock in the afternoon of October 30, near the present town of Ohio. Willett, marching up the creek's east bank, arrived just as Ross's men were crossing to the west. Captain Walter Butler, of Cherry Valley infamy, headed the Rangers covering Ross's rear. An Oneida sniper spotted him from across the creek and shot him through the head; then he crossed over to dispatch him with another bullet and rip off his scalp. Willett, short of provisions, gave up the pursuit and returned to Fort Dayton.

Ross's men, living on half a pound of horsemeat a day per man, wet, chilled, traveling in Indian file at a constant trot, arrived at Carleton Island November 7. Tice, at the head of the Indians, returned the way they had come, repaired one of the boats sunk at Oneida Creek, and arrived at Oswego later that day. Reported losses on both sides were inexact. Ross lost seventy-four, including three Indians killed and four wounded. Fifty men were missing, many of whom later turned up. Willett estimated that he had lost ten killed and thirty wounded.[30]

*

With the news in November 1781 of Lord Charles Cornwallis's surrender at Yorktown, it became clear that the reconquest of the Iroquois homeland was out of Haldimand's power. Defense of Canada from invasion now became his prime concern. On February 18, 1782, he sent Ross instructions to occupy and rebuild Fort Oswego as a bulwark against rebel armies. The Iroquois had been pleading for this move for years, and Brant brought a force of tribesmen to assist in the work. "He rules his Indians as he pleases," Ross told Haldimand. "I never saw men work so hard."

In view of this service, Ross had no alternative but to grant Brant's request to lead another "great Stroke" against the Mohawk Valley. It could hardly be more than an exercise in defiance. It would comprise a joint force of 43 Royal Greens light infantrymen under Captain George Singleton and 460 Indians.[31]

They left Oswego on July 5. On the thirteenth, they arrived at Fort Stanwix, abandoned by the rebels, and two days later reached Fort Herkimer. With a small party of twenty, they decoyed forty of the garrison to emerge and killed eight or nine, but most of the rebels recognized the ruse in time to run back into the fort. At noon, unable to lure the rebels out again, the expedition proceeded to Fort Dayton, where they encountered as little success. Of a total of 224 cattle they seized, with difficulty Brant and Singleton persuaded the Indians to relinquish 25 to the Greens. The Indians were proving increasingly unruly and split into scavenging parties to hunt for prisoners. Before further action could be attempted, a dispatch arrived from Ross, announcing that negotiations were under way for an accommodation with the rebels. They must limit further operations to defense. The expedition was aborted. Brant and Singleton marched their men back to Oswego.[32]

Whatever hope the Indians had retained of controlling their own destiny seemed gone. "We think the rebels will ruin us at last if we go on as we do one year after another," Brant wrote Sir John Johnson. The Indians, he declared, found themselves caught "between two Hells" of rebel annihilation and British retrenchment.[33]

CHAPTER 13

✦ ✦ ✦ ✦ ✦ ✦ ✦ ✦ ✦ ✦ ✦

BETRAYAL

Three thousand miles across the ocean, in Paris, negotiators at the conference table dealt the Iroquois a blow more fatal than any they had ever suffered on the battlefield. The preliminary articles of peace, signed November 30, 1782, assigned to the United States all territory west to the Mississippi and north to the Great Lakes. True, the British had attempted to include an article permitting the Indians to maintain armed forces in forts contiguous with the water line until Congress ordered them to evacuate, but the Americans countered with an equally unsuccessful proposal for evacuation of the forts within three months after the signing of the document. For the Indians, the treaty was a sentence of death for their civilization.[1]

When the preliminary articles came before the House of Lords on February 17, 1783, only one member spoke at length for the "return and peaceable possession" of the Indians' lands. Lord Walsingham dwelt on the faithful service rendered by the Indians during the rebellion, rewarded by "shameful and unpardonable" abandonment of promises given to them in 1701, 1726, and 1746 that "they should be for ever protected." The prime minister, Lord Shelburne, answered with steely logic. It was not a matter of morality, he declared, but of hard reality. Treaties cannot last in perpetuity. They endure only "as long as the parties are able to perform the conditions."[2] How could the Indians' lands be guaranteed when they were to become part of American territory? He might have added that the Indians had already lost their sovereignty in the 1763 Peace of Paris, which ended the French and Indian War, awarding Canada and the Ohio territory to Britain "in full right," also never mentioning the Indians and totally disregarding their claims.[3]

News of the preliminary articles arrived in Canada in late April 1783 and was met with the apprehension of the Indians "that if it was really true that the English had basely betrayed them by pretending to give up their country to the Americans without their consent or consulting them, it was an act of cruelty and injustice that Christians *only* were capable of doing." They asked for reassurance from Sir John Johnson (Owassighsishon, he who makes the roof to tremble), and Haldimand ordered him immediately to hasten for a conference with them at Niagara. It was a painful task, and Sir John attempted to buck it to John Butler, "who has reaped the benefit and gained the credit of almost everything that has been done in the Department." Haldimand tartly rejoined that "The sooner you depart for Niagara, the better."[4]

Sir John found 1,685 Indians waiting for him at Niagara on July 23. The best relief he could offer them was the hope that the definitive treaty, or perhaps a secret agreement, would yet prove more favorable. Failing that, he could not "harbour an idea that the United States will act so unjustly or impolitically as to endeavor to deprive you of any part of your country under the pretext of having conquered it."[5]

For Britain had no intention of intervening, or in effect resuming the war to benefit the Indians. Haldimand, as much as he sympathized with their plight, made this clear. He urged them to negotiate treaties with the Americans. If the Americans refused, he would offer land in Canada on which they could settle. Lord North, who succeeded Shelburne, agreed.[6]

But the immediate concern was to prevent the unleashing of a great Indian war that might repeat the horrors of Pontiac's Revolt of 1763. In order to keep alive the Indians' hope of restoration of the 1768 Fort Stanwix dividing line and to persuade them of the continuing support of Britain, Haldimand recommended British retention of the frontier forts—Oswegatchie, Oswego, Niagara, Detroit, and

Mackinac. The provisional articles, and the definitive treaty that followed, provided for evacuation "with all convenient speed." The British did not comply until the Jay Treaty of 1795.[7]

If the Indians were to negotiate, they would be most effective if they spoke with one voice, and to this end Brant secured the approval of Sir John Johnson for a meeting at Sandusky to create a confederacy of the northern and southern tribes, which the Six Nations had proposed two years earlier. Supervised by Detroit-based Alexander McKee, deputy agent for Indian affairs, representatives of thirty-five nations assembled on September 5 at Sandusky. The Shawnees and the Cherokees agreed to join in spite of their resentment toward the Iroquois for having given away in 1768 their claims to territory comprising the present Kentucky, West Virginia, Tennessee, and northern Alabama.

Brant addressed the Hurons, the Delawares, the Shawnees, the Mingoes, the Ottowas, the Chippewas, the Potawatomis, the Creeks, and the Cherokees: "We the Six Nations with this Belt bind your Hearts and Minds with ours, that there may be never hereafter a Separation between us, let there be Peace or War, it shall never disunite us, for our Interests are alike, nor Should any Thing ever be done but by the Voice of the whole, as we make but one with you." The chiefs approved, Sindatton speaking for the Lake Indians, Ryneck for the Shawnees, Deyonquat the Half King for the Delawares. Afterward a deputation left for Niagara, where on October 6 the confederacy was formalized.[8] Little Beard and Good Peter were dispatched to Schuyler at Schenectady, bearing a strongly worded request from Brant that he "appoint a place, somewhere between us and you, where we will meet and kindle a Council-fire," but it must be upon a "fixed principle," the inviolability of the lands "which were acknowledged to be ours at the treaty held at Fort Stanwix in the year 1768."[9]

The authority of the United States national government under the newly ratified Articles of Confederation needed definition. Article 9 gave the Congress "the sole and exclusive right and power" of "entering into treaties and alliances" and of "managing all affairs with the Indians, not members of any of the states, provided that the legislative right of any state within its own limits be not infringed or violated." This vague language did not deter the Indians from asserting sovereignty, or New York State from claiming jurisdiction, based on a 1701 treaty between the Crown and the Five Nations.

Time was running out. The Americans did not yet know that the British would not relinquish the northwest forts; it was feared that they might be seized by the Indians who were simmering over white encroachments beyond the dividing line of the Stanwix Treaty of 1768. New York State had taken independent action by attempting to expel the Senecas and resettle the Oneidas and Tuscaroras on their western territory and by granting a large portion of Onondaga and Cayuga country to war veterans as bounty lands. The Council of Appointment had named three Indian commissioners, who, with the governor, would enter into negotiations with the Indians for a separate treaty with New York.[10]

"What think you of the State of New York undertaking to hold a treaty of its own Authority with the Six Nations in defiance of our Resolves and the Clause of the Confederation restricting the individual states?" wrote South Carolina Congressman Jacob Read to Washington. "If this Conduct is to be pursued our Commissioners are rendered useless." As Virginia Congressman James Madison acknowledged, however, his state had already asserted, on June 9, 1779, "the exclusive right of a pre-emption, from the Indians, of all lands within the limits of its own chartered territory," thus supporting New York's authority to contract with the Indians in disregard of the 1768 Stanwix Treaty line. And Governor Clinton rejected the proposal of congressional Indian commissioners Arthur Lee and Richard Butler that New York's negotiations "be more properly transacted at the same time with, and in subordination to the General Treaty."[11]

Before it would attempt to negotiate peace with the Indians, the Congress wanted assurances that they were amenable. For this purpose it instructed Secretary at War Benjamin Lincoln to send agents to sound out the Indians. He sent Major Ephraim Douglass, his former aide-de-camp and an Indian trader, to meet with the western Indians, and John Joseph Bull, a Moravian missionary whose son and daughter had been killed in a white massacre of Indians at Fort Pitt, to meet with the Iroquois. Although the British commandants at Detroit and Niagara would not permit the agents to address general gatherings of the Indians, they did speak to enough chiefs and British officials to bring back vital information. Douglass was told by General Allan Maclean, the new commandant at Niagara, that if the Indians did not cease their attacks on American settlements, British troops would join the Americans to punish them. Bull employed a Pennsylvania trader, Ebenezer Allen, to confer with the Indians, who informed him that "as they have been the Agressors, they will readily give up a part of their Country and engage never more to wage War or join the enemies of the United States, nor trespass over the Boundary which may be agreed upon."[12]

Given these assurances, a five-man committee of Congress turned to the guidelines that had been submitted in letters from Schuyler and Washington. Schuyler, writing on July 29, 1783, had advised that, although the Indians might be expelled into Canada, it would involve an expense "infinitely beyond the value of the object," for in time the advance of white settlement would reduce the availability of game and thus peacefully force them to retire further. Furthermore, if driven into Canada, they might resume hostilities in the future, harass American settlements, and disrupt the fur trade.[13] Washington had toured the Hudson and Mohawk country in July and had visited Schuyler at his Albany mansion. He wrote Congressman James Duane that his sentiments "coincide precisely" with Schuyler's, but he sent a proposal to the Congress that went beyond Schuyler's in its severity. He would ignore the Indians' insistence on the Ohio River as the western limit of American settlement, according to the Stanwix Treaty of 1768, and set up most of the present state of Ohio for exclusive white settlement, ultimately to constitute one or more states.[14] The committee conferred with him in person and submitted a report that was virtually a copy of his recommendations, even incorporating some of his wording.

On October 15, 1783, the Congress adopted the committee's report with minor changes. The provisional treaty of peace, Congress resolved, had relinquished to the United States "the sovereignty of this country" westward to the Mississippi and north to the Great Lakes. Rather than provoke another Indian war, the report nevertheless proposed to establish a dividing line, protecting the Indians' property rights in the lands where they resided but voiding their claims to territory west of the Ohio River. As "atonement for the enormities which they have perpetrated," the Indians were to cede to the United States the territory between the Ohio and Miami rivers and north to Lake Erie, to be used as bounty for war veterans, revenue for payment of the public debt, and an outlet for immigration.[15] The question remained whether the Senecas, who claimed the western land but allowed allied tribes to occupy it, would agree to such a punitive demand. That would have to wait for a conference, at least until August 20 of 1784, after the season of corn planting and maturation. Meanwhile, on March 12, the Congress appointed five commissioners to conduct the negotiations. Only two, Oliver Wolcott and Richard Butler, actually served.[16]

New York's Governor Clinton jumped the gun on the Congressional commissioners. On April 12, 1784, he invited the Mohawks, the Onondagas, the Cayugas, and the Senecas to a council at German Flatts sometime in May. Brant, bent on action by a united Indian confederacy, replied in the name of a Six Nations meeting at Loyal Village on June 6 that they awaited the arrival of southern Indian delegates who had been delayed by a dispute with Virginians who had crossed the Ohio River boundary line of the 1768 Stanwix Treaty. Also, they preferred to meet at Stanwix, rather than German Flatts. Finally, and this might negate the New York proposal, Brant concluded with the reservation that the Indians "wish to see proper persons from the different States present and we Expect to make one peace with the whole."[17]

Clinton promptly recognized Brant as an obstacle and even launched a futile effort to unseat him. He sent his reply by the hand of an Albany trader, Peter Ryckman, whom he instructed to mingle with the Indians and "to hint, as from yourself," that they replace him with the Onondagas, the Fire Keepers of the Iroquois league, as their negotiators. He was to investigate whether there was any jealousy or envy of Brant "and promote it as much as you prudently can."[18]

Fanciful as were Clinton's machinations, there were nevertheless very real divisive factors within the Indians' ranks that kept Brant from speaking for them as a united confederation. The Oneidas and the Tuscaroras, in any case, would find it difficult to accept Brant's leadership. Besides, their minister, Kirkland, warned of New York's scheme to dispossess them of their eastern lands and expel them to the west. They were reluctant to send delegates to the conference at Stanwix. The western Indians refused to meet the Americans within enemy territory and would negotiate only at British-held Niagara.[19]

The council met only nominally at Fort Stanwix, for it was burnt and abandoned; the conferees assembled a half mile below in three small blockhouses and several cabins. Brant and nine war chiefs arrived on August 30, including Cornplanter and one each from the pro-British Oneida and Tuscarora factions. Governor Clinton, Abraham Cuyler, Peter Schuyler, and Henry Glen represented New York, assisted by seven associates and accompanied by James Monroe as an observer for the Continental Congress. On September 1, the second day of the meeting, before any business could be attempted, a three-man committee was dispatched to the Oneidas and the Tuscaroras to request their presence. Two days later a delegation of six sachems and ten war chiefs arrived, accompanied by Kirkland.

In effect, the deliberations separated themselves into two councils. On September 4, Clinton delivered to the Oneidas and the Tuscaroras a conciliatory speech prepared by a committee of the New York associates, assuring them that New York had no intention of appropriating any of their lands but wished only to establish their precise boundaries. The Indians reassuringly replied that they were in no way influenced by troublemakers who had attempted to alarm them, but that they viewed the 1768 Fort Stanwix Treaty line as their boundary. They stipulated their territory as reaching some fifty miles from the Unadilla River to the Owego River in the west and from Lake Ontario and the St. Lawrence River south to the Pennsylvania border.

On September 5, Clinton delivered a speech to the Mohawks, the Onondagas, the Cayugas, and the Senecas, also prepared by the New York associates. He bluntly told them that, "considering our Losses, the Debts we have incurred, and our former Friendship, it is reasonable that You make to Us such a Cession of your Lands as will aid Us in repairing and discharging the same." Deceptively, Brant agreed, adding, though, that the Indians were "sent in order to make peace" and were "not authorized to stipulate any particular cession of Lands." No signed treaty resulted, but at least all parties had agreed on a declaration of peace. They could attempt nothing further until the forthcoming meeting with the congressional commissioners.[20]

That meeting took place without Brant. He seemed in no hurry to resume negotiations. He returned to Niagara to promote property arrangements and considered a conference at Stanwix in the spring. He was even planning a second voyage to England to verify the Indian territorial claims. Therefore, Cornplanter headed the Iroquois delegation that met with the commissioners. Sidetracked by the negotiations with New York and delayed by an outbreak of sickness at Niagara, the Indians were slow to assemble, and they were riven by smoldering antagonism between the two sides of the late conflict. They arrived on October 7 and found themselves virtual prisoners of a company of Continentals. Four days later the council convened.[21]

A third congressional commissioner, Arthur Lee, had been assigned to Wolcott and Butler, and accompanying them as observers were Monroe, another Virginia congressman, James Madison, the marquis de Lafayette, and two representatives from Pennsylvania. Two agents of New York, Peter Schuyler and Peter Ryckman, were expelled for trafficking in liquor. Lafayette was popular among the Iroquois, who retained a predilection for the French; he had won their esteem seven years before during his leadership of an aborted invasion of Canada. The commissioners at first viewed him as an interloper but then decided to employ him to break the ice with a strong speech to prepare the Indians for harsh concessions.[22]

Butler opened by announcing to the Indians that the United States were the "sole sovereigns" of the territory in North America ceded by Britain in the treaty of peace. Thus, as a precondition to any agreement, the Indians must deliver up all their prisoners, "white and black," and including the three Oneida chiefs imprisoned at Niagara. After that, the Indians must present a statement of the boundaries they wished to establish.

The Indians determined to respond with bravado and assigned the Mohawk Aaron Hill to deliver a pugnacious keynote. "We are free and independent," he declared. "I speak in the name of the Six Nations, . . . but also in the name of all the other tribes, . . . the Ottawas, Chippewas, Hurons, Potowatomas, Messasagas, Miamis, Delawares, Shawanees, Cherokees, Chicasas, Choctas, and Creeks." As for the prisoners, the Americans should send a task force to collect them, in order to insure that none were being held back. It was a performance that Griffith Evans, secretary of the Pennsylvania delegation, found "abounding with ridiculous ostentation and arrogance."

After this, Cornplanter took over to define the boundaries. The essence of his reply, although more temperate in tone than Hill's diatribe, was a defense of the Indians' covenant with the king as the justification for fighting the Americans and a reassertion of the 1768 Fort Stanwix Treaty line.[23]

The congressmen reacted with unconcealed fury. They were commissioners to deal not only with the Iroquois, they said, but with the western tribes as well, and their agenda reached westward to the Mississippi. Their strategy was to sever the confederacy that Brant had formed and deal separately with the leagues of the east and west. "We summoned the Six Nations only to this treaty," Lee told them; "that Nations not called should send their voices hither is extraordinary. You have not shown us any authority either in writing or by belts, for your speaking in their names." The Iroquois, Lee warned, were a "subdued people" and now "stand out *alone* against our whole force." Their proposal for the Americans to collect their prisoners did not give the "smallest satisfaction," exposing the American deputation as it would to murder by the prisoners' captives. Cornplanter's boundary line made no concessions, supposedly ceding lands already given up in 1768.

Lee then laid down a boundary line that would cede to the United States a four-mile strip stretching from Niagara on Lake Ontario to Buffalo Creek on Lake Erie, and a six-mile-square area around Fort Oswego. From the mouth of Buffalo Creek (the present Buffalo River), a line would be drawn south to the northern boundary of Pennsylvania and then westward along that boundary to the Ohio River, which would be the western limit of Iroquois territory. In effect this would exclude the Senecas from the western section of New York State comprising the present Chautauqua County and a strip of Cattaraugus County. And the Iroquois would be surrendering the jurisdiction they had traditionally claimed over the vast domain west of the Ohio River. Nothing was said about the Onondaga and Cayuga territory appropriated by New York as veterans' bounty land.[24]

Aaron Hill's pugnaciousness disappeared. The Iroquois, he told a confidant, "were obliged to comply with whatever the Commissioners dictated—that in short they were as prisoners." A prisoner indeed he became, when the Continental troops present, under orders from the commissioners, seized Hill and five other chiefs, to be held as hostages until the Indians returned their captives.[25]

One further negotiation took place at Stanwix. The commissioners for Pennsylvania, Samuel Atlee, William McClay, and Francis Johnston, told the Iroquois that the Treaty of Peace had given Pennsylvania sovereignty over Indian claims to the northwestern sector of the state. Nevertheless, Pennsylvania, in the interest of harmony, was prepared to pay four thousand dollars in goods for it. The Indians demanded an additional thousand, and the commissioners agreed.[26]

EPILOGUE

✦ ✦ ✦ ✦ ✦ ✦ ✦ ✦ ✦ ✦ ✦

The Iroquois found themselves powerless to resist the post-Revolutionary takeover and peopling of their heartland by the new American nation.[1]

New York State, in disregard of its promises and in violation of the prohibitions of the Articles of Confederation, and afterward of the national Constitution, systematically set about dispossessing even the loyal Indians of their territory through a policy of threats, deception, and guile. At the Treaty of Fort Herkimer on June 28, 1785, the Oneidas and the Tuscaroras ceded, over the protests of their spokesman, Good Peter, the territory comprising the present counties of Chenango, Broome, and Tioga, in return for $11,500 in goods and money. Next, in a treaty at Fort Schuyler [Stanwix] on September 12, 1788, the Onondagas ceded all their lands for 1,000 French crowns in money, 200 in clothing, and 500 silver dollars annually. Ten days later, another treaty was concluded there with the Oneidas, ceding the remainder of their lands, save for a small reservation, for $1,000 in money to be used for the construction of a gristmill and a sawmill and an annuity of $600 in silver. On February 25, at Albany, came the Cayugas' turn. They ceded all their territory, from Lake Ontario to the Pennsylvania border, except for a small reservation, in return for 2,125 silver dollars and an annuity of 500 silver dollars. There still remained the claims of the Mohawks, the exiles from Fort Hunter and Canajoharie who had settled on grants donated by the Canadian government along the Grand River and the Bay of Quinté. In a treaty signed at Albany on March 29, 1797, with Brant and John Deserontyon representing them, they ceded their claims for $1,000 and $600 in expenses. New York could not attempt appropriation of Seneca lands because of a prior claim of Massachusetts by the 1629 royal charter, which was acknowledged by an agreement of the two states at Hartford on December 16, 1785.[2]

National considerations forced the federal government to step in with assertion of control over the Seneca territory. In 1794, the Ohio tribes had revolted against the United States, and there was danger that the Senecas would join them. In order to forestall this, Timothy Pickering, appointed by Washington as a special commissioner to the Iroquois, negotiated the Treaty of Canandaigua on November 11, 1794. Although by that time the western Indians had been defeated at the Battle of Fallen Timbers, the Treaty of Greenville would not be concluded until well into the following year. The Canandaigua treaty restored to the Senecas the New York lands they had lost in the Treaty of Fort Stanwix and promised protection against interference by New York. It confirmed to the Oneidas, the Onondagas and the Cayugas the reservation lands New York had negotiated with them. The Senecas ceded all claims to the Ohio Valley.[3]

But the treaty did not protect the Senecas from rapacious speculators. A group of Dutch bankers known as the Holland Land Company had purchased a huge Genesee tract of 3,300,000 acres from the financier Robert Morris, who had obtained it from the State of Massachusetts for $333,333, on condition that he first acquire the Indian title. He secured an appointment as federal commissioner and under that authority concluded a treaty with the Senecas at Big Tree on the Genessee River, on September 15, 1797. The Seneca chiefs, Cornplanter, Red Jacket, and Little Billy, were bribed with annuities, and the women were won over with gifts of clothing and trinkets and the prospect of money to hire white men to plough their fields. For $100,000, the Senecas surrendered all their territory except 200,000 acres for eleven village reservations.[4]

Unlike the rest of the Six Nations, who sold off their remaining lands, the Senecas retained enough of theirs to continue until this day as one of the few eastern tribes whose descendants still occupy a fraction of their ancestral territory. Totaling seventeen hundred according to the U.S. census of 1792, they elected to return to land allotted to them in New York—one-third in the Genesee Valley, one-third at Buffalo Creek Reservation, and one-third at reservations at Allegany, Cattaraugus, and Tonawanda. The Oneidas, numbering six hundred, returned for a short time to a reservation at their former territories in western Oneida and northern Madison counties. Between 1795 and 1846, they sold all their lands to New York State. But the state had not obtained approval for the purchases from the national government as required by the Congressional Indian Trade and Intercourse Act of 1790. In 1985, the United States Supreme Court ruled that the Oneidas' lands had been illegally disposed of. In December 1998, after New York State had stalled on restitution, the Federal Government joined with the Oneidas (now grown to about 1,000 in New York State, 15,000 in Wisconsin and 3,000 in Ontario) in filing a suit in Federal court in Syracuse against 20,000 frantic landowners as well as the state and the counties for the return of 270,000 acres between Syracuse and Utica. On February 24, 1999, Judge Neal McCurn appointed Ronald J. Riccio to mediate.[5]

The remaining tribes stayed in Canada on tracts purchased for them by Haldimand from the resident Mississauga Indians. The Mohawks from Fort Hunter, numbering 200, settled in Canada on 92,000 acres on the northern shore of the Bay of Quinté at Lake Ontario's northeastern end (the area of the present Tyendinaga Reserve, between Shannonville and Deseronto). The Mohawks from Canajoharie, numbering 448, settled along the Grand River, on a grant estimated as between 570,000 and 675,000 acres, six miles deep on each bank, between lakes Ontario, Huron, and Erie. Joining them there were 381 Cayugas, 245 Onondagas, 162 Oneidas, 129 Tuscaroras, and 78 Senecas. With a scattering from the western tribes, the total number of Indians on the Grand River, according to a census of 1785, came to 1,843.[6] At present there are fifteen dispersed Iroquois settlements in North America, including one of Oneidas in Wisconsin and another of Senecas and Cayugas in Oklahoma.

The dispossession of the Iroquois spelled the severance of their league and the demise of the warrior way of life. After the peace, under the leadership of Brant, they attempted to reconstitute their league, but geographical divisions proved discordant. A Canadian and an American confederacy resulted, each with its own governing body of fifty sachems. The two leagues continue, one centered at Onondaga Reservation, south of Syracuse, and the other at Six Nations Reserve near Brantford, northwest of Toronto.[7]

Among the preserved letters of soldiers in Sullivan's expedition is a collection by a young officer writing to his fiancée of "the great Loneliness which is creeping into my Soul with every hour and every mile which separates me from you," days before he was killed. "I really feel guilty," he confesses, "as I applied the torch to huts that were Homes of Content until we ravagers came spreading desolation everywhere." Yet he senses a world beyond: "Our mission here is ostensibly to destroy but may it not transpire that we pillagers are carelessly sowing the seeds of Empire?"[8]

ABBREVIATIONS

✦ ✦ ✦ ✦ ✦ ✦ ✦ ✦ ✦ ✦

AHWD [Andrew Hunter War Diary]. Princeton University Library.

BOB *The Order Book of Capt. Leonard Bleeker, Major of Brigade in the Early Part of the Expedition under Gen. James Clinton, against the Indian Settlements of Western New York, in the Campaign of 1779.* New York, 1865.

CP Claus Papers. Public Archives of Canada, C–1478–1485, vols. 1, 2, 14, 25, 26.

DAB Allen Johnson and Dumas Malone, eds. *Dictionary of American Biography.* New York, 1928–58.

DAR K. G. Davies, ed. *Documents of the American Revolution, 1770–1783.* Dublin, Ireland, 1972–78.

DCB George W. Brown, ed. *Dictionary of Canadian Biography.* Toronto, 1966–.

DCNY E. B. O'Callahan, ed. *Documents Relative to the Colonial History of the State of New-York.* Albany, N.Y., 1857.

DMS R. W. G. Vail, ed. "The Western Campaign of 1779: The Diary of Quartermaster Sergeant Moses Sproule of the Third New Jersey Regiment in the Sullivan Expedition of the Revolutionary War, May 17–October 17, 1779." *New-York Historical Society Quarterly* 41 (Jan. 1957).

DSC Pierre E. Du Simitière Collection. Historical Society of Pennsylvania, v. Yi 1411 Q. Philadelphia.

HD Henry Dearborn. *Revolutionary War Journals of Henry Dearborn, 1775–1783.* Ed. Lloyd A. Brown and Howard H. Peckham. Chicago, 1939; reprint, Freeport, N.Y., 1969.

HGP James Gregory, ed. *The Horatio Gates Papers, 1726–1828.* Glen Rock, N.J., 1978. Microfilm.

HMSA Paul Lawrence Stevens. "His Majesty's 'Savage' Allies: British Policy and the Northern Indians during the Revolutionary War.

The Carleton Years 1774–1778." Ph.D. diss., State University of New York at Buffalo, 1984.

HP   Frederick Haldimand Papers. British Library. London.

IAP   Maryly B. Penrose, ed. *Indian Affairs Papers, American Revolution*. Franklin Park, N.J., 1981.

IAR   Barbara Graymont. *The Iroquois in the American Revolution*. Syracuse, N.Y. 1972.

IDH   Francis Jennings and Wiliam N. Fenton, eds. *Iroquois Indians: A Documentary History of the Diplomacy of the Six Nations and their League*. Research Publications, Woodbridge, Conn., 1985. Microfilm.

JB   Isabel Thompson Kelsay. *Joseph Brant, 1743–1807: Man of Two Worlds*. Syracuse, N.Y., 1984.

JBP   Joseph Brant Papers. Draper Manuscripts, ser. F. State Historical Society of Wisconsin, Alexandria, Va., 1983. Microfilm.

JCC   Worthington C. Ford, ed. *The Journals of the Continental Congress, 1774–1789*. Washington, D.C., 1904–37.

JMEJS George S. Conover, compiler. *Journals of the Military Expedition of Major General John Sullivan against the Six Nations of Indians in 1779*. Albany, N.Y., 1887; reprint, Freeport, N.Y., 1972.

KRR   Ernest A. Cruikshank. "The King's Royal Regiment of New York." In *Ontario Historical Society Papers and Records*. Toronto, 1931.

NS   Alexander C. Flick, ed. "New Sources on the Sullivan-Clinton Campaign in 1779." *Quarterly Journal of the New York State Historical Association* 10 (July 1929).

OBFB "The Order Book of Lieut. Colonel Francis Barber." *Proceedings of the New Jersey Historical Society* 65 (Apr. 1947).

OBNY Almon W. Lauber, ed. *Orderly Books of the Fourth New York Regiment, 1778–1780, the Second New York Regiment, 1780–1783, by Samuel Talmadge and Others, with Diaries of Samuel Talmadge, 1780–1782 and John Barr, 1779–1782*. Albany, N.Y., 1932.

OG   R. W. G. Vail, ed. "Diary of Lieut. Obadia Gore, Jr., in the Sullivan-Clinton Campaign of 1779." *Bulletin of the New York Public Library* 33 (Oct. 1929).

PA   Samuel Hazard, ed. *Pennsylvania Archives* 6, Harrisburg, Pa. 1853–.

PCC   Papers of the Continental Congress. National Archives, Washington, D.C. Microfilm ed., 1957–59.

PGC   Hugh Hastings, ed. *Public Papers of George Clinton.* New York
and Albany, 1900.

PGW   Papers of George Washington. Library of Congress, 1964. Microfilm.

PJS   Otis G. Hammond, ed. *Letters and Papers of Major-General John
Sullivan.* Concord, N.H., 1930–39.

PMHB   *Pennsylvania Magazine of History and Biography.*

PNG   Richard K. Showman, ed. *The Papers of General Nathanael
Greene.* Chapel Hill, N.C., 1976–.

PRO   British Public Record Office. London.

SCC   Alexander C. Flick, ed. *The Sullivan-Clinton Campaign in 1779:
Chronology and Selected Documents.* Albany, N.Y., 1929.

W-B   Oscar Jewell Harvey. *A History of Wilkes-Barré.* Wilkes-Barré,
Pa., 1909.

WGW   John C. Fitzpatrick, ed. *The Writings of George Washington,
1745–1799.* Washington, D.C., 1931–40.

NOTES

✦ ✦ ✦ ✦ ✦ ✦ ✦ ✦ ✦ ✦

Notes to the Prologue

1. Richard Aquila, *The Iroquois Restoration: Iroquois Diplomacy on the Colonial Frontier, 1701–1754* (Detroit, 1983), 30; George T. Hunt, *The Wars of the Iroquois: A Study in Intertribal Trade Relations* (Madison, Wis., 1940), 66.

2. Daniel K. Richter, *The Ordeal of the Longhouse: The Peoples of the Iroquois League in the Era of European Colonization* (Chapel Hill, N.C., 1992), 1, 39–41; Francis Jennings, ed., *The History and Culture of Iroquois Diplomacy: An Interdisciplinary Guide to the Treaties of the Six Nations and Their League* (Syracuse, N.Y., 1985), 7–16; Bruce Johansen, *Forgotten Founders: How the American Indian Helped Shape Democracy* (Boston, 1982), passim; William A. Starna and George R. Hamell, "History and the Burden of Proof: The Case of Iroquois Influence on the U.S. Constitution," *New York History* 77 (Oct. 1996): 427–52.

3. Aquila, *Iroquois Restoration*, 34–39; Hunt, *Wars of the Iroquois*, 145–61.

4. Richard White, *The Middle Ground: Indians, Empires, and Republics in the Great Lakes Region, 1650–1815* (Cambridge, Eng., 1991), 352–53; Francis S. Philbrick, *The Rise of the West: 1754–1830* (New York, 1965), 30–31; Ian K. Steele, *Warpaths: Invasions of North America* (New York, 1994), 120–21, 148.

5. Max M. Mintz, *The Generals of Saratoga: John Burgoyne and Horatio Gates* (New Haven, Conn., 1990), 115–16.

6. Speech of Cornplanter, Dec. 1, 1790, in Franklin B. Hough, ed., *Proceedings of the Commissioners of Indian Affairs, Appointed by Law for the Extinguishment of Indian Titles in the State of New York* (Albany, N.Y., 1861), 1:160.

Notes to Chapter 1

1. William L. Stone, *The Life and Times of Sir William Johnson* (Albany, N.Y., 1865), 2:375–76; James Thomas Flexner, *Mohawk Baronet: Sir William Johnson of New York* (New York, 1959), 347.

2. Milton W. Hamilton, *Sir William Johnson: Colonial American, 1715–1763* (Port Washington, N.Y., 1976), 3–124, 297–310, 376; Anne Grant, *Memoirs of an American Lady* (New York, 1901; reprint, Freeport, N.Y., 1972), 14–15; Cadwallader Colden to Earl of Dartmouth, Aug. 2, 1774, in "The Colden Letter Books," *Collections of the New-York Historical Society* 2 (1877): 350.

3. Arthur Pound and Richard E. Day, *Johnson of the Mohawks* (New York, 1930), 455–56.

4. Daniel Claus to [?], Aug. 30, 1779, *CP*, vol. 2, f. 131; Daniel Claus to Frederick Haldimand, Sept. 6, 1779, *CP*, vol. 25; Alexander Fraser, quoted in Barbara Graymont, "Konwatsitsiaenni," *DCB*, 4:418; J. Howard Hanson and Samuel Ludlow Frey, eds., *The Minute Book of the Committee of Safety of Tryon County* (New York, 1905), 96.

5. Joseph Priest, *The Captivity and Sufferings of Gen. Freegift Patchin of Blenheim, Schoharie County, among the Indians, under Brant* (Albany, N.Y., 1833), 34; on average Indian height, see Thomas Hughes, *A Journal by Thos. Hughes,* ed. E. A. Benians (Cambridge, Eng., 1947), 175; *JB*, 52–53, 73–75, 115–16; Dean R. Snow, *The Iroquois* (Cambridge, Mass., 1994), 65, 145; John Norton, *The Journal of Major John Norton, 1816,* ed. Carl F. Klinck and James J. Talman (Toronto, 1970), 271; G. A. Rawlyk, "The Reverend John Stuart, Mohawk Missionary and Reluctant Loyalist," in Esmond Wright, ed., *Red, White, and True Blue: The Loyalists in the Revolution* (New York, 1976), 59–63. As an example of the priority of the female line, the eldest son of the renowned Mohawk chief Captain David Hill could not succeed in 1792 to the chiefdom even though he had been the top scholar at Harvard College. Patrick Campbell, *Travels in the Interior Inhabited Parts of North America in the Years 1791 and 1792* (Toronto, 1937), quoted in Charles M. Johnston, ed., *The Valley of the Six Nations: A Collection of Documents on the Indian Lands of the Grand River* (Toronto, 1964), 61.

6. Brant to Evan Nepean, [1786], in William L. Stone, *Life of Joseph Brant — Thayendanegea* (New York, 1838), 2: 257; speech of Brant, [1804], ibid., 420.

7. [John Strachan], "Life of Capt. Brant," *The Christian Recorder* (Kingston, Upper Canada) (May–June 1819): 108–10; Nicholas B. Wainwright, ed., "Turmoil at Pittsburgh: Diary of Augustine Prevost, 1774," *PMHB* 85 (Apr. 1961): 112–17; Alan Taylor, *William Cooper's Town* (New York, 1995), 48. On close Indian male friendships, see Joseph Francois Lafitau, *Customs of the American Indians Compared with the Customs of Primitive Times,* ed. William N. Fenton and Elizabeth L. Moore (Toronto, 1974), 1: 7, 364–65; Walter L. Williams, *The Spirit and the Flesh: Sexual Diversity in American Indian Culture* (Boston, 1986), 91–92.

8. Daniel Claus to John Blackburn, Oct. 21, 1778, *CP,* vol. 14, f. 263; John Johnson to Tryon County Committee of Safety, [Oct. 1775], in William W. Campbell, *Border Warfare of New York, during the Revolution; or, the Annals of Tryon County* (New York, 1849), 76.

9. Jonathan G. Rossie, "Johnson, Guy," *DCB,* 4:393–94; James F. Vivian and Jean H. Vivian, "Congressional Indian Policy during the War for Independence," *Maryland Historical Magazine* 63 (Sept. 1968): 243.

10. Jonathan G. Rossie, "Daniel Claus: A Personal History of Militant Loyalism in New York," in James Kirby Martin, *The Human Dimensions of Nation Making: Essays on Colonial and Revolutionary America* (Madison, Wis., 1976), 147–67; Claus to Society for Propagation of the Gospel, June 27, 1778, in John Wolfe Lydekker, *The Faithful Mohawks* (New York, 1938; reprint, Port Washington, N.Y., 1968), 154.

11. Earl of Dartmouth to Thomas Gage, Aug. 2, 1775, in Thomas Gage, *The Correspondence of General Thomas Gage,* ed. Clarence E. Carter (New Haven, Conn., 1933), 2:204; Earl of Dartmouth to Guy Johnson, July 24, 1775, *DAR,* 11:56; Guy Johnson, quoted in *JB,* 70.

12. Horace O. Gillette, reminiscences of an Oneida chief who spoke to John Skenandon, *Chicago Times,* Mar. 28, 1874, as quoted in Draper Manuscripts microfilm, ser. U, vol. 11, reel 57, 218–19.

13. *JB,* 34–47; Proceedings of the Commissioners of the Twelve United Colonies with the Six Nations, Aug. 31, 1775, *DCNY,* 8:622.

14. Mintz, *Generals of Saratoga,* 72–73, 94; Douglas Leighton, "Campbell, John," *DCB,* 4:130; Daniel Claus, "A General Detail of Col. Claus's Service since the Commencement of the War 1755 to 1783," *CP,* vol. 14, f. 26.

15. Guy Johnson to Daniel Claus, Aug. 9, 1776, *CP,* vol. 1, f. 216; John Johnson to Daniel Claus, Jan. 20, 1777, in Arent Schuyler De Peyster, *Miscellanies,* ed. J. Watts De Peyster (Dumfries, Scotland, 1813), xlix–li;

Richard K. McMaster, "Parish in Arms: A Study of Father John McKenna and the Mohawk Valley Loyalists, 1773–1778," *United States Catholic Historical Society Historical Records and Studies* 45 (1957): 107–25; Charles Miner, *History of Wyoming, in a Series of Letters, from Charles Miner to His Son William Penn Miner* (Philadelphia, 1845), 236.

16. Claus to [John] Vardill, Oct. 15, 1778, *CP*, vol. 25, f. 24; R. Arthur Bowler and Bruce G. Wilson, "Butler, John," *DCB*, 4:117–20.

17. *JB*, 158–62; Harold P. Clunn, *The Face of London* (London, [1956]), 96, plate 62.

18. Johnson to Germain, Jan. 26, 1776, *DCNY*, 8:657; George Germain to Lords of Treasury, Mar. 8, 1776, *DAR*, 10:237; Daniel Claus, memorandum, Sept. 10, 1780, in Milton W. Hamilton, ed., *The Papers of Sir William Johnson* (Albany, N.Y., 1962), 13:728.

19. *JB*, 165; speech of Thayendenegh, Mar. 14, 1776, *DCNY*, 8:671; Brant speech to Six Nations, Dec. 1776, *PRO*, CO 42/87, f. 222; answer of Thayendenegh and of Ohranti, May 7, 1776, *DCNY*, 8:671.

20. Charles Ryskamp and Frederick A. Pottle, eds., *Boswell: The Ominous Years, 1774–1776* (New York, 1931), 341–42; [James Boswell], "An Account of the Chief of the Mohock Indians Who Lately Visited England (with an Exact Likeness)," *London Magazine* (July 1776): 339.

21. *JB*, 167–69; [Strachan], "Life of Capt. Brant," 148.

22. Guy Johnson to George Germain, Aug. 9, 1776, *DAR*, 10:350; Daniel Claus, "Anecdotes of the Mohawk Chief Captn. Joseph Brant alias Tayendanegea," Sept. 1778, *IAP*, 318; Germain to Howe, Mar. 28, 1776, *DAR*, 12:95.

23. Colin G. Calloway, *The American Revolution in Indian Country: Crisis and Diversity in Native American Communities* (Cambridge, Eng., 1995), 108–23; John Butler to Guy Carleton, Feb. 2, 1778, *DAR*, 15:36; Daniel Claus, "Observations of J. Brant's Distinguished Genius & Character from other Indians," *CP*, vol. 2, ff. 207–9; Norton, *Journal of Major John Norton*, 271–72; Walter Butler, memoir, June 4, 1778, in Howard Swiggett, *War out of Niagara: Walter Butler and the Tory Rangers* (New York, 1933; reprint, Port Washington, N.Y., 1963), 119.

24. Claus, "Observations of Brant," ff. 209–11; Claus, "Anecdotes of Brant," 319; Don R. Gerlach, *Proud Patriot: Philip Schuyler and the War of Independence, 1775–1783* (Syracuse, N.Y., 1987), 183–85.

25. Paul L. Stevens, *A King's Colonel at Niagara, 1774–1776: Lt. Col.*

John Caldwell and the Beginnings of the American Revolution on the Frontier (Youngstown, N.Y., 1987), 68.

26. Claus, "Anecdotes of Brant," 319.

27. Claus to the Mohawks, Dec. 28, 1776, Frederick Haldimand Papers, Public Archives of Canada, quoted in *JB,* 187.

28. Claus, "Observations of Brant," f. 210; William Sturtevant, ed., *Handbook of North American Indians,* vol. 15, *Northeast* (Washington, D.C., 1978), 473–75, 481–84, 491, 495, 500–501, 507, 519–20.

29. *JB,* 190–96; Pomroy Jones, *Annals and Recollections of Oneida County* (Rome, N.Y., 1851), 140; Richard McGinnis, "A 'Loyalist' Journal," ed. Carol Lind, *New York Genealogical and Biographical Record* 105 (Oct. 1974): 196–97; Claus, "Anecdotes of Brant," 319–20; *Journals of the Provincial Convention, Committee of Safety, and Council of Safety of the State of New York, 1775–1777* (Albany, N.Y., 1842), 1:996, July 21, 1777, quoted in Ralph T. Pastore, "Congress and the Six Nations, 1775–1778," *Niagara Frontier* 20 (1973): 88; Gerlach, *Proud Patriot,* 239; Nicolas Herkimer to Philip Schuyler, July 2, 1777, *IAP,* 81.

30. Germain to Carlton, Mar. 26, 1777, *DAR,* 14:53–55; [Hertel de Rouville], "L'expedition du Fort Stanwix," *Le Canada Français* 33 (1945–46): 219.

31. Carleton to John Butler, May 18, 1777, *DAR,* 13:127; Butler to Carleton, June 15, 1777, *DAR,* 14:115–16.

32. Governor Blacksnake, *Chainbreaker: The Revolutionary War Memoirs of Governor Blacksnake, as told to Benjamin Williams,* ed. Thomas S. Abler (Lincoln, Nebr., 1989), 59–80; Elizabeth Cometti, ed., *The American Journal of Lt. John Enys,* quoted in Colin G. Calloway, *Crown and Calumet: British Indian Relations, 1783–1815* (Norman, Okla., 1986), 120; James E. Seaver, *A Narrative of the Life of Mrs. Mary Jemison,* ed. June Namias (Norman, Oka., 1992), 99–100; Butler to Carleton, July 28, 1777, *PRO,* CO 42/37, f. 97.

NOTES TO CHAPTER 2

1. Claus to Evan Nepean, Mar. 8, 1787, *PRO,* CO 42/19, ff. 106–7; Claus to Lord North, May 8, 1776, *CP,* vol. 14, ff. 212–13; Claus memorandum, Sept. 10, 1780, in Hamilton, *Papers of Sir William Johnson,* 13: 728–30; Claus to Frederick Haldimand, Oct. 15, 1778, *CP,* vol. 25, ff. 37–38; Germain to Carleton, Feb. 19, 1777, *PRO,* CO 42/36, ff. 41–42.

2. Claus to John Vardill, Oct. 15, 1778, *CP*, vol. 25, ff. 23–24; Claus to William Knox, Oct. 16, 1777, *DAR*, 14:219–20.

3. Penrose, *Mohawk Valley in the Revolution: Committee of Safety Papers & Genealogical Compendium* (Franklin Park, N.J., 1978), 121–23.

4. Pierre Pouchot, *Memoirs of the Late War in North America between France and England*, ed. Brian Leigh Dunnigan, trans. Michael Cardy (Youngstown, N.Y., 1994), 371; Peter Gansevoort to Philip Schuyler, July 4, 1777, *IAP*, 84.

5. Max von Eelking, *The German Allied Troops in the North American War of Independence, 1776–1783*, ed. J. G. Rosengarten (Albany, N.Y., 1893; reprint, Bowie, Md., 1987), 133, 141; Claus to William Knox, Oct. 16, 1777, *DAR*, 14:220–21; St. Leger to Carleton, Aug. 27, 1777, *DAR*, 14: 171; Butler to Carleton, July 28, 1777, *PRO*, CO 42/37, f. 98; Claus, "General Detail of Col. Claus's Service," ff. 28–32; Blacksnake, *Chainbreaker*, 62, 75.

6. St. Leger General Order, July 12, 1777, *CP*, vol. 14, f. 251; John F. Luzader, Louis Torres, and Orville W. Carroll, *Fort Stanwix: History, Historic Furnishing, and Historic Structure Reports* (Washington, D.C., 1976), 82–83, 125–26.

7. Description of Peter Gansevoort by his granddaughter, Catherine Gansevoort Lansing, in John Albert Scott, *Fort Stanwix (Fort Schuyler) and Oriskany* (Rome, N.Y., 1927), 87–90; Larry Lowenthal, *Days of Siege: A Journal of the Siege of Fort Stanwix in 1777* (N.Y. 1983), 15; Gansevoort to Schuyler, July 4, 1777, *IAP*, 84–85; Herkimer to Schuyler, [July 15, 1777], *IAP*, 89–90.

8. St. Leger to Carleton, Aug. 27, 1777, *DAR*, 14:171; Lowenthal, *Days of Siege*, 24.

9. Jones, *Oneida County*, 312, 338–39; Lowenthal, *Days of Siege*, 26.

10. *HMSA*, 1225–28.

11. Penrose, *Mohawk Valley in the Revolution*, 121–24; Herkimer proclamation, July 17, 1777, in Campbell, *Annals of Tryon County*, 91–92; Goose Van Schaick to Schuyler, Aug. 4, 1777, *PGC*, 2:169; Gansevoort to Goose Van Schaick, July 28, 1777, in Jeptha R. Simms, *The Frontiersmen of New York* (Albany, N.Y., 1882), 2:30–31; Spencer to Tryon County Committee of Safety, July 29, 1777, in Campbell, *Annals of Tryon County*, 92.

12. T. Wood Clarke, The Bloody Mohawk (New York, 1940), 214–15.

13. Stone, *Life of Joseph Brant*, 1:234–40; Timothy Dwight, *Travels in*

New England and New York, ed. Barbara Miller Solomon (Cambridge, Mass., 1969), 3:132.

14. Claus, "Anecdotes of Brant," 321; St. Leger to Carleton, Aug. 27, 1777, *DAR,* 14:171; St. Leger to Butler, Aug. 4, 1777, *CP,* vol. 14, f. 252.

15. Claus, "General Detail of Col. Claus's Service," 31–32; Jones, *Oneida County,* 344; Blacksnake, *Chainbreaker,* 128.

16. Freeman H. Allen, "St. Leger's Invasion and the Battle of Oriskany," *Proceedings of the New York State Historical Association* 12 (1913): 164; Dwight, *Travels,* 3:132–33; St. Leger to Carleton, Aug, 27, 1777, *DAR,* 14: 171–72; Butler to Carleton, Aug. 15, 1777, *PRO,* CO 42/37, ff. 103–4; Robert W. Venables, ed., " 'Genl. Harkemer's Battle,': A Poetic Account of the Battle of Oriskany," *New York History* 58 (Oct. 1977): 474–76; Simms, *Frontiersmen of New York,* 2:93; Barbara Graymont, "The Oneidas and the American Revolution," in Jack Campisi and Laurence M. Hauptman, eds., *The Oneida Indian Experience: Two Perspectives* (Syracuse, N.Y., 1988), 36–37.

17. Jonathan Trumbull, Jr., to Jonathan Trumbull, Aug. 11, 1777, in "The Trumbull Papers," *Collections of the Massachusetts Historical Society,* 7th ser., 2 (1902): 111–12; examination of Adam Helmer, Aug. 11, 1777, in *Journals of the Provincial Convention of New York,* 1:1038; Campbell, *Annals of Tryon County,* 125.

18. Marinus Willett to *Connecticut Courant,* Aug. 11, 1777, in William W. Willett, *A Narrative of the Military Actions of Colonel Marinus Willett, Taken Chiefly from His Own Manuscript* (New York, 1831), 131–33.

19. *HMSA,* 1250–52; Simms, *Frontiersmen of New York,* 2:91, 114–15; Butler to Carleton, Aug. 15, 1777, *PRO,* CO 42/37, f. 104; deposition of Moses Younglove, n.d., in Stone, *Life of Joseph Brant,* 1:appendix, xxxiv; O. Turner, *Pioneer History of the Holland Purchase of Western New York* (Buffalo, N.Y., 1850), 262.

20. *HMSA,* 1252–54.

21. Claus, "Anecdotes of Brant," 321; St. Leger to Gansevoort, Aug. 9, 1777, in Luzader, Torres, and Carroll, *Fort Stanwix,* 48.

22. Willett, *Narrative of Willett,* 55–58.

23. St. Leger to Gansevoort, Aug. 9, 1777, and Gansevoort to St. Leger, Aug. 9, 1777, in Luzader, Torres, and Carroll, *Fort Stanwix,* 48; Jonathan Trumbull, Jr., to Jonathan Trumbull, Aug. 11, 1777, "Trumbull Papers," 112.

24. Gansevoort to Horatio Gates, Dec. 12, 1777, in Luzader, Torres, and Carroll, *Fort Stanwix,* 78.

25. Willett, *Narrative of Willett,* 58–61; James Kirby Martin, *Benedict Arnold, Revolutionary Hero: An American Warrior Reconsidered* (New York, 1997), 363.

26. Mintz, *Generals of Saratoga,* 90–92, 99–108, 119–30, 178–80; "Report of Council of War of German Flatts," Aug. 21, 1777, Horatio Gates Papers, New-York Historical Society, in Luzader, Torres, and Carroll, *Fort Stanwix,* 51; Martin, *Benedict Arnold,* 365.

27. Stone, *Life of Joseph Brant,* 1:258–60.

28. *HMSA,* 1265–70; St. Leger to Burgoyne, Aug. 11, 1777, *PRO,* CO 42/37, f. 170; St. Leger to Carleton, Aug. 27, 1777, *DAR,* 14:173–74; Stone, *Life of Joseph Brant,* 1:261; Mary Brant to Claus, Oct. 5, 1779, *CP,* vol. 2, f. 135; Jean-Baptiste-Melchior Hertel de Rouville, "L'enterprise manquée," *Le Canada Français* 33 (1945–46): 219; Claus to Knox, Oct. 16, 1777, *DAR,* 14:223.

29. Unsigned, "Affair at Bennington," Sept. 4, 1777, in Historical Manuscripts Commission, *Report on the Manuscripts of Mrs. Stopford-Sackville* (London, 1910; reprint, Boston, 1972), 2:76; Lowenthal, *Days of Siege,* 51–52; Hertel de Rouville, "L'enterprise manquée," 228.

30. Arnold to Gates, Aug. 23, 1777, *PGC,* 2:255; Arnold to Gates, Aug. 28, 1777, Gates Papers.

31. Ernest Cruikshank, *The Story of Butler's Rangers and the Settlement of Niagara* (Welland, Ont., 1893; reprint, Owen Sound, Ont., 1975), 37–39.

32. Claus, "General Detail of Col. Claus's Service," f. 28.

33. *HMSA,* 1383–88; Claus, "Anecdotes of Brant," 322.

34. Claus, "Anecdotes of Brant," 322; Jelles Fonda to Commissioners of Indian Affairs, Apr. 21, 1778, *IAP,* 134; Claus to [?], Aug. 30, 1779, *CP,* vol. 2, f. 132; Claus to Guy Johnson, Jan. 4, 1779, *CP,* vol. 14, f. 266; *HMSA,* 1461–66.

NOTES TO CHAPTER 3

1. Butler to Carleton, Feb. 2, 1778, *DAR,* 15:35; Claus, "Anecdotes of Brant," 322–23; report of council at Niagara by Mason Bolton and John Butler with Senecas, Cayugas, Onondagas, Tuscaroras, Oneidas, Mohawks, Delawares, Tideiroonas, Munsies, and Conoys, [Dec. 1777], *PRO,* CO 42/38, ff. 108–11.

2. *HMSA*, 1476–78.

3. Bolton and Butler, council at Niagara, CO 42/38, ff. 108–11; "The Journal of Adam Crysler," in James J. Talman, *Loyalist Narratives from Upper Canada* (Toronto, 1946), 58; Butler to Carleton, Feb. 2, 1778, *DAR*, 15:35–36.

4. McGinnis, " 'Loyalist' Journal," 106 (Jan. 1975): 14; R. Arthur Bowler and Bruce C. Wilson, "Butler, John," *DCB*, 4:118; Butler to Carleton, May 15, 1778, *HP*; *W-B*, 2:971; Bolton and Butler to Henry Clinton or William Howe, Nov. 23, 1777, *DAR*, 13:249–50. See also the unverified letter Butler to Howe, June 7, 1778, in James Armitage's deposition, July 6, 1778, *PGC*, 3:527.

5. Butler to Carleton, Feb. 2, 1778, *DAR*, 15:36.

6. C. Hale Sipe, *The Indian Wars of Pennsylvania* (Harrisburg, Pa., 1929; reprint, New York, 1971), 527–31, 537–49; James Deane to Schuyler, May 19 and 25, 1778, in Caleb Stark, *Memoir and Official Correspondence of Gen. John Stark* (Concord, N.H., 1860; reprint, Boston, 1972), 145, 152; Peter C. Mancall, *Valley of Opportunity: Economic Culture along the Upper Susquehanna, 1700–1800* (Ithaca, N.Y., 1991), 134; Richard Reuben Forry, "Edward Hand: His Role in the American Revolution," Ph.D. diss., Duke Univ., 1976, 141–43; Edward Hand to Jasper Ewing, Mar. 7, 1778, and recollections of Samuel Murphy, n.d., in Reuben Gold Thwaites and Louise Phelps Kellogg, eds., *Frontier Defense on the Ohio, 1777–1778* (Madison, Wis., 1912), 215–21. For a discussion of widespread butchery of Indians in Pennsylvania, see Alden T. Vaughan, "Frontier Banditti and the Indians: The Paxton Boys' Legacy," *Pennsylvania History* 51 (Jan. 1984): 1–29.

7. Butler to Carleton, Apr. 10, 1778, *PRO*, CO 43/14, in *W-B*, 2:966; Cruikshank, *Butler's Rangers*, 39–40.

8. McGinnis, " 'Loyalist' Journal," 106 (Jan. 1975): 14; Samuel Kirkland to Schuyler, May 23, 1778, in Stark, *John Stark*, 148–50; *HMSA*, 1569–78.

9. Jeptha R. Simms, *History of Schoharie County, and the Border Wars of New York* (Albany, N.Y., 1845), 273–80; William Dietz, Thomas Cheson, Jost Becker to John Stark, May 30, 1778, *PGC*, 3:377; Jacob Klock to George Clinton, June 5, 1778, ibid., 402–4; Abraham Wempel, June 6, 1778, ibid., 413; military pension application of David Freemoyer, 1834, in John C. Dann, ed., *The Revolution Remembered: Eyewitness Accounts of the War for Independence* (Chicago, 1980), 288–91.

10. Jacob Klock to George Clinton, June 5, 1778, *PGC*, 3:402–4; Samuel Campbell and Samuel Clyde, June 5, 1778, ibid., 409–10; Jacob Klock to

Abraham Ten Broeck, June 6, 1778, ibid., 414–15; deposition of Hendrick X. Warmwood, June 5, 1778, ibid., 415–16; Frederick Fisher, Zephaniel Bachelder, James Veden, Thomas Romea, C. F. M. Adams, and Giles Fonda to John Stark, June 4, 1778, in Stark, *John Stark*, 158–59.

11. Robert Jones's statement, July 10, 1778, *PGC*, 3:543–44.

12. Pastore, "Congress and the Six Nations, 1775–1778," 93; Vivian and Vivian, "Congressional Indian Policy," 258; *JCC*, 11:587–91.

13. Max M. Mintz, "Horatio Gates, George Washington's Rival," *History Today* 26 (July 1976): 427; Allan S. Everest, *Moses Hazen and the Canadian Refugees in the American Revolution* (Syracuse, N.Y., 1976), 58; Paul David Nelson, *General Horatio Gates, A Biography* (Baton Rouge, La., 1976), 197–98; Gates to Timothy Bedel, June 26, 1778, *HGP*.

14. Gates to Henry Laurens, June 17 and 23, 1778, *PCC*; Willett, *Narrative of Willett*, 65–66.

15. Joseph Klock to George Clinton, June 22, 1778, *PGC*, 3:475–76; *JB*, 223–24.

16. Isaac A. Chapman, *A Sketch of the History of Wyoming* (Wilkes-Barre, 1830), 6–8; extract, *Connecticut Courant*, Sept. 29, 1772, in Robert J. Taylor, ed., *The Susquehanna Company Papers* (Ithaca, N.Y., 1968), 5:39; Julian P. Boyd, ed., *The Susquehanna Company Papers* (Ithaca, N.Y., 1962), 1:lxxxiv–lxxxv; Thomas Penn to John Penn, Jan. 31, 1769, and to James Tilghman, Jan. 31, 1769, ibid., 64–67; extract, record of a conference with the Six Nations at Albany, Aug. 31, 1775, ibid., 6:348; Paul A. W. Wallace, *Indians in Pennsylvania*, revised by William A. Hunter (Harrisburg, Pa. 1981), 157–59; Mancall, *Valley of Opportunity*, 76–78, 92–94, 140–41.

17. C. E. Cartwright, *Life and Letters of the Late Hon. Richard Cartwright* (Toronto, 1876), 30; James R. Williamson and Linda A. Fossler, *Zebulon Butler, Hero of the Revolutionary Frontier* (Westport, Conn., 1995), 57; Daniel Washburn's account of the Massacre of Wyoming, and narrative of Elisha Harding of the Massacre of Wyoming, in Horace Edwin Hayden, ed., "Echoes of the Massacre of Wyoming," *Proceedings and Collections of the Wyoming Historical and Geological Society* 7 (1901): 82, 88–90; Norton, *Journal of Major John Norton*, 274–75; McGinnis, "A 'Loyalist' Journal," 106 (Jan. 1975): 14–15; *W-B*, 2:983–95; Nathan Denison to Jonathan Trumbull, July 28, 1778, in Taylor, *Susquehanna Papers*, 7:47. In May 1785, in support of Loyalist compensation claims to Parliament, John Butler submitted a narrative of his services in which he concocted an account that his expedition to Wyoming was a response to an invitation from Colo-

nel Nathan Denison and Judge John Jenkins to the chiefs of the Six Nations for a council. On the expedition's arrival, Denison repudiated the invitation and declared that he was "determined to fight, and that he would have all our Scalps before Night." Narrative of Lieut. Col. Butler's Services in America, *HP*, Add. 21,875, ff. 191–92.

18. John Butler to Mason Bolton, July 8, 1778, *DAR*, 15:165; McGinnis, " 'Loyalist' Journal," 106 (Jan. 1975): 15–16; Norton, *Journal of Major John Norton*, 275; Martha B. Clark, "Lazarus Stewart," *Lancaster County Historical Society Papers* 14 (Dec. 1910): 306; Frank J. Cavaioli, "A Profile of the Paxton Boys: Murderers of the Conestoga Indians," *Journal of the Lancaster County Historical Society* 87, no. 3 (1983): 88–105; Williamson and Fossler, *Zebulon Butler*, 62; James H. Hutson, *Pennsylvania Politics, 1746–1770* (Princeton, N.J., 1972), 84–85; Thomas P. Sloughter, "Interpersonal Violence in a Rural Setting: Lancaster County in the Eighteenth Century," *Pennsylvania History* 58 (Apr. 1991): 112–13, 121–22 n. 29; Boyd, *Susquehanna Papers,* 4:vi–viii, xi–xii, xx, 122–23, 148, 165; *W-B,* 2:1003–11; John B. B. Trussell, "The Battle of Wyoming and Hartley's Expedition," *Historic Pennsylvania Leaflet No. 40* (Harrisburg, 1976), 1–3.

19. Butler to Bolton, July 8, 1778, *DAR,* 15:165–66; *W-B,* 2:991–1029; Zebulon Butler to Board of War, July 10, 1778, in Henry B. Dawson, *Battles of the United States* (New York, 1858), 1:429–30; Miner, *History of Wyoming,* 220–28, 244; John Franklin, Jan. 19, 1828, "Wyoming Battle," Wyoming Herald, Wilkes-Barre, Pa., Sept. 19, 1828, State Library of Pa., Harrisburg, Pa.; Johann Ewald, *Diary of the American War: A Hessian Journal,* ed. and trans. Joseph P. Tustin (New Haven, Conn., 1979), 166–67.

20. John Butler to Mason Bolton, July 8, 1778, *DAR,* 15:166; *IAR,* 171; *W-B,* 2:1032, 1035, 644; William Maclay to Timothy Matlack, July 12, 1778, Taylor, *Susquehanna Papers,* 7:44.

NOTES TO CHAPTER 4

1. Butler to Carleton, Aug. 15, 1777, *PRO,* CO 42/37, f. 104; Trumbull to Washington, Aug. 27, 1778, George Washington Papers microfilm, Library of Congress, Washington, D.C., reel 51; *JCC,* 11:721, 827–29; Washington to Board of War, Aug. 3, 1778, *WGW,* 12:261–66.

2. Hazel C. Mathews, *The Mark of Honor* (Toronto, 1965), 56.

3. Peter Bellinger to George Clinton, Sept. 19, 1778, *PGC,* 4:47–49; Robert Cochran to Volckert P. Douw, Sept. 28, 1778, ibid., 132; William

Caldwell to John Butler, Sept. 21, 1778, HP; Taylor and Duffin to Claus, Nov. 15, 1778, *IAP*, 172–73; *IAR*, 178–79; Stone, *Life of Joseph Brant*, 1: 363–66.

4. Robert B. Roberts, *New York's Forts in the Revolution* (Rutherford, N.J., 1980), 380; Gansevoort to Schuyler, July 10, 1778, Gansevoort Papers, New York Public Library, vol. 4, f. 19.

5. Stark to Gates, July 1, 1778, in Stark, *John Stark*, 174; Nelson, *General Horatio Gates*, 199–200; Washington to Stark, Aug. 5, 1778, *WGW*, 12:284.

6. George Clinton to Washington, Oct. 15 and 17, 1778, *PGC*, 4:163–64 and 168; William Butler to George Clinton, Sept. 27 and Oct. 28, 1778, and extracts from his journal, Oct. 1–16, 1778, ibid., 104 and 222–28; depositions of William Thomson and Henry Main, Oct. 22, 1778, ibid., 185; William Gray to Robert Erskine, Oct. 28, 1778, in Albert H. Heusser, *George Washington's Map Maker: A Biography of Robert Erskine* (New Brunswick, N.J., 1928; reprint, 1966), 184–85; Marjory Barnum Hinman, *Onaquaga: Hub of the Border Wars of the American Revolution in New York State* (Windsor, N.Y., 1975), 53–61; Jay Gould, *History of Delaware County and Border Wars of New York* (Roxbury, N.Y., 1856), 92n–93n; David Freemoyer's pension application, in Dann, *Revolution Remembered*, 291.

7. Hartley to Executive Council of Pennsylvania, Oct. 8, 1778, *PA* 6 (1853): 3; Hartley to Zebulon Butler, Aug. 22, 1778, in "Correspondence of Col. Zebulon Butler, Wyoming, June–December, 1778," *Proceedings and Collections of the Wyoming Historical and Geological Society* 7 (1901): 137.

8. David Craft, "The Expedition of Col. Thomas Hartley against the Indians in 1778, to Avenge the Massacre of Wyoming," *Proceedings and Collections of the Wyoming Historical and Geological Society* 9 (1905): 188–213; Trussell, "Battle of Wyoming and Hartley's Expedition," 3–4; Walter Butler to James Clinton, Feb. 11, 1779, *IAP*, 185; Hartley to the Indians of Chemung, Oct. 1, 1779 [1778], and Hartley to Continental Congress, Oct. 8, 1778, *PCC*, roll 183; *PA*, first ser., 7 (1853): 5–9.

9. John Butler to Mason Bolton, July 8, 1778, *DAR*, 15:166; four Indian chiefs to John Cantine, Dec. 13, 1778, *PGC*, 4:364; James Deane to Philip Schuyler, Oct. 10, 1778, *IAP*, 156; Bolton to Haldimand, Nov. 11, 1778, *Historical Collections Made by the Michigan Pioneer and Historical Society*

19 (1892): 364; Walter Butler to Mason Bolton, Nov. 17, 1778, *DAR*, 15: 262; *HMSA*, 1739–46.

10. Cruikshank, *Butler's Rangers,* 51–54; Taylor and Duffin to Claus, Nov. 11, 1778, *CP*, vol. 25, ff. 37–38; Claus to Haldimand, Nov. 20, 1778, ibid., ff. 53–55; Taylor and Duffin to Claus, Nov. 15, 1778, *IAP*, 173; Blacksnake, *Chainbreaker*, 104; *JB*, 228–32; Walter Butler to Mason Bolton, Nov. 17, 1778, *DAR*, 15:261; *IAR*, 186–90.

11. Walter Butler to Mason Bolton, Nov. 17, 1778, *DAR*, 15:261–62; Abraham Ten Broeck to George Clinton, *PGC*, 4:267; Daniel Whiting to Edward Hand, Nov. 13, 1778, ibid., 286; four Indian chiefs to John Cantine, Dec. 13, 1778, ibid., 364; letter from an officer at Cherry Valley, in *Boston Gazette and Country Journal*, Dec. 7, 1778, in Mrs. William S. Little, "The Massacre at Cherry Valley," *Rochester Historical Society Publication Fund* 6 (1927): 127; *IAR*, 184–89; Campbell, *Annals of Tryon County*, 250.

12. David E. Alexander, ed., "Diary of Captain Benjamin Warren at Massacre of Cherry Valley," *Journal of American History* 3 (July 1909): 383; Cartwright, *Cartwright*, 33.

13. George Clinton to John Jay, Nov. 17, 1778, *PGC*, 4:289–90; George Clinton to New York Delegates in Congress, Nov. 18, 1778, *PGC*, 4:294.

NOTES TO CHAPTER 5

1. Washington to d'Estaing, Oct. 2, 1778, *WGW*, 13:10–11; Washington to Gates, Oct. 20, 1778, *WGW*, 13:112; Washington to President of Congress, Oct. 26, 1778, *WGW*, 13:159.

2. Washington to John Armstrong, May 18, 1779, *WGW*, 15:97; Washington to John Jay, Aug. 15, 1779, *WGW*, 16:107.

3. Lachlan McIntosh to Washington, Apr. 27, 1779, in Jared Sparks, ed., *Correspondence of the American Revolution* (Boston, 1853), 2:288–89; Harvey H. Jackson, *Lachlan McIntosh, and the Politics of Revolutionary Georgia* (Athens, Ga., 1979), 42–43, 46–47, 78. See also Almon W. Lauber, "The Valleys of the Susquehanna and the Delaware," in Alexander C. Flick, ed., *History of the State of New York* (New York, 1934; reprint, Port Washington, N.Y., 1962), 5:125–26; Joshua V. H. Clark, *Onondaga: or Reminiscences of Earlier and Later Times* (Syracuse, N.Y., 1849), 1:327.

4. *NS*, 191–94; *SCC*, passim; John Butler to Frederick Haldimand, July 21, 1779, *NS*, 270; Victor Leroy Johnson, *The Administration of the Amer-*

ican Commissariat during the Revolutionary War (Philadelphia, 1941), 151, 157–58; E. Wayne Carp, *To Starve the Army at Pleasure: Continental Army Administration and American Political Culture, 1775–1783* (Chapel Hill, N.C., 1984), 113, 118, 125–26; Richard Buel, Jr., *Dear Liberty: Connecticut's Mobilization for the Revolutionary War* (Middletown, Conn., 1980), 143–51, 160–69; Richard Buel, Jr., "Time: Friend or Foe of the Revolution?" in Don Higginbotham, ed., *Reconsiderations on the Revolutionary War* (Westport, Conn., 1978), 136–38; *WGW*, 14, 15, 16, passim.

5. Washington to Marquis de Lafayette, July 4, 1779, *WGW*, 15:370; speech of Corn Planter, Half Town, and Great Tree to Washington, Dec. 1, 1790, in Hough, *Proceedings of the Commissioners of Indian Affairs*, 1: 161.

6. Mintz, *Generals of Saratoga*, 228–30; *PNG*, 3:28 n–31 n.

7. Washington to President of Congress, Nov. 11, 1778, and to Henry Laurens, Nov. 14, 1778, *WGW*, 13:223–44 and 254–57; *JCC*, 13:12–13.

8. Gates to Jay, Mar. 15, 1778, in John Jay, *John Jay: The Making of a Revolutionary*, ed. Richard B. Morris (New York, 1975), 1:576–77; Jay to Washington, Apr. 6 and 21, 1778, ibid., 577 n, 585; Washington to Jay, Apr. 14, 1778, *WGW*, 14:381–86.

9. Joseph Reed to Zebulon Butler, Apr. 2, 1779, *W-B*, 2:1161.

10. Nathanael Greene to Washington, Jan. 5, 1779, *PNG*, 3:144–45.

11. Washington to Schuyler, Jan. 18 and 25, 1779, *WGW*, 14:19 and 45–46; Schuyler to Henry Laurens, Mar. 15, 1778, and Schuyler to Washington, Feb. 4, 1779, *IAP*, 119 and 183.

12. Washington to Schuyler, Jan. 18 and Feb. 11, 1779, *PGW*.

13. Schuyler to Washington, Mar. 1, 1779, *PGW*.

14. Washington to Schuyler, Feb. 16, 1779, *WGW*, 14:121–22; Schuyler to Washington, Mar. 1 [3], 1779.

15. Schuyler to Duane, Mar. 7, 1779, quoted in Gerlach, *Proud Patriot*, 371.

16. Greene to Washington, Mar. 17–20, 1779, *PNG*, 3:346–50.

17. Washington to Schuyler, Mar. 21, 1779, *WGW*, 14:268–72.

18. James Clinton to Washington, Apr. 8 and 29, 1779, in "New York during the Revolution: Selections from the Clinton Correspondence, 1776–83," *Magazine of History* 24 (Mar. 1917): 123 and 125.

19. T. W. Egly, Jr., *Goose Van Schaick of Albany, 1736–1789: The Continental Army's Senior Colonel* ([United States], 1992), 2–3, 10, 60, 106–7; Thomas McClennan to (?), Apr. 30, 1779, in Albert Hazen Wright,

ed., *Sullivan Expedition of 1779: Contemporary Newspaper Comment and Letters, Studies in History no. 5* (Ithaca, N.Y., 1943), 50–51.

20. "Lieut. Erkuries Beatty Journal: Part First," in Wright, *Sullivan Expedition: Newspaper Comment and Letters,* 41–43; Goose Van Schaick, minutes and proceedings of the Onondaga expedition, Apr. 24, 1779, enclosed in Schuyler to Washington, Apr. 27, 1779, PCC, reel 169, ff. 258–59; John Butler to Mason Bolton, [late Apr. 1779], SCC, 83; Clark, *Onondaga,* 1:329–32; Egly, *Van Schaick,* 59–63. For a description of an Onondaga longhouse, see Richter, *Ordeal of the Longhouse,* 260–61.

21. George Clinton to James Clinton, May 2, 1779, and Van Schaick to James Clinton, May 22, 1779, in Wright, *Sullivan Expedition: Newspaper Comment and Letters,* 45 and 53; John Butler to [Mason Bolton], May 21, 1779, SCC, 89.

NOTES TO CHAPTER 6

1. Washington to Jay, Apr. 14, 1779, WGW, 14:384–85; Washington to Gates, Mar. 6, 1779, WGW, 14:198–201; Washington to Sullivan, Mar. 6, 1779, WGW, 14:201; Gates to Washington, Mar. 16, 1779, in James Gregory, ed., *The Horatio Gates Papers, 1726–1828* (Glen Rock. N.J., 1878), microfilm.

2. Sullivan to Gates, Mar. 17 and 23, 1779, *PJS,* 2:535–36 and 542.

3. Charles P. Whittemore, *A General of the Revolution: John Sullivan of New Hampshire* (New York, 1961), 1–116, 226–27, 245; Washington to President of Congress, July 17, 1776, quoted in Charles P. Whittemore, "John Sullivan: Luckless Irishman," in George Athan Billias, ed., *George Washington's Generals* (New York, 1964), 142; Sullivan to Washington, Feb. 1778, *PJS,* 2:21; Washington to Sullivan, Mar. 15, 1777, WGW, 7:290.

4. Greene to Washington, Apr. 26, 1779, PNG, 3:430; Washington to John Armstrong, May 18, 1779, WGW, 15:99; Benjamin Rush, "Historical Notes of Dr. Benjamin Rush," PMHB 27 (1903): 147; Greene to Jeremiah Wadsworth, Apr. 14, 1779, PNG, 3:403; Greene to John Brown, Sept. 6, 1778, PNG, 2:512.

5. Thomas G. Amory, *The Military Services and Public Life of Major-General John Sullivan* (Boston, 1868; reprint, Port Washington, N.Y., 1968), 252–57.

6. Greene to Jeremiah Wadsworth, Apr. 14, 1779, PNG, 3:403; Sullivan

to Washington, Apr. 15, 1779, *PJS*, 3:1–5; Sullivan to Washington, Apr. 16, 1779, *PJS*, 3:5–8; Schuyler to Washington, Apr. 3, 1779, *PCC*, roll 183.

7. Washington to Schuyler, Apr. 19, 1779, *WGW*, 14:407; Sullivan to Gates, Apr. 28, 1779, *PJS*, 3:10; Sullivan to George Clinton, Apr. 29, 1779, *PJS*, 3:10–11; Sullivan to Jay, July 21, 1779, in Jay, *John Jay*, 1:616; Washington to Sullivan, May 4, 1779, *WGW*, 14:492–93.

8. Sullivan to Greene, May 12 and 16, 1779, *PJS*, 3:19 and 23; Washington to Sullivan, May 31, 1779, *WGW*, 15:189–192; Joseph R. Fischer, *A Well-Executed Failure: The Sullivan Campaign against the Iroquois, July–September 1779* (Columbia, S.C., 1997), 40–41.

9. Sullivan to Washington, June 2, 1779, *PCC*, roll 169, ff. 540–41; Washington to Sullivan, June 4, 1779, *WGW*, 15:226–27; Sullivan to Jay, *PJS*, 3:81.

10. Forry, "Edward Hand," 1–161; Washington to Hand, Apr. 1 and 9, 1779, *WGW*, 13:321 and 354; A. Tiffany Norton, *History of Sullivan's Campaign against the Iroquois* (Lima, N.Y., 1879), 88; *W-B*, 2:1165–68; journal of Ebenezer Elmer, *JMEJS*, 81.

11. Hughes, *A Journal by Tho. Hughes*, 65.

12. Harry M. Ward, *General William Maxwell and the New Jersey Continentals* (Westport, Conn., 1997), 1–124; William S. Stryker, *General Maxwell's Brigade of the New Jersey Continental Line in the Expedition against the Indians, in the Year 1779* (Trenton, N.J., 1888), 10; Officers' Memorial and Remonstrance to Council and General Assembly of New Jersey, Apr. 17, 1779, *PCC*, roll 169, ff. 325–27; William Maxwell to Washington, May 6, 1779, *PCC*, roll 169, ff. 315–16.

13. Washington to Maxwell, May 10, 1779, *WGW*, 15:33.

14. Washington to President of Congress, May 11, 1779, *WGW*, 15:44; James Kirby Martin and Mark Edward Lender, *A Respectable Army: The Military Origins of the Republic, 1763–1789* (Arlington Heights, Ill., 1982), 148–49; Charles Royster, *A Revolutionary People at War: The Continental Army and American Character, 1775–1783* (New York, 1979), 299; Don Higginbotham, *The War of American Independence: Military Attitudes, Policies, and Practice, 1763–1789* (Bloomington, Ind., 1971), 403–4.

15. Journals of George Grant, Thomas Roberts, and Samuel M. Shute, *JMEJS*, 107, 240, 262–63; Robert K. Wright, Jr., *The Continental Army* (Washington, D.C., 1989), 321–25; William Malcom to Washington, Apr. 25, 1779, and Washington to Malcom, Apr. 29, 1779, *PGW*, roll 57.

16. Edward E. Curtis, "Poor, Henry Varnum," *DAB,* 15:69–70; Mintz, *Generals of Saratoga,* 189, 193–94, 209–11.

17. Washington to Alexander McDougall, May 6, 1779, *WGW,* 15:2; journals of Thomas Blake, Daniel Gookin, and Daniel Livermore, *JMEJS,* 38, 102–3, 178–80.

18. Summary of intelligence concerning the Susquehanna expedition against Indians of the Six Nations, *IAP,* 205; Washington to Sullivan, May 4, 1779, and Sullivan to Washington, May 8, 1779, *PJS,* 3:12–13 and 15–16; "Autobiography of Philip Van Cortlandt," *Magazine of American History* 2 (May 1878): 279, 289; Garrick M. Harding, *The Sullivan Road* (Wilkes-Barre, Pa., 1899), 6–21; *OBFB,* 78; *W-B,* 2:1170–76; journals of John L. Hardenbergh and Charles Nukerck, *JMEJS,* 115–21 and 214–15; Sullivan to Washington, May 31, 1779, *PJS,* 3:47; *PNG,* 3:98 n, 213 n; *PNG,* 4:25 n–26 n, 45 n, 53 n–54 n, 59 n–60 n, 70 n–71 n, 92 n.

19. Sullivan to Jay, July 21, 1779, *PJS,* 3:83; Joseph Reed to Sullivan, June 3, 1779, *PJS,* 3:54–55; Hand to Sullivan, May 20, 1779, *PJS,* 3:24; *OBFB,* 65–74, 82; journal of Thomas Roberts, *JMEJS,* 241; *DMS,* 48; Moravian diary, June 15, 1779, in *W-B,* 2:1181.

20. Sullivan to Jay, July 21, 1779, *PJS,* 3:81; *OBFB,* 72, 74–76; journals of Ebenezer Elmer, Moses Fellows, and William Rogers, *JMEJS,* 80–81, 86, 247–48; entries of June 18, 19, 20, 21, 22, 23, *AHWD.*

21. Journals of James Norris, William Rogers, and Samuel M. Shute, *JMEJS,* 225, 248–51, and 268 n.

22. "Joseph Elliott's Story of His Escape from Queen Esther's Fury, July 3 and 4, 1778. Taken down by Washington Lung," *Proceedings and Collections of the Wyoming Historical and Geological Society* 13 (1914): 128; *W-B,* 2:1018–24, 1060–77.

23. Kirkland to Jerusha Kirkland, July 5, 1779, Samuel Kirkland Papers, Hamilton College Burke Library, 78a, quoted in Christine Sternberg Patrick, "The Life and Times of Samuel Kirkland, 1741–1808," Ph.D. diss., State University of New York at Buffalo, 1993, 328; Samuel K. Lothrop, "Samuel Kirkland," in Jared Sparks, ed. *The Library of American Biography* (Boston, 1837), 248.

24. *W-B,* 2:1189; *HD,* 158–59; journal of James Norris, *JMEJS,* 226; entries of July 14 and 27, 1779, *AHWD.*

25. Entry of June 29, 1779, *AHWD;* Adam Hubley to Sullivan, July 2, 1779, *PJS,* 3:70; Reed to Board of War, Aug. 12, 1779, *PA,* first ser., 7

(1853): 640; *OBFB*, 53; Sullivan to Jay, July 21, 1779, *PJS*, 3:82; Sullivan to William Shreve, Aug. 24, 1779, *PJS*, 3:102.; *OBFB*, 48–49.

26. James Clinton to George Clinton, June 15, 1779, *PGC*, 5:86; James Clinton to Washington, June 26 and 30, 1779, *PCC*; Washington to James Clinton, June 27, 1779, *WGW*, 15:325–26; Washington to Sullivan, July 1, 1779, *PJS*, 3:66–69.

27. Sullivan to Washington, July 10, 1779, *PJS*, 3:75–77; Sullivan to James Clinton, July 11, 1779, *PJS*, 3:78; Sullivan to Jay, July 21, 1779, *PJS*, 3:80–84.

28. Washington to President of Congress, Aug. 15 and 21, 1779, *WGW*, 16:98–108 and 140–42; Greene to Jay, Sept. 19, 1779, *PNG*, 4:395–98, 398 n–400 n; *JCC*, 5:332 and 15:1169; Octavius Pickering, *The Life of Timothy Pickering* (Boston, 1867), 1:238–41.

29. *OBFB*, 146, 213, 219, and 66 (Jan. 1948): 49–50; journal of William Rogers, *JMEJS*, 252, 254; entries of July 14 and 27, *AHWD*.

30. Journals of Ebenezer Elmer, Thomas Roberts, and William Rogers, *JMEJS*, 82, 241, and 253; John B. B. Trussell, Jr., *The Pennsylvania Line: Regimental Organization and Operations, 1776–1783* (Harrisburg, Pa., 1977), 159; William Maclay to Joseph Reed, July 26, 1779, *PA* 7 (1853): 586; Ephraim Blaine to Jeremiah Wadsworth, Aug. 22, 1779, *PJS*, 3:101; entry of July 24, 1779, *AHWD*; Sullivan to Timothy Pickering, July 26, 1779, *PJS*, 3:85–86; Pickering to Jay, Aug. 4, 1779, in Jay, *John Jay*, 621–23; *OBFB*, 214–16; Sullivan to Clinton, July 30, 1779, *PJS*, 3:90.

31. Entry of July 29, 1779, *AHWD*; journal of William Rogers, *JMEJS*, 254; *W-B*, 2:1197–98.

Notes to Chapter 7

1. *OBFB*, 54, 57, 122; Albert Hazen Wright, *The Sullivan Expedition of 1779: Regimental Rosters of Men, Studies in History no. 34* (Ithaca, N.Y., 1965), 2–4; journals of William Barton, Henry Dearborn, Thomas Grant, Adam Hubley, James Norris, and William Rogers, *JMEJS*, 5, 68, 137, 146–47, 227, 255; Whittemore, *Sullivan*, 265.

2. Greene to Robert L. Hooper, Jr., July 10, 1779, *PNG*, 4:221; Sullivan to President of Congress, Nov. 9, 1779, *PJS*, 3:161; Sullivan to Samuel Hunter, July 30, 1779, *PJS*, 3:89.

3. Journal of James Norris, *JMEJS*, 228; *W-B*, 2:1205.

4. *OBFB*, 123; journal of William Rogers, *JMEJS*, 258.

5. Sullivan to President of Congress and to Washington, Aug. 15, 1779, *PJS*, 3:95 and 100; journal of John L. Hardenbergh, *JMEJS*, 124–25.

6. Journals of William Barton, Henry Dearborn, Ebenezer Elmer, Thomas Grant, and Adam Hubley, *JMEJS*, 6, 69, 85, 138, 150–51; *OG*, 728.

7. Entry of Aug. 11, 1779, *AHWD;* journals of Thomas Grant and William Rogers, *JMEJS*, 139, 260.

8. *OBFB*, 159; Journals of James Norris, Erkuries Beatty, and William Rogers, *JMEJS*, 229, 26, 260.

9. Journal of Jabez Campfield, *JMEJS*, 54.

10. "Narrative of Lieut. Moses Van Campen," in J. Pritts, ed., *Mirror of Olden Time Border Life* (Abington, Va., 1849), 482.

11. Sullivan to Washington, Aug. 15, 1779, *PJS*, 3:98–100; Norton, *Sullivan's Campaign*, 93–94; journal of Henry Dearborn, *JMEJS*, 69–70; Joseph Brant [to Mason Bolton, Aug. 9, 1779], *SCC*, 130.

12. John Butler to [Mason Butler], Aug. 26, 1779, *NS*, 280–81; Francis Barber to George Clinton, Aug. 15, 1779, Historical Society of Pennsylvania, Philadelphia, Pa.; Norton, *Journal of Major John Norton*, 277; James Edward Brady, "Wyoming: A Study of John Franklin and the Connecticut Settlement into Pennsylvania," Ph.D. diss., Syracuse Univ., 1972, 136–38; [Elihu] Marshall to his brother, Aug. 15, 1779, in Wright, *Sullivan Expedition: Newspaper Comment and Letters*, 46; *OBFB*, 202; "Personal Narrative of the Services of Lieut. John Shreve of the New Jersey Line of the Continental Army," *Magazine of American History* 2 (1879): 571; Philip Van Cortlandt to [Gilbert Van Cortlandt], Aug. 22, 1779, in Philip Van Cortlandt, *The Revolutionary War Memoir and Selected Correspondence of Philip Van Cortlandt*, ed. Jacob Judd (Tarrytown, N.Y., 1976), 141–42.

13. Journal of James Norris, *JMEJS*, 229.

14. Sullivan to President of Congress, Aug. 15, 1779, *PJS*, 3:97–98.

15. William W. Campbell, "Life and Services of General James Clinton," in Campbell, *Annals of Tryon County*, 339; John Allison, "A Short Memorandum of the names and distances that the 4th Pennsa. Regt. march'd thro' in the year 1779, in the western expedition against the Savages, commanded by Major Genl. Sullivan," *DSC;* James Clinton to Mary Clinton, June 13, 1779, *PGC*, 5:82–83.

16. James Clinton to George Clinton, June 15, 1779, *PGC*, 5:86–87; Nelson Greene, ed., *History of the Mohawk Valley*, (Chicago, Ill. 1925) 1: 928–48.

17. James Clinton to Washington, June 14 and 19, 1779, in "New York

during the Revolution," 178–79; Wright, *Sullivan Expedition: Regimental Rosters*, 4–7.

18. John Fea, "Clinton's Overland Portage March from the Mohawk to Otsego Lake," in Greene, *History of the Mohawk Valley*, 1:922–49; *BOB*, 49–50; journal of William McKendry, *JMEJS*, 200.

19. Journals of Erkuries Beatty and William McKendry, *JMEJS*, 19, 199.

20. Journal of William McKendry, *JMEJS*, 200; "A Chaplain of the Revolution: Memoirs of the Reverend John Gano," *Historical Magazine* 5 (Oct. 1861): 332; *BOB*, 74, 80, 26 n; Simms, *Schoharie County*, 299–300; on blacks in the rebel armies, see Charles Patrick Neimeyer, *America Goes to War: A Social History of the American Army* (New York, 1996), 82–83.

21. *BOB*, 66, 87, 101–4; journals of Erkuries Beatty and William McKendry, *JMEJS*, 20, 200; Howard Thomas, *Marinus Willett: Soldier, Patriot, 1740–1830* (Prospect, N.Y., 1954), 106; Lewis Dubois to James Clinton, July 29, 1779, *OBNY*, 69.

22. "Chaplain of the Revolution," 333; Thomas R. Bard, ed., "Journal of Lieutenant Robert Parker, of the Second Continental Artillery, 1779," *PMHB* 27 (1903): 410; journals of Erkuries Beatty and William McKendry, *JMEJS*, 22, 201; James Clinton to George Clinton, Aug. 10, 1779, *PGC*, 5: 189.

23. Copy of diary of Charles Macarthur, *DSC*; *OBNY*, 796.

24. Journals of Erkuries Beatty, Jeremiah Fogg, John L. Hardenbergh, and William McKendry, *JMEJS*, 22–26, 92–93, 125–26, 201–3; *OBNY*, 798–807; David Craft, "Historical Address," *JMEJS*, 355.

25. Articles of Agreement, Aug. 25, 1779, New York State Historical Association Library, Cooperstown, N.Y.

NOTES TO CHAPTER 8

1. Washington to Brodhead, Mar. 5 and 21, 1779, *WGW*, 14:194–96, 421–22.

2. Jackson, *McIntosh*, 90–92; Brodhead to Washington, Sept. 16, 1779, *SCC*, 152–55; Obed Edson, "Brodhead's Expedition against the Indians of the Upper Allegheny, 1779," *Magazine of American History* 3 (Nov. 1879): 654–71; Eber L. Russell, "The Lost Story of the Brodhead Expedition," *Quarterly Journal of the New York State Historical Association* 11 (April 1930): 252–63; William Turner Brady, "Brodhead's Trail up the Allegheny, 1779," *Western Pennsylvania Historical Magazine* 37 (March 1954): 19–

31. There were unconfirmed reports of American casualties. The Seneca warrior Blacksnake heard that four stragglers were killed. According to local tradition, eighteen Americans were killed. Blacksnake, *Chainbreaker*, 117.

3. Speech of Teaquanda, June 19, 1779, *HP*, Add. 21,771, ff. 114–115v.; Mason Bolton to Frederick Haldimand, Aug. 16, 1779, *SCC*, 129.

4. John O. Dendy, "Frederick Haldimand and the Defense of Canada, 1778–1784," Ph.D. diss., Duke Univ., 1972, 127–46; *HMSA*, 1782, 1792–93, 2411–44; John Butler to Bolton, [late April 1779], *SCC*, 83–84; John Butler to Bolton, May 13 and July 3, 1779, *NS*, 217, 266–67.

5. John Butler to Bolton, July 3, 1779, *NS*, 266–67.

6. John Johnson to Daniel Claus, July 16, 1779, quoted in Cruikshank, *Butler's Rangers*, 38.

7. Johnson to Haldimand, May 4, 1779, *KRR*, 216; Earle Thomas, *Sir John Johnson, Loyalist Baronet* (Toronto, 1986), 80; Haldimand to Bolton, July 23, 1779, *NS*, 274.

8. Cruikshank, *Butler's Rangers*, 62–66; John Butler to Bolton, June 18, 1779, *NS*, 265.

9. Brant to Bolton, July 29, 1779, *SCC*, 108–9; Nathan Ker to George Clinton, July 29, 1779, *SCC*, 109–10; Brant [to Bolton, Aug. 19, 1779], *SCC*, 129–30; *IAR*, 199–202; *JB*, 249–52; Frederick W. Cook, "Marauders in the Minisink," *Proceedings of the New Jersey Historical Society* 82 (Oct. 1964): 278–80.

10. Cartwright, *Cartwright*, 36–37; John Macdonell to [John Butler], July 24 and Aug. 5, 1779, *NS*, 275–77; *PA* 7 (1853): 589–92, 611; J. F. Meginness, *Otzinachson; A History of the West Branch Valley of the Susquehanna* (Philadelphia, 1857), 248–55; James R. Williamson, "McDonald's Raid along the West Branch, July, 1779," *Daughters of the American Revolution Magazine* 114 (June, 1980): 824–26.

11. John Butler to Walter Butler, Aug. 11 and 12, 1779, *NS*, 278–79; John Butler to [Mason Bolton], Aug. 26, 1779, *NS*, 281; Joseph Brant to [Mason Bolton], [Aug. 19, 1779], *SCC*, 130; Bolton to Haldimand, Oct. 2, 1779, *HP*; Cartwright, *Cartwright*, 38; Cruikshank, *Butler's Rangers*, 70.

12. John Butler to [Mason Bolton], Aug. 31, 1779, *NS*, 282–83; Richard Cartwright, "Continuation of Journal of an Expedition into the Indian Country, 1779," *JBP*, series F, vol 6, ff. 30–36; Blacksnake, *Chainbreaker*, 108.

13. Hand to Jasper Yeates, Aug. 26, 1779, *OG*, 33:740–41; journal of Jeremiah Fogg, *JMEJS*, 94.

14. *BOB*, 123–29.

15. Entry of Aug. 26, 1779, *AHWD;* journals of Moses Fellows, Jeremiah Fogg, Adam Hubley, James Norris, and William Rogers, *JMEJS*, 87, 94, 154, 231, 264–65.

16. Journals of William Barton, Erkuries Beatty, Jabez Campfield, Jeremiah Fogg, Adam Hubley, and Samuel M. Shute, *JMEJS*, 7, 26, 55, 94, 154–55, 271.

17. Journal of William Barton, *JMEJS*, 7; entry of Aug. 28, *AHWD*.

18. Journals of Adam Hubley and William McKendry, *JMEJS*, 155–56, 203.

19. James Clinton to George Clinton, Aug. 30, 1779, *SCC*, 132–33; John Butler to [Mason Bolton], Aug. 31, 1779, *NS*, 283.

20. Sullivan to Washington, Aug. 30, 1779, *PJS*, 3:107–13; *HD*, 176–79, 183; journals of Daniel Gookin, William Barton, and James Norris, *JMEJS*, 105, 8, 232; *DMS*, 56; Cartwright, *Cartwright*, 39–40; entry of Aug. 29, 1779, *AHWD;* entry of Aug. 29, 1779, journal of Charles Macarthur [McCarter], *DSC;* John Butler to [Mason Bolton], Aug. 31, 1779, *NS*, 284.

21. Anonymous to (?), Aug. 31, 1779, *SCC*, 139; John Butler to [Mason Bolton], Aug. 31, 1779, *NS*, 284; Historical address of David Craft, *JMEJS*, 361–62; *HD*, 178–79, 183; journal of James Norris, *JMEJS*, 233.

22. Entry of Sept. 1, 1779, journal of William Pierce, *DSC; HD*, 178–79; entry of Aug. 31, journal of Charles Macarthur [McCarter], *DSC;* journals of Thomas Roberts, Rudolphus Van Hovenburgh, and William Barton, *JMEJS*, 244, 279, 8.

23. Entries of Sept. 1–4, 1779, journal of William Pierce, *DSC;* journals of William Barton, Erkuries Beatty, John Burrowes, Jabez Campfield, and Jeremiah Fogg, *JMEJS*, 9, 28, 45, 57, 96; *DMS*, 58; Robert S. Rantoul, ed., "The Narrative of Major Thompson Maxwell," *Historical Collections of the Essex Institute* 7 (June 1865): 112.

24. Anonymous American soldier to (?) Stagg, Sept. 6, 1779, *NS*, 310; journal of Jabez Campfield, *JMEJS*, 56.

25. John Butler to [Mason Bolton], Aug. 31, 1779, *NS*, 284; Sullivan to John Jay, Sept. 30, 1779, *PJS*, 3:125; journals of William Barton, Erkuries Beatty, John Burrowes, Jabez Campfield, and Jeremiah Fogg, *JMEJS*, 9, 28, 45, 56–57, 96–97; *DMS*, 58.

NOTES TO CHAPTER 9

1. Sullivan to Jay, Sept. 30 and Oct. 2, 1779, *PJS*, 3:123–28, 135, 140; Anon. to Miranda ?, Aug. 30, 1779, "The Love Letters of Soldier on Battle-

field," *Telegram*, Mar. 10, 1929, reprint of article in *Hornell Daily Times*, Aug. 1879, clipping in Chemung County Historical Society Museum, Elmira, N.Y.

2. Simcoe to Henry Dundas, Feb. 23, 1794, quoted by Brian Leigh Dunnigan in Richard Merritt, Nancy Butler, and Michael Power, eds., *The Capital Years: Niagara-on-the Lake, 1792–1796* (Toronto, 1991), 71; Bolton to Haldimand, Aug. 16 and Sept. 7, 1779, NS, 279–80, 290; David, a Mohawk, to Haldimand, Aug. 22, 1779, *DAR*, 16:174.

3. Haldimand to Germain, Sept. 14 and 25, 1779, *DAR*, 17:213, 220; Haldimand to John Butler and to Mason Bolton, Sept. 3, 1779, NS, 286–88.

4. Johnson to Haldimand, Sept. 6 and 9, 1779, and Haldimand to Johnson, Sept. 9, 1779 (two letters), *KRR* 27 (1931): 221–22.

5. Ibid., 224–26; Haldimand to Germain, Nov. 1, 1779, *DAR*, 17:238–39.

6. Sullivan to Jay, Sept. 30, *SCC*, 159; Joseph R. Fischer states that the crops of the Iroquois fields could have supplied the army's dietary needs for the period of an offensive against Niagara. However, he considers Sullivan's artillery to have been inadequate for a siege, despite the fort's personnel shortage. Fischer, *Well-Executed Failure*, 213–14, 229.

7. Sullivan's address to the army, Aug. 30, 1779, *PJS*, 3:112–13; Nathan Davis, "History of the Expedition against the Five Nations, Commanded by General Sullivan, in 1779," *Historical Magazine*, 2nd ser. 3 (April 1868): 201.

8. Davis, "History of the Expedition," 203.

9. Journals of Jeremiah Fogg, Henry Dearborn, Moses Fellows, John Jenkins, James Norris, Thomas Roberts, William Barton, Erkuries Beatty, John Burrowes, Jabez Campfield, George Grant, Adam Hubley, and William McKendry, *JMEJS*, 95–96, 73, 89, 173, 232, 247, 8–12, 27–28, 45, 56–57, 110, 157–58, 204; entry of Sept. 1, 1779, *AHWD*.

10. Entries of Sept. 1–4, 1779, journal of William Pierce, *DSC;* entry of Sept. 23, 1779, *AHWD;* journals of William Barton, Erkuries Beatty, John Burrowes, Jabez Campfield, Jeremiah Fogg, and George Grant, *JMEJS*, 9, 28, 45, 57, 96, 111; Rantoul, "Narrative of Major Thompson Maxwell," 112.

11. Journals of Jeremiah Fogg, Adam Hubley, and Erkuries Beatty, *JMEJS*, 96–97, 160, 30; entry of Sept. 7, 1779, journal of William Pierce, *DSC*.

12. Journal of Jeremiah Fogg, *JMEJS*, 98.

13. Journals of Adam Hubley and William McKendry, *JMEJS*, 160, 205.

NOTES TO CHAPTER 10

1. Journal of Jabez Campfield, *JMEJS*, 58.

2. Entry of Sept. 10, 1779, journal of William Pierce, *DSC*; journals of Erkuries Beatty, George Grant, and John Jenkins, *JMEJS*, 30, 111, 174; William Gordon, *The History of the Rise, Progress, and Establishment of the Independence of the United States of America* (London, 1788), 311.

3. Nathan Davis, "History of the Expedition," 202; *OG*, 735 n; journals of Jeremiah Fogg and Adam Hubley, *JMEJS*, 98, 160.

4. Sullivan to Jay, Sept. 30, 1779, *PJS*, 3:128–29; "Chaplain of the Revolution," 334.

5. Journals of John Burrowes, George Grant, and John L. Hardenbergh, *JMEJS*, 47, 111, 130.

6. Journal of Thomas Grant, *JMEJS*, 141; *OG*, 735 n; *HD*, 185.

7. Sullivan to Jay, Sept. 30, 1779, *PJS*, 3:134, 129; Guy Johnson's map of 1771, in William M. Beauchamp, *A History of the New York Iroquois, Now Commonly Called the Six Nations* (New York State Museum Bulletin 78, Archaeology 9; reprint, Port Washington, N.Y., 1962), 286–87; Simms, *Schoharie County*, 300 n; Adam Hoops to John Greig, Sept. 18, 1841, *JMEJS*, 311.

8. John Butler to Bolton, Sept. 8 and 10, 1779, *NS*, 291, 293.

9. Notes and map, "Groveland Escapade" of John S. Clark, *JMEJS*, 131; John Butler to [Bolton], Sept. 14, 1779, *NS*, 295.

10. Blacksnake, *Chainbreaker*, 113, 140–41; journals of Erkuries Beatty, John Burrowes, Thomas Grant, and John Jenkins, *JMEJS*, 31–32, 48, 142, 174–75; Bard, "Journal of Lieutenant Robert Parker, [continued] of the Second Continental Artillery, 1779," PMHB, 28 (1904), 14–15; pension application of David Freemoyer, in Dann, *Revolution Remembered*, 292–96; Patrick Frazier, *The Mohicans of Stockbridge* (Lincoln, Nebr., 1992), 228–29.

11. Sullivan to Jay, Sept. 30, 1779, *PJS*, 3:131; journals of Henry Dearborn and Adam Hubley, *JMEJS*, 75, 161–62; John Salmon to James Everett Seaver, Jan. 24, 1824, in James Everett Seaver, *A Narrative of the Life of Mary Jemison, the White Woman of the Genesee*, ed. Charles Delameter Vail (New York, 1942), 152–56; Edward Hand to Jasper Yeates, Sept. 25, 1779, *OG*, 741–42.

12. Entry of Sept. 13, 1779, *AHWD*; "Journal of Lieutenant Robert Parker," PMHB 28 (1904): 15.

13. "Journal of Robert Parker," 15; journals of Charles Nukerck, Jabez Campfield, Henry Dearborn, John Burrowes, James Norris, and Jeremiah Fogg, *JMEJS*, 218, 75, 48, 59, 235, 99; entry of Sept. 14, 1779, journal of William Pierce, *DSC*.

14. Moses Van Campen to Committee at Rochester, Sept. 10, 1841, in Henry O'Rielly, ed., *Notes of Sullivan's Campaign, or the Revolutionary Warfare in Western New York* (Rochester, N.Y., 1842), 187–88; Lockwood R. Doty, *History of Livingston County, New York* (Jackson, Mich., 1905), 175; entry of Sept. 14, 1779, journal of William Pierce, *DSC*; journal of William McKendry, *JMEJS*, 206; entry of Sept. 14, 1779, *AHWD*; Cartwright, *Cartwright*, 41–42; journal of Rudolphus Van Hovenburgh, *JMEJS*, 281; *HD*, 188; "Bucktooth's Recollections," *JBP*, 16 F, 105–8; John Butler to [Mason Bolton], Sept. 14, 1779, *SCC*, 148–49; Norton, *Journal of Major John Norton*, 277–78; Seaver, *Mary Jemison*, ed. Vail, 72–73.

15. Sullivan to Jay, Sept. 30, 1779, *PJS*, 3:131; Davis, "History of the Expedition," 203; journal of Jabez Campfield, *JMEJS*, 60.

16. "Orderly Book of Hand's Brigade from Wyoming to Tioga," *PA*, 6th ser., 14 (1907): 103; journal of John Burrowes, *JMEJS*, 48; *HD*, 188.

17. *HD*, 188; *OG*, 737n; "Sullivan's Campaign—Intended Ambuscade," *JBP*, 16 F, 39–40; Arthur C. Parker, "The Indian Interpretation of the Sullivan-Clinton Campaign," *Rochester Historical Society Publication Fund Series* 8 (1929): 56; William N. Fenton, "Problems Arising from the Historic Northeastern Position of the Iroquois," in *Essays in Historical Anthropology of North America*, Smithsonian Miscellaneous Collections, vol. 100 (Washington, D.C., 1940), 211.

NOTES TO CHAPTER 11

1. Journals of Erkuries Beatty, John Burrowes, and Charles Nukerck, *JMEJS*, 32–33, 49, 218.

2. Entry of Sept. 18, 1779, *AHWD*; entry of Sept. 18, 1779, journal of William Pierce, *DSC*; Oneiga, Indian messenger, to Sullivan, Sept. 1779, *PJS*, 3:115–16.

3. Gerlach, *Proud Patriot*, 376; Washington to Sullivan, May 31 and Sept. 15, 1779, *PJS*, 3:51, 121; Sullivan to the Oneida Indians, 1779, *PJS*, 3: 117–19.

4. *DMS*, 64.

5. *HD*, 190–92; journal of William Barton, *JMEJS*, 13.

6. Journals of James Norris, Jeremiah Fogg, Adam Hubley, Erkuries Beatty, and William Barton, *JMEJS*, 236–37, 100, 165, 34, 13; *OBNY*, 802.

7. *DMS*, 65–66; journal of Thomas Grant, *JMEJS*, 142–44.

8. Entry of Sept. 28, 1779, *AHWD;* journals of William Barton, Erkuries Beatty, John Livermore, and Charles Nukerck, *JMEJS*, 13, 34, 189, 219.

9. Sullivan to Peter Gansevoort, Sept. 20, 1779, and Sullivan to Jay, Sept. 30, 1779, and Schuyler to Gansevoort, Oct. 7, 1779, and Gansevoort to Sullivan, Oct. 8, 1779, *PJS*, 3:122–23, 132–33, 143–44; Washington to Schuyler, Oct. 12, 1779, *WGW*, 16:460–61; Washington to Gansevoort, Oct. 25, 1779, *WGW*, 17:27.

10. Davis, "History of the Expedition," 205; journal of Adam Hubley, *JMEJS*, 166.

11. "Orderly Book of Edward Hand," *PA*, 14 (1907): 112–13; journals of Erkuries Beatty, John Burrowes, Charles Nukerck, and William McKendry, *JMEJS*, 35, 50, 208, 219; *DMS*, 66.

12. Washington to Sullivan, Oct. 3, 1779, *PJS*, 3:142–43.

13. Sullivan to Washington, Sept. 28, 1779, *PCC;* Sullivan to Jay, Sept. 30, 1779, *PJS*, 3:123–36; Davis, "History of the Expedition," 205; Gordon, *History*, 3:312 n; *IAR*, 218; Blacksnake, *Chainbreaker*, 115.

14. Washington to Jay, Oct. 4, 1779, *WGW*, 16:407; Washington to Sullivan, Nov. 1779, *PJS*, 3:160–61; Washington to Jay, Oct. 9, 1779, *PCC;* Gordon, *History*, 3:312; Washington to Sullivan, Oct. 8, 1779, *PJS*, 3:147; General Orders, Oct. 17, 1779, *WGW*, 16:479.

15. William Plumer, "John Sullivan," in Albert Stellman Batchellor, ed., *Early State Papers of New Hampshire* (Concord, N.H., 1892), 21:823; Sullivan to Washington, Nov. 6, 1779, *PJS*, 3:158; Sullivan to President of Congress, Nov. 9, 1779, *PJS*, 3:161–62; Journals of the Continental Congress, Nov. 13, 1779, *PJS*, 3:162–63.

16. Bolton to (?), May 1780, quoted in Cruikshank, *Butler's Rangers*, 78; Sayengeraghta speech, council at Niagara, 1779, *HP*, add. mss. 21,779, f. 21., quoted in Calloway, *American Revolution in Indian Country*, 132–33.

17. *WGW*, 15: 370.

NOTES TO CHAPTER 12

1. Guy Johnson to George Germain, Nov. 11, 1779, *DAR*, 16:213; Calloway, *American Revolution in Indian Country*, 133–35; "Return of the

Several Indian Nations and Equipment . . . for the Year 1780," *HP*, Add. Mss. 21,769, f. 93.

2. Hughes, *A Journal by Thos. Hughes*, 151; Brian Leigh Dunnigan, "Fort Niagara in 1781," in John L. Field, ed., *Bicentennial Stories of Niagara-on-the-Lake* (Lincoln, Ont., 1981), 2–5; Brian Leigh Dunnigan, "Military Life at Niagara, 1792–1796," in Merritt, Butler, and Power, *The Capital Years,* 73; Roberts, *New York's Forts,* 360.

3. Simcoe to Henry Dundas, Feb. 23, 1794, and report of Capt. Gother Mann, Oct. 29, 1792, quoted in Dunnigan, "Military Life at Niagara," 71.

4. E. A. Cruikshank, ed., "Records of Niagara: A Collection of Documents Relating to the First Settlement, 1778–1783," *Publications of the Niagara Historical Society* 38 (1927): 9; Blacksnake, *Chainbreaker,* 114; Seaver, *Mary Jemison,* ed. Namias, 84.

5. Bruce G. Wilson, *The Enterprises of Robert Hamilton: A Study of Wealth and Influence in Upper Canada, 1776–1812* (Ottawa, 1983), 11–17; *HMSA,* 2039–43; Calloway, *American Revolution in Indian Country,* 133–37, 144–47.

6. Indian Records, vol. 10, f. 94, Public Archives of Canada, Ottawa, Canada, microfilm.

7. Indian Records, vol. 12, ff. 140–74, Public Archives of Canada, microfilm; Draper Manuscripts, series U, vol. 11, State Historical Society of Wisconsin, microfilm reel 57, ff. 240–41.

8. Cruikshank, *Butler's Rangers,* 78; Haldimand to Germain, Oct. 24, 1779, *PRO,* CO 42/39, f. 388.

9. Guy Johnson to Haldimand, May 3, 1780, *HP,* Add. Mss. 21,766; *IAR,* 224–25.

10. Indian Records, vol. 12, ff. 180, 183; Haldimand to Germain, Oct. 25, 1780, *DAR,* 18:208; *JB,* 285.

11. Priest, *Captivity and Sufferings of Gen. Freegift Patchin,* 1–14; Examination of Walter Elliot, Apr. 12, 1780, *PGC,* 5:632–33; Brant to the Americans, Apr. 10, 1780, in Mathews, *Mark of Honor,* 70; Alexander Harper to Mrs. Harper, Apr. 8, 1780, *PGC,* 5:579–80.

12. *JB,* 287–88.

13. Simms, *Schoharie County,* 334–36.

14. Mathews, *Mark of Honor,* 71.

15. Sir John Johnson to Haldimand, Mar. 27 and Apr. 3, 1780, and Haldimand to Johnson, Mar. 23 and 30, Apr. 4 and 17, and May 4, 1780,

KRR, 227–32; Mary Beacock Fryer, *King's Men: The Soldier Founders of Ontario* (Toronto, 1980), 93.

16. Sir John Johnson to Haldimand, May 16, 1780, *KRR,* 232–33; Goose Van Schaick to George Clinton, May 17, 1780, *PGC,* 5:716.

17. Sir John Johnson to Haldimand, June 3, 1780, *KRR,* 233–34.

18. Egly, *Van Schaick,* 81–82; Van Schaick to George Clinton, May 27, 1789, *PGC,* 5:761–62.

19. Guy Johnson to Haldimand, Aug. 1, 1780, *HP,* Add. Ms. 21,766; *JB,* 293–95; *IAR,* 235–37; Cornelius Van Dyck to Goose Van Schaick, July 3, 1780, *PGC,* 5:913–14; Samuel Kirkland to Volkert P. Douw, [July] 3, 1780, *IA,* 258–59; John Graham to George Clinton, July 27, 1780, *PGC,* 6: 59; Abraham Wemple to George Clinton, Aug. 2, 1780, *PGC,* 6:80–82; George Clinton to Albert Pawling, Aug. 10, 1780, *PGC,* 6:93–94.

20. Frank H. Severence, "The Tale of Captives at Fort Niagara," *Publications of the Buffalo Historical Society* 9 (1906): 251.

21. Haldimand to Sir John Johnson, Aug. 24, 1780, *KRR,* 236; Haldimand to Germain, Oct. 25, 1780, *DAR,* 18:210.

22. Fryer, *King's Men,* 101; Clark, *Onondaga,* 1:333–34; Sir John Johnson to Haldimand, Oct. 31, 1780, *HP,* Add. Ms. 21,818, ff. 205–7; Volkert Veeder to Henry Glen, Oct. 17, 1780, *PGC,* 6:303.

23. Robert Van Rensselaer to George Clinton, Oct. 13 and 18, 1780, *PGC,* 6:291, 302; George Clinton to Washington, Oct. 30, 1780, *PGC,* 6: 351–55; Haldimand to Germain, Oct. 25, 1780, *DAR,* 16:420; Franklin B. Hough, *The Northern Invasion of October, 1780* (New York, 1866), 53– 62.

24. Narration of militiaman Thomas Sammons, in Greene, *History of the Mohawk Valley,* 2:1036; court-martial of Robert Van Rensselaer, Mar. 12, 1781, *PGC,* 6:692–703.

25. Jonathan Lawrence to Samuel Drake, Oct. 24, 1780, *PGC,* 6:332– 33; Cruikshank, *Butler's Rangers,* 87; George Clinton to Washington, Oct. 30, 1780, *PGC,* 6:354.

26. John Munro to Sir John Johnson, Oct. 24, 1780, *KRR,* 246–48; Adiel Sherwood to Henry Livingston, Jr., Oct. 17, 1780, *PGC,* 6:408; Stephen Lush to George Clinton, Oct. 12, 1780, *PGC,* 6:288–89; William Malcomb to Robert Van Rensselaer, Oct. 13, 1780, *PGC,* 6:292; Haldimand to Germain, Oct. 25, 1780, *DAR,* 16:420.

27. Germain to Haldemand, July 26 and Nov. 18 and 23, 1781, *DAR,* 20:195, 261–65; Haldimand to Henry Clinton, Sept. 13, 1781, *KRR,* 268;

Michael A. Bellesiles, *Revolutionary Outlaws: Ethan Allen and the Struggle for Independence on the Early American Frontier* (Charlottesville, Va., 1993), 197–99; Henry Watson Powell to Haldimand, Sept. 26, 1781, *KRR*, 270.

28. John Ross to Haldimand, [Nov.] 7, 1781, *KRR*, 271–72; journal of Gilbert Tice, Oct. 5–Nov. 12, 1781, *HP*, Add. Mss. 21,767; narration of William Wallace, in Greene, *History of the Mohawk Valley*, 2:1078; Willett to George Clinton, Nov. 7, 1781, *PGC*, 7:488.

29. Narration of militiaman William Wallace, in Greene, *History of the Mohawk Valley*, 2:1078–80.

30. Willett to George Clinton, Nov. 2, 1781, *PGC*, 7:472–75; Mathews, *Mark of Honor*, 75; narration of militiaman Philip Graff, in Greene, *History of the Mohawk Valley*, 2:1080; journal of Gilbert Tice, *Ontario Historical Society Papers and Records*, 21 (1924): 196–97; *KRR*, 275.

31. Haldimand to Ross, Feb. 18 and Mar. 2, 1782, *KRR*, 276–77; Ross to Robert Mathews, June 26 and July 7, 1782, KRR, 281–82.

32. Journal of George Singleton, [July 5–15, 1783], *HP*, Add. Mss. 21,785, ff. 148–148v.; Haldimand to Earl of Shelburne, July 17, 1782, *DAR*, 21:97; Ross to Haldimand, Aug. 3, 1782, *KRR*, 283.

33. Brant to Sir John Johnson, Dec. 25, 1782, *BP*, Add. Mss. 21,775.

NOTES TO CHAPTER 13

1. *IAR*, 262; Richard B. Morris, ed., *John Jay, the Winning of the Peace: Unpublished Papers 1780–1784* (New York, 1980), 578.

2. William Cobbett, ed., *Parliamentary History of England from the Earliest Period to the Year 1803* (London, 1806–20), 23:410.

3. *Journals of the House of Commons* (London, 1803), 29:361; Michael N. McConnell, *A Country Between: The Upper Ohio Valley and Its Peoples, 1724–1774* (Lincoln, Nebr., 1992), 181.

4. Allan Maclean to Haldimand, May 18, 1783, *DAR*, 21:171; Haldimand to Sir John Johnson, May 26, 1783, and June 2, 5, 23, 1783, and Sir John Johnson to Haldimand, June 2, 1783, in Thomas, *Sir John Johnson*, 106–8.

5. Speech of Sir John Johnson, [July 23, 1783], "Haldimand Papers," *Michigan Pioneer and Historical Society Historical Collections* 20 (1892): 177.

6. Haldimand to Sir John Johnson, April 1784, in Henry S. Manley, *The*

Treaty of Fort Stanwix, 1784 (Rome, N.Y., 1932), 21; Lord North to Haldimand, Aug. 8, 1783, *DAR,* 21:206.

7. "Preliminary Terms of Peace between Britain and the United States, November 30, 1782," in Jonathan R. Dull, *A Diplomatic History of the American Revolution* (New Haven, Conn. 1985), 170; Haldimand to North, Nov. 27, 1783, *DAR,* 19:452; A. L. Burt, "A New Approach to the Problem of the Western Posts," *Canadian Historical Association Annual Report* (1931): 65–68; J. Leitch Wright, Jr., *Britain and the American Frontier, 1783–1815* (Athens, Ga., 1975), 16–29.

8. Minutes of Transactions with Indians at Sandusky, Aug. 26 to Sept. 8, 1783, *PRO,* CO 42/45, ff. 10–152; *JB,* 344–46; meetings of chiefs of Six Nations, Shawnees, Delawares, and Cherokees at Niagara, Oct. 2, 4, and 6, 1783, *PRO,* CO 42/15, ff. 370–73.

9. Brant to Schuyler, Oct. 23, 1783, in "Joseph Brant or Thayeadane-gea," *American Historical Record* 2 (Aug. 1873): 355–56.

10. Manley, *Treaty of Fort Stanwix,* 28–32; Barbara Graymont, "New York State Indian Policy after the Revolution," *New York History* 56 (Oct. 1976): 444–45.

11. Jacob Read to Washington, Aug. 13, 1784, in Paul H. Smith, ed., *Letters of Delegates to Congress* (Washington, D.C., 1994), 21:768–69; Robert A. Rutland, ed., *The Papers of James Madison* (Chicago, 1973), 8: 158 n. 2; Arthur Lee and Richard Butler to George Clinton, Aug. 19, 1784, *PGC,* 8:340.

12. Ephraim Douglass to Benjamin Lincoln, Aug. 18, 1783, *PCC,* roll 163, no. 3, f. 150; Ebenezer Allen to Continental Congress, Aug. 12, 1783, in Manley, *Treaty of Fort Stanwix,* 41.

13. Schuyler to President of Congress, July 29, 1783, IA, 289–90.

14. Washington to James Duane, Sept. 7, 1783, *WGW,* 27:133–40.

15. *JCC,* 25:680–95; Reginald Horsman, *Expansion and American Indian Policy, 1783–1812* (East Lansing, Mich., 1967), 6–20; Francis Paul Prucha, *American Indian Policy in the Formative Years: The Indian Trade and Intercourse Acts, 1790–1834* (Cambridge, Mass., 1962), 32–35.

16. *IAR,* 266–67.

17. Brant to George Clinton, June 6, 1784, *PGC,* 8:323–25.

18. Clinton to Ryckman, [Aug. 14, 1784], *PGC,* 8:335.

19. Peter Ryckman to Henry Glen, Aug. 23, 1784, *PGC,* 8:342; Jellis Fonda to George Clinton, Aug. 31, 1784, *PGC,* 8:348; John Dease to Sir John Johnson, Sept. 5, 1784, *IDH.*

20. "Journal of Griffith Evans, Clerk to the Pennsylvania Commissioners at Fort Stanwix and Fort McIntosh, 1784–1785," *PMHB* 65 (Apr. 1941): 206; Hough, *Proceedings of the Commissioners of Indian Affairs*, 1:35–62.

21. *JB*, 361–62; Lafayette to Washington, Oct. 8, 1784, in Stanley J. Idzerda and Robert Rhodes Crout, eds., *Lafayette in the Age of the American Revolution: Selected Letters and Papers, 1776–1790* (Ithaca, N.Y., 1979), 5:264–65.

22. "Treaty of Fort Stanwix, in 1784," in Neville Craig, ed., *Olden Time* 2, no. 9 (Sept. 1847): 411–13; account of Lafayette's meeting with the Six Nations, Oct. 3–4, 1784, in Idzerda and Crout, *Lafayette*, 5:255–59.

23. Craig, *Olden Time*, 414–21; "Journal of Griffith Evans," 207–12.

24. Craig, *Olden Time*, 423–27; "Captain Brant's Account of What Passed at Fort Stanwix, in October 1784," *IDH*.

25. John Dease to Alexander Fraser, Nov. 26, 1784, Indian Records, vol. 15, ff. 158–61, printed in Manley, *Treaty of Fort Stanwix*, 98–99.

26. Commissioners for treating with the Indians to John Dickinson, Nov. 15, 1784, *PA*, 1st ser., 10:357.

Notes to the Epilogue

1. William Wyckoff, *The Developer's Frontier: The Making of the Western New York Landscape* (New Haven, Conn., 1990), 103–31; James W. Darlington, "Peopling the Post-Revolutionary New York Frontier," *New York History* 74 (1993): 341–81.

2. Commissioner of Indian Affairs, *Treaties between the United States of America and the Several Indian Tribes, from 1778 to 1837* (Washington, D.C., 1837), 41–48; Graymont, "New York State Indian Policy after the Revolution," 452–71; Jack Campisi, "From Stanwix to Canandaigua: National Policy, States' Rights, and Indian Land," in Christopher Vecsey and William A. Starna, eds., *Iroquois Land Claims* (Syracuse, N.Y. 1988), 57–60; Jennings, *History and Culture of Iroquois Diplomacy*, 201–3; J. David Lehman, "The End of the Iroquois Mystique: The Oneida Land Session Treaties of the 1780s," *William and Mary Quarterly* 47 (1990): 526–47.

3. Campisi, "From Stanwix to Canandaigua," 60–64.

4. Anthony F. C. Wallace, *The Death and Rebirth of the Seneca* (New York, 1970), 179–83; Jennings, *History and Culture of Iroquois Diplomacy*, 204; Commissioner of Indian Affairs, *Treaties between the U.S. and Indian Tribes*, 73–78.

5. Hough, *Proceedings of the Commissioners of Indian Affairs,* 1: 198n–99n; Campisi, "From Stanwix to Canandaigua," 60; *New York Times,* Dec. 12, 1998, Jan. 30, 1999, and Feb. 25, 1999; *Oneida Daily Dispatch,* Feb. 26, 1999.

6. Johnston, *Valley of the Six Nations,* xli, 52; E. A. Cruikshank, "The Coming of the Loyalist Mohawks to the Bay of Quinté," *Ontario Historical Society Papers and Records* 26 (1930): 398–402.

7. *IAR,* 285; Laurence M. Hauptman, *The Iroquois Struggle for Survival: World War II to Red Power* (Syracuse, N.Y., 1986), x.

8. "The Love Letters of Soldier on the Battlefield," *Telegram,* Mar. 10, 1929.

INDEX

✦ ✦ ✦ ✦ ✦ ✦ ✦ ✦ ✦ ✦ ✦

ABOUT THE AUTHOR

✦ ✦ ✦ ✦ ✦ ✦ ✦ ✦ ✦ ✦ ✦ ✦

Max M. Mintz is professor emeritus of history at Southern Connecticut State University. He is the author of *Gouverneur Morris and the American Revolution* and *The Generals of Saratoga: John Burgoyne and Horatio Gates*.